W9-ABN-396

ONLY JOKING

ONLY JOKING

What's So Funny About Making People Laugh?

JIMMY CARR &
LUCY GREEVES

Red Wing Public Library
225 East Avenue
Red Wing, MN 55066

GOTHAM BOOKS
Published by Penguin Group (USA) Inc.
375 Hudson Street, New York, New York 10014, U.S.A.
Penguin Group (Canada), 90 Eglinton Avenue East, Suite 700, Toronto, Ontario M4P 2Y3, Canada (a division of Pearson Penguin Canada Inc.); Penguin Books Ltd, 80 Strand, London WC2R 0RL, England; Penguin Ireland, 25 St Stephen's Green, Dublin 2, Ireland (a division of Penguin Books Ltd); Penguin Group (Australia), 250 Camberwell Road, Camberwell, Victoria 3124, Australia (a division of Pearson Australia Group Pty Ltd); Penguin Books India Pvt Ltd, 11 Community Centre, Panchsheel Park, New Delhi – 110 017, India; Penguin Group (NZ), cnr Airborne and Rosedale Roads, Albany, Auckland 1310, New Zealand (a division of Pearson New Zealand Ltd); Penguin Books (South Africa) (Pty) Ltd, 24 Sturdee Avenue, Rosebank, Johannesburg 2196, South Africa

Penguin Books Ltd, Registered Offices: 80 Strand, London WC2R 0RL, England

Published by Gotham Books, a division of Penguin Group (USA) Inc.

First printing, September 2006
10 9 8 7 6 5 4 3 2 1

Copyright © 2006 by Jimmy Carr and Go Tiger Ltd.
All rights reserved

Gotham Books and the skyscraper logo are trademarks of Penguin Group (USA) Inc.

LIBRARY OF CONGRESS CATALOGING-IN-PUBLICATION DATA

Carr, Jimmy (Jimmy Anthony)
Only joking : what's so funny about making people laugh? / Jimmy Carr and Lucy Greeves.
p. cm.
Includes bibliographical references and index.
ISBN 1-592-40235-6 (hardcover)
1. Wit and humor—History and criticism. I. Greeves, Lucy. II. Title.
PN6147.C37 2006
809.7—dc22
2006015495

Printed in the United States of America
Set in Goudy with Bodoni MT • Designed by Sabrina Bowers

Without limiting the rights under copyright reserved above, no part of this publication may be reproduced, stored in or introduced into a retrieval system, or transmitted, in any form, or by any means (electronic, mechanical, photocopying, recording, or otherwise), without the prior written permission of both the copyright owner and the above publisher of this book.

The scanning, uploading, and distribution of this book via the Internet or via any other means without the permission of the publisher is illegal and punishable by law. Please purchase only authorized electronic editions, and do not participate in or encourage electronic piracy of copyrighted materials. Your support of the author's rights is appreciated.

While the author has made every effort to provide accurate telephone numbers and Internet addresses at the time of publication, neither the publisher nor the author assumes any responsibility for errors, or for changes that occur after publication. Further, the publisher does not have any control over and does not assume any responsibility for author or third-party Web sites or their content.

For the Unknown Joker

CONTENTS

Preface **ix**

1. Joking Matters
Why jokes are important **1**

2. Tickling the Naked Ape
The science of laughter **13**

3. Send in the Clowns
The early evolution of the stand-up comic **35**

4. Only Kidding
How children learn to joke **59**

5. Nuts, Bolts and Hydraulic Brains
Dissecting the joke **77**

6. No Way to Make a Living
How to be a professional joker **101**

7. Take My Wife . . . No, Please: Take My Wife
Joking across the gender divide **139**

8. Beyond the Pale?
Offensive jokes and why we laugh at them **163**

9. An Englishman, an Irishman and a Rabbi . . .
The checkered history of ethnic jokes **187**

10. Sometimes the Joke Gets Elected
Why we need political jokes **215**

11. Knock Knock.
Who's There?
The Police.
When jokes get taken to court **237**

12. The Last Laugh **261**

Acknowledgments **277**

Notes **279**

Further Reading/Viewing **287**

Index **291**

PREFACE FOR THE AMERICAN EDITION

This is a book about jokes and the people who tell them. Here's how it came about.

We've been best friends since we met at university in 1992, and for the past fourteen years jokes have been a constant presence in our relationship. It was Lucy who first encountered comedy in a professional capacity (we use the term loosely), selling tickets for comedy shows at the Edinburgh Festival. By the time Jimmy announced he was going to be a comedian, Lucy had long ago wearied of the late nights, breadline income and monstrous egos, and got herself a proper job as a copywriter. She begged Jimmy to reconsider; nobody becomes a stand-up without losing all his money and gaining a drug problem. It's a job you wouldn't wish on your worst enemy. What kind of person gets his kicks from standing, alone, facing a room full of strangers who have paid to laugh at him? We all like a joke, but liking them enough to write hundreds, then tell them over and over again, surely moves you from "funny guy" territory into the realm of "pathological obsessive." Despite the fact that he was quite good at the whole joke thing, she knew it would end in tears. . . .

Unfortunately, Jimmy's subsequent comedy career dealt something of a blow to Lucy's reputation as a trend-spotter. But we're still friends. We're a bit busier now than we were in those happy days of student grants and eight-week semesters, but underneath we haven't changed a bit. Some people let fame go to their heads. They get all puffed up and start talking about themselves in the third person. Jimmy Carr would never let that happen to him.

Honestly, he wouldn't.

Unfortunately when we decided to write a book together, talking about ourselves in the third person became unavoidable. Our individual identities had to be submerged in a pool of "we." Don't be fooled by our apparent unanimity, though. It conceals a number of bitter differences of opinion. For example, Jimmy thinks that pun about "a pool of 'we'" is really, really poor and potentially damaging to his professional reputation; it makes Lucy snort with laughter. But on the whole, we found ourselves in agreement. Let's just say that after fourteen years of terrible puns, you know when to compromise.

We may not always agree about what's funny, but we both understand that jokes matter. It's easy for people to dismiss jokes as trifling and insignificant because they are designed to be laughable, and because they are such short, sharp shots of pure entertainment. In fact, although a joke on the page is a fairly straightforward proposition, as soon as it gets out into the open it's quite a different matter. The context in which the joke is heard can change it from an innocent riddle to a complex, coded social message, one that is usually ambivalent and open to a range of interpretations. The act of telling a joke can be profoundly serious.

Fortunately, this book is not. Despite Jimmy's professional interest in jokes, and Lucy's tendency to take *everything* slightly too seriously, we wrote this book as enthusiasts, not academics. It's unapologetically personal, and it's steeped in the kind of humor that we love. There are almost as many theories about humor as there are theorists—one scholar alone identifies eighty different "theories of laughter."[1] We didn't think anyone needed another one. Good jokes, on the other hand, you can

[1] *Readers intent on counting them may turn to Edmund Bergler's 1956 book,* Laughter and the Sense of Humour.

never have too many of. So this book isn't just about jokes, it's a joke book too.

We've scoured the widest possible range of sources to bring you 450 of the best jokes we could find. Some of them are by Jimmy—but not as many as there would have been if he had written this book on his own.[2] Some are genuinely ancient—fifteen hundred years old in one case—others are the latest gems from some of our favorite modern comedians. Where possible, we have credited jokes to their original author. But the genealogy of a joke doesn't always work that way, so many remain anonymous. (If you are a comic and find a joke here that you are sure is yours, please let us know via the publisher.)

[2] *All of them. Probably.*

Some of these jokes may be familiar, like old friends who aren't quite as funny as you used to think they were. Others will certainly make you groan. A few may offend you. But we hope that many more of them will surprise and delight you. They'll tickle some mysterious neural circuit, triggering a visceral response that makes you laugh out loud and store them up to retell to your friends. That's the hit all of us joke junkies are looking for.

When we were preparing this U.S. edition of the book, we had to consider very carefully the question of how well jokes travel between nations and cultures. We are both big fans of American comedy, and we hope that's duly reflected in these pages. We think you guys are *funny*. But we're not natives, so we make no apologies for the crass generalizations and bizarre cultural misunderstandings that no doubt litter these pages, despite the best efforts of our patient editors. Happily, it has been our experience that you can get away with a lot in the U.S. if you talk "like the Queen," and we can assure you that one does.

George Bernard Shaw famously described Britain and America as "two nations divided by a common language."

The intricacies of translating between the two cultures are such that some jokes just won't export. For example, you'll find this one in the UK edition:

> *—Doctor, doctor, I can't pronounce my Fs, Ts and Hs.*
> *—Well, you can't say fairer than that then.*
> ***—Tim Vine***

The joke is lost if you don't recognize "you can't say fairer than that" as a common phrase meaning, "that's a good deal, don't you think?" As in, "I'll wash if you dry—you can't say fairer than that." Except that's a bad example—is "the washing up" a familiar household chore in America? In fact, don't you "wash up" before dinner? It's an idiomatic minefield.

Another one we just couldn't translate is this one:

> *I have a nut allergy. When I was at school the other children used to make me play Russian roulette by force-feeding me a packet of Revels.**—Milton Jones***

That joke makes little sense to a U.S. audience because you're missing one crucial reference point. A packet of Revels is a popular but peculiarly old-fashioned little box of assorted chocolate-covered sweets—candy, to you. Beneath the chocolate, some of them are raisins, some are caramels, some are a particularly revolting sort of orange paste and some are peanuts. It's hard to tell which is which until you put them in your mouth. So now you get the joke, but it's not funny. Whereas for us, the Revels brand name evokes an instant glow of school-yard nostalgia. When we hear that joke in Britain, every one of us can see the retro orange-and-brown-striped cardboard packaging, can taste the cheap, slightly chalky chocolate and reexperience the strange tension of trying to guess what's lurking underneath. In fact, Milton Jones's analogy is so instantly and universally resonant that it's become official: the latest Revels advertising campaign features a pastiche of the Russian roulette scene from *The Deer Hunter.*

In the space between hearing a joke and bursting into laughter, there's no time to undertake a reasoned analysis of what makes it funny. For the duration of the burst of laughter that follows a joke you enjoy, you're not the least bit conscious of why you're laughing—it's as though the laughter drowns out rational thought. In fact, that's the condition for laughing at a joke: if you have to stop and puzzle out why, the magic is lost.

But these "untranslatable" jokes—the ones that need footnotes—are remarkably few and far between. Of the four-hundred-odd jokes in this book, fewer than twenty were deemed "too British" for a U.S. audience, mainly for reasons of local idiom or references to brands or personalities not well known outside the UK. The occasional problems we have in understanding each other's jokes tend to be caused by superficial differences in our "common language" and not by the underlying substance of the joke. We may have different confectionary, but our sense of humor is essentially similar enough for most jokes to manage the transatlantic commute quite happily. There's a rich tradition of cultural exchange between our two countries. No, really. And nowhere is it more cordial or more reciprocal than in the world of comedy. It's the one "special relationship" that never seems to sour, no matter that for every Chaplin, we also send you a Benny Hill. And for every *Seinfeld*, you give us a *Joey*. If our common language divides us, our common sense of humor brings us back together.

Not everyone agrees with us about the similarities between the U.S. and UK joking cultures. One particularly popular misconception is that British humor is entirely defined by our class system. Certainly the contemporary preoccupations of any culture are reflected in its jokes. There are all sorts of examples of twentieth-century British humor that feed off the comic potential of class anxiety, from

Monty Python to *Fawlty Towers*. But most of these jokes can readily be enjoyed by an American audience. In fact, if you substitute the words "social standing" for "class," you'll see that our two humor cultures have this underlying concern in common. Anxiety about how we're perceived by our neighbors finds expression in many of the jokes we make on both sides of the pond, even if the local customs are different.

The other cliché is that Americans don't understand irony. We realize that's completely unfounded: your humorists display an acute grasp of the fine art of comic misdirection. (Particularly the numerous "ringers" who turn out to be Canadian.) It's just that this art is not as widely respected in the U.S. as it is in Britain. Irony is slippery. It's smart-assed. Simple, honest folk don't trust irony—and with good reason. Simple, honest folk in the UK don't trust it either; it's just that we don't have as many of them as you do, and ours are neither quite so honest nor, it has to be said, quite so simple. But joking apart—and you'd be forgiven for doubting our earnestness—Americans are not so much worse at irony as better at sincerity. You can sometimes get through a public speaking engagement without feeling the terrible pressure to say something snide and witty. You lack our compulsion to puncture every weighty moment with a joke, and British comedy can look awfully mean-spirited in comparison. Often when we unleash some casually biting wit on our American friends, we worry at first that you have misunderstood and have taken offense. We're rather affronted when you chuckle indulgently and say, "I just love that dry British humor."

Taboo topics for humor on either side of the pond show a similar pattern: there are local peculiarities but enough common ground for us to share our guilty pleasures in the jokes that result. American jokes reveal a far greater preoccupation with race than British jokes—this has been true for a hundred years and more. Conversely, there's a rich strand of British humor that draws on camp innuendo—

from Kenneth Williams to Graham Norton—and which has no exact parallel in the U.S. As we'll see later on, Sigmund Freud and his followers might draw some fairly far-reaching conclusions about our respective psychosexual hang-ups from the dirty jokes we tell. But what's a complex or two between friends? Some of the best jokes are the ones we laugh at because we know we shouldn't, and jokes that milk a sacred cow in America still retain much of their ghoulish freshness for us in the UK. We didn't really know who O. J. Simpson was before the infamous car chase, but we gleefully lapped up the scurrilous stream of e-mail jokes nonetheless.

If you really want to understand a culture other than your own, pay close attention to what it does for laughs. Jokes are a shortcut to the innermost depths of the nation's psyche, and they offer even more privileged access to closely related strangers like the Americans and the British. Here's the thing: Jokes are partly an expression of the alienated outsider that lives in all of us. They show us the world through a prism of otherness. In a sense, every joke expresses something about what it feels like to see things from an extraordinary point of view: what it feels like to be a foreigner. Comedians like Woody Allen, Steve Martin or Chris Rock fascinate a British audience partly because they each represent a different way of being American. But they each also occupy an observer's role, standing slightly outside the mainstream of everyday American life and pointing out its absurdities. They are our tour guides to the USA's interior landscape: they acknowledge the strangeness of American life and help us to get the measure of it. We can only hope that this book goes some small way toward returning the favor on behalf of Britain.

So join us, if you please, on a scenic tour of the joking

landscape where we live. Along the way, we'll introduce a broad and scintillating spectrum of UK comedy that may be new to you, from the eccentric battiness of Tim Vine to the gleeful misanthropy of Les Dawson. We'll explode a few myths, but we'll probably confirm some prejudices too. We'll be dry, we'll be ironic, we'll seldom be quite sincere. And by the end, you'll not only know what makes us laugh: you'll probably understand—far better than we intended—what makes us tick.

ONLY JOKING

CHAPTER ONE

Joking Matters

The reason angels can fly is that they take themselves lightly.

G. K. CHESTERTON

As far as we're concerned, there are three enduring mysteries of human existence: sex, death and jokes.

Frankly the first two have been overanalyzed—Plato and Dr. Ruth have it pretty much sewn up between them, it would seem—so for the purposes of this book we thought we'd concentrate on the jokes. Because jokes are just fascinating, once you start to turn them around and look at them from different angles. Pretty much everyone that we've ever met knows at least one joke. Admittedly in a large number of cases it transpires that people know the setup from one joke and the punch line from a completely different one, but that's another story. Jokes spread around the world and embed themselves in our shared culture; the most resonant of them get lodged in the language in the same way as clichés or old wives' tales do. Why do we store them and recall them, these tiny folk tales, these wonderful lies? Why is there a constant demand for fresh ones, while the old ones survive for centuries? Why *did* the chicken cross the road?

A joke, for the purposes of this book, is defined primarily as something you say deliberately to evoke amusement.

This summer I'm going to go to the beach and bury metal objects that say "Get a life" on them.—*Demetri Martin*

It's a thing of words, a unit of communication. Not simply slapstick, not just storytelling, not mere wordplay—although it undoubtedly can contain elements of all of these. It's a formulaic verbal construction designed to elicit a response—laughter. Beyond that, it gets more complicated. A joke usually revels in its brevity, getting its business done in few words, whether it's a "one-liner," a riddle, a pun or a very short story; yet quite often we also recognize as a joke quite a long story with very little point, which may or may not involve a hirsute canine. A joke will usually incorporate a setup and a punch line—in fact, the punch line might be said to be the defining feature of a joke—but not always: for example, the kind of "in-joke" where so much is implied by the teller, and understood by the listener, that the setup or the punch line can go unspoken; or the aforementioned shaggy dog story, where what we laugh at is the last line's lack of punch. A joke might bear a close resemblance to its backward first cousin, the practical joke, which ends in a physical payoff rather than a verbal punch line. It doesn't have to be told by a professional comedian, or heard in a comedy club. A good joke is footloose; it takes on a life of its own as it passes from person to person, through playground, pub and e-mail in-box.

Jokes rightly belong to an oral culture: they live out loud, not on the page. Anyone who tries to capture and analyze these elusive little stories treads a fine line. On the one hand, the moment you take a joke out of context and start to unpick its meaning or its cultural significance, you risk losing the "funny." It's like dismantling a football into a sad little heap of its component parts—leather, catgut, wadding, rubber, air—then trying to hoof it into the goal. On the other hand, jokes do carry more complex and sub-

I was a ballerina, but I had to quit after I injured a groin muscle. It wasn't mine.—*Rita Rudner*

tle significance than we sometimes allow them, and a heightened appreciation of the craft that goes into them, the history of their origins and uses, and a certain curiosity about why they matter makes us appreciate even more keenly the magic moment when a well-struck joke hits the back of the net.

So let's try not to get too stodgy about it: jokes, by definition, are not to be taken seriously. We brush off their effects by saying, "It's just a joke," or "I'm only joking." We dismiss individuals we don't respect in the same way: "He's a total joke." When telling jokes, we agree that they are best delivered lightly, off-the-cuff—however much effort may go into this appearance of levity. And that's the extraordinary thing about jokes, really: trivial as we insist they are, still we treasure them. We commit them carefully to memory and share them with people we love or people we want to love us. We support a massive and increasingly global joke-manufacturing industry of stand-up comedians and all sorts of backroom gag-smiths: sitcom writers, radio DJs, journalists. A sense of humor is one of our most valued social assets; have you met a single person who will cheerfully admit that they don't have one?

Children, with their natural anarchy and love of nonsense, are practically born joking. As we grow older, our joking becomes more restricted. We absorb with varying degrees of success the complex unwritten rules that govern where, when and to whom a particular joke can be told. Almost all of us learn to "take a joke," whether or not we're any good at telling them. And not getting a joke, or not getting a laugh when you tell one, are excruciating experiences. It seems that being able to prove you have a sense of humor is a matter of peculiar social importance—particularly in Britain,

I was out last week collecting for a sponsored walk. I ended up raising so much money I was able to afford a taxi.
—Jimmy Carr

where we take the art of joking very seriously indeed, although we try not to let it show. Jokes oil the wheels of our social encounters in so many useful ways: breaking the ice at the office party; establishing that the sister's new boyfriend is a good bloke; lightening the mood at Uncle Ted's wake. This sort of use may go some way to explaining why jokes and joking loom so large in British culture—a nation so profoundly ill at ease with itself socially is bound to be particularly in need of the crutch that a joke provides. Sociologists have measured the silences in conversations between English speakers and concluded that we cannot bear a pause of longer than four seconds—we would rather fill the gap with anything. Having exhausted the weather as a topic, we often move straight on to trying to make each other laugh. We store little witticisms up our sleeves like handkerchiefs, just in case.

Jokes can also be gloriously intimate things. Finding someone with the same sense of humor is a little bit like finding a compatible sexual partner. The same things turn you on. Each of us knows there are things that we're a little bit ashamed to laugh at, just as we all have sexual proclivities we'd rather not reveal on a first date. But we just can't help it—we can't decide what makes us laugh any more than we can decide what gets us off. And when you do find a date who laughs at the same off-color jokes, that first taboo that you break together leads to the shedding of other inhibitions, hang-ups and, quite often, pants. There's further evidence of this connection between joking and dating in the personal ads, where G.S.O.H. (for "Good Sense Of Humor") is an almost universal requirement. Although perhaps the sort of people who place these ads are just being realistic about the

The world is a dangerous place; only yesterday I went into a drugstore and punched someone in the face.—*Jeremy Limb*

mental attitude required in anyone who's planning to get into bed with them.

One of the greatest delights of a close-knit social unit, be it a family or a group of old friends, is a shared sense of humor. Often the anticipation of a good joke is enough to start the laughter bubbling up long before the punch line. When we hear a joke that tickles us, one of our first thoughts is, so-and-so would love that one. We memorize it and preserve it as a gift to bestow on so-and-so next time we meet, or else we e-mail it to him there and then. It's a roundabout way of telling someone, "I like you. I would like to think that you are like me. I want you to like me too, and I want to make you happy." Which is hard to say, in so many words, to your mates from the rugby club. Yet these jokes wear out quickly. A few old favorites might hang around, but most are done for after two or three tellings. Almost as soon as we've passed them on we need fresh material.

Of course it's important to recognize that jokes aren't always offered as gifts, and that the net result isn't always laughter. It's not just that there are good jokes and bad jokes; a huge number of jokes are hilarious and violently cruel *at the same time*, depending on where you're standing. They're strangely ambivalent things. A single joke can mean a hundred different things to different people, depending on who tells it, when, where and to whom—even something as slight as a raised eyebrow can radically alter its meaning. A joke is hardly ever "simply" a sunny celebration of wit, a *jeu d'esprit*. Like any other thing made of words, a joke can be a force for good, and a force for . . . less good. There are even some jokes that are downright evil, whether we like it or not. A joke can be little more than an insult, a socially sanctioned cruelty. Jokes can make people

Introducing "lite," the new way to spell "light" but with 20 percent fewer letters.—*Jerry Seinfeld*

feel threatened and they can make people very angry—sometimes so angry that they lead to a court case, imprisonment, even death for the people who tell them. But it's this edge of danger, this shadow side that gives jokes their power. A joke is anarchic, a little scrap of chaos from beyond the boundaries of the rational, a toe dipped in the shallow end of antisocial behavior.

In the normal run of things, we ignore the joke's dark underbelly. We laugh jokes off without much thought, but the jokes we tell and the jokes we respond to reveal a great deal about us. They can function at once to conceal and to expose our deepest beliefs and bigotries. Joke-telling can betray a human need to feel included and accepted in a social group, while uncovering at the same time our love of the shocking and the subversive.

Our ability to joke about things that are painful or forbidden is a valuable asset, a handle on sanity in a mad world. We tell jokes because human existence is an unforgiving slog; we tell them in the face of overwhelming odds and despite the ravages of time and fate. Notwithstanding the fact that our natural good humor may be soured by the blows life aims at us, we joke and laugh all the more. Wherever human beings are oppressed—by corrupt government, poverty or merely the specter of disease and death—jokes thrive. In these circumstances, the fundamental human insistence on laughing despite it all makes the joke a noble thing. According to U.S. stand-up comic Albert Brooks, "When the time comes where there literally is no ability to extract laughs from a subject, it's really the end of the world. I mean, people with horrible diseases make jokes till the end. It's like the armor against being completely eaten and gone from the planet."

If it wasn't for Venetian blinds, it would be curtains for us all.—*Eric Morecambe*

We put this book together as a celebration of the noble art of joking, and as a tribute to all the men and women who ever put on the armor of jokes and went out to fight against the void. And because we had a few questions to ask: Why did human beings start telling jokes? How do jokes work? How do we learn to tell them? Why do some people go to jail to defend their right to joke? Do jokes help us to understand the human condition? Are there things you really can't, ever, joke about? Where do jokes come from, and who owns them? Why can't women remember punch lines? Was Buddha funnier than Jesus? And above all, do jokes really matter?

If you're being chased by a police dog, try not to go through a tunnel, then onto a little seesaw, then jump through a hoop of fire. They're trained for that.—*Milton Jones*

2.6 PERCENT OF JOKES ARE ABOUT STATISTICS

A newspaper has come up with a new survey. Apparently, three out of four people make up 75 percent of the population.—*David Letterman*

Experts say you're more likely to get hurt crossing the street than you are flying, but that doesn't make me feel any less frightened of flying. If anything, it makes me more afraid of crossing the street.—*Ellen DeGeneres*

According to official statistics one third of all accidents in the workplace go unreported. How on earth do they know? —*Jimmy Carr*

Eighty-two point six percent of statistics are made up on the spot.—*Vic Reeves*

Smoking is one of the leading causes of statistics.—*Fletcher Knebel*

There are three kinds of people. Those who can count, and those who cannot.—*George Carlin*

THE PETTING ZOO

A man buys a parrot but discovers too late that it is extremely foul-mouthed and bad-tempered. The bird keeps shouting obscenities at the man, who is forced to lock it in his garden shed to try to shut it up. This doesn't work and he can still hear the filthy-mouthed bird from the house. In desperation the man retrieves the parrot and shuts it in a cupboard, but the bird still keeps screaming at him, and now the neighbors are starting to complain about the noise. As a last resort the man shoves the parrot into the fridge. Miraculously, the parrot suddenly shuts up, so the man takes the bird out of the fridge and puts it back on its perch. The parrot then apologizes for its appalling behavior and asks to be forgiven. "That's okay," says the man. "As long as you don't do it again." "I won't," says the parrot, casting a nervous eye at the fridge. "By the way . . . what did the chicken do?"

I was thinking of sending my dog to one of those pet psychiatrists. The trouble is, he knows he's not allowed on the couch.

What has four legs and says "Boo"?
A cow with a cold.

What has four legs and says "Aaaa"?
A sheep with no lips.

A man sees a farmer walking a pig and notices that the animal has a wooden leg. Curious, he asks the farmer how the pig lost its limb. "Well," says the farmer. "One night the wife and me were asleep when the pig spotted the house was on fire. It broke down the door, ran up the stairs and dragged me to safety. Then it went back in and carried out my wife, then it went in a third time and rescued my four children. We'd all be dead if it weren't for this pig." "So did the pig get its leg burned in the fire?" asks the man. "Oh, no," says the farmer. "But when you've got a pig like this, you don't eat it all at once."

Two fish are in a tank. One turns to the other and says, "Do you know how to drive one of these things?"

Two fish swim into a concrete wall. One turns to the other and says, "Dam!"

A man loses his dog, so he puts an ad in the paper. And the ad says, "Here, boy!"—*Spike Milligan*

CHAPTER TWO

Tickling the Naked Ape

In which we ask some men with Ph.D.s why jokes are good, then willfully misinterpret the results of numerous careful scientific studies.

Dogs laugh, but they laugh with their tails. What puts man in a higher state of evolution is that he has got his laugh on the right end.

MAX EASTMAN

Why do human beings tell jokes? Well, why did the chicken cross the road? In keeping with the willfully literal punch line to that particular riddle, we answer thus: to make each other laugh. And to understand why provoking laughter is something that so many citizens of the world aspire to, we need to start by looking at the nature of laughter itself.

We're assuming that everyone reading this book agrees, to some extent, with Darwin's notion that human beings evolved from ape-like ancestors through a process of natural selection, characterized by the "survival of the fittest."[1] That means agreeing that most, if not all, of our fundamental characteristics—our large brains, opposable thumbs, capacity to form pair-bonds—have a role in furthering the success of our species. Evolutionary theory suggests that a near-universal behavior like laughing must serve some purpose; otherwise all the funny people would have died out a very long time ago. Man is arguably the planet's most successful species, barring the cockroach. We're top dogs, kings of the jungle, mammalian overlords. So does our ability to

[1]Not necessarily a safe assumption these days. Creationists, for example, believe that everything Genesis says is literally true. We don't even think Phil Collins is a very good drummer.

Why is it that the winner of the Miss Universe contest always comes from Earth?—*Rich Hall*

laugh make humans fitter to survive, and has it helped us to become the number one ape?

From Aristotle onward, and probably long before him too, mankind has arrogantly assumed that he's the only animal that laughs. More recent research suggests that may not be true; what the scientific literature calls "repetitive vocalizations in response to pleasure stimuli" have been observed in several other creatures. Both Dian Fossey and Jane Goodall describe how gorillas chuckle when tickled (although the alternative theory that the gorillas' "chuckles" actually signified "crazy lady go now never touch Bobo again" remains untested). More recently, animal behaviorists at the University of Plymouth observed smiling and laughter in baby chimps as young as one month old. The apes responded to their human handlers' smiles and laughed out loud when tickled, just as human babies would. A chimp's "laugh" is not quite the same as a human's, however. The ape makes its characteristic "play face"—mouth open, lower teeth exposed, upper teeth covered—and makes a panting sound on both inward and outward breaths.[2] When students of neuropsychologist Robert Provine were played a recording of chimp "laughter" and asked to guess what it was, their answers included a dog panting, sanding wood and masturbating.

[2] *If you're reading this on the bus, we recommend you wait until you get home to experiment with your "play face."*

Actually, perhaps that should read, "a person sanding wood, a person masturbating *or* a dog panting." It's anyone's guess what an out-of-breath, horny canine carpenter would sound like.

Meanwhile, in a lab somewhere in Boston, grown men and women have been tickling rats in the name of science, and making them laugh—or at least chirrup happily. Surely

Cats have nine lives. Which makes them ideal for experimentation.—*Jimmy Carr*

that's the kind of animal testing we can all approve of. Above and beyond the response to tickling, it seems that some more sophisticated beasts may have a rudimentary sense of humor that allows them to appreciate simple practical jokes. Researcher Roger Fouts claimed that one of his subjects, a chimpanzee name Washoe, once urinated down his neck while riding on his shoulders, then made the sign for "funny."

In the face of this evidence, we'll grudgingly relinquish the notion that laughter is ours alone. But even if we allow the great apes a sense of humor, the verbal complexity of jokes like the ones in this book would put them beyond the reach of even the most intensively trained signing chimp. The ability to *make jokes* in order to make each other laugh is surely safe to claim as exclusively human property. Deriving amusement from a story or riddle that depicts an external situation or event—a concept, not a practical joke—*is* a uniquely human habit. More than that, it's a fundamental element of the mystery of consciousness. If gorillas were better at telling jokes, they might not get such a raw deal with the zoos and the poachers and the shrinking natural habitat. Maybe it's not the opposable thumb thing holding them back, after all. No one's denying that apes are funny: making faces, throwing poo—you can tell they're making an effort. What they lack is a really good script editor.

Laughter has always been part of our repertoire of noises. Like crying, whimpering and moaning, it's an instinctive and universal mode of human expression. These noises mean the same in all cultures and we develop them in our

A computer once beat me at chess, but it was no match for me at kickboxing.—*Emo Philips*

very early life, long before language gets a look-in. For example, rhythmic crying is a communication tool available to us from birth. Few babies need much incentive to pick it up and run with it. The smile appears a long and weary five weeks later, on average, with laughter and tantrums following at three to four months. Note that these two strike simultaneously, like thunder and lightning; we learn both to be furious and to laugh it off at around the same stage of our development. With all of these signals, the infant is broadcasting its emotional state. Adults are no different: when we laugh, we are telling each other something whether we are conscious of communicating or not.

The generally accepted evolutionary explanation for the development of laughter argues that it evolved from a threat response or warning. To paraphrase slightly: Early man, the theory goes, thought he saw a woolly mammoth charging across the tundra. He bared his teeth, narrowed his eyes and prepared to scream the alarm to the rest of his tribe. Suddenly the woolly mammoth slipped[3] and fell down, out cold. Early man's grimace of fear softened into a wide smile and his scream of alarm became a hearty laugh as he ran to fetch his mammoth-disemboweling hook and his brothers.

[3]This sort of accident was, sadly, all too common during the Ice Age.

In other words, laughter is a release of tension on discovering that a perceived threat is not, in fact, a threat at all. Think of a child's first experiences of laughter, which generally occur at around the same time as it learns to distinguish its parents by sight from other adults, and develops a fear of strangers. Imagine the dilemma: Large hairy adult looms threateningly over me. Will it attack? No, thank goodness. It is merely running its fingers lightly over my tummy. Most of us experience our first laugh through being tickled.

Experiments in neuroscience appear to support the

It's a small world, but I wouldn't want to have to paint it.
—Steven Wright

"threat diffused" theory of laughter too. Neuroscientist V. S. Ramachandran used his work with brain-damaged patients to identify a "laughter circuit" in the brain: a network deep in the limbic system, the seat of our emotions, which fires up when we find something funny. Or, in the case of some of Dr. Ramachandran's patients, when we are in pain. Patients with damage to a particular region of the insular cortex suffer from pain asymbolia: instead of feeling fear and agony when the good doctor repeatedly pricks a pin into their fingers, they find it excruciatingly funny. (We only have his word for that, but he is quite a distinguished scientist.) What we can take this to mean is that the neural pathways for pain, fear and laughter are intimately interconnected. It makes neurological sense that an aborted fear response would end up as a laugh, and perhaps also helps to explain why the spectacle of somebody falling, hard, upon their arse is probably the single funniest thing in the world. We empathize with the pain, but in the end it's someone else's arse. Phew!

The notion that laughter is a response to a conceptual shift, a change in our perception of the state of the world around us, is closely mirrored by the classic joke structure. First, the setup: we are presented with a universe of facts and characters. This universe can be surreal, but it has internal logic.

> *A traffic policeman stops a speeding car, and is surprised to discover six live penguins in the trunk.*
>
> *"Yes, Officer—I'm in a terrible state. I won these penguins in a raffle and I don't know what to do with them."*
>
> *Replies the policeman, "If I were you, I'd take them to the zoo."*

A woman with a clipboard stopped me in the street. She said, "Could you spare a couple of minutes for cancer research?" I said, "All right, but we won't get much done."—*Jimmy Carr*

The following day, the policeman notices the same car, and flags it down again. The six penguins are still huddled in the trunk, but now they're wearing sunglasses. "I thought I told you to take them to the zoo," says the policeman.

"Yes, you did—and they enjoyed it so much I'm taking them to the seaside today."

The setup of the joke creates a vivid word picture which, for all its absurdity, nevertheless conforms to certain expectations. We identify with the baffled traffic policeman, who is somewhat surprised to find live penguins in a man's car and instructs him to do the sensible thing and take them to the zoo. So far, it's just a zany story in the *National Enquirer:* "PENGUIN FREAK IN HIGHWAY ARREST." And then, with the punch line, comes a paradigm shift. That one line forces you to reinterpret all the facts that went before, presenting an entirely different picture of events, with a different internal logic. Suddenly you're in a world where penguins are two-foot-tall tourists with communication skills and aesthetic judgment, where they treat humans as their chauffeurs. And they *wear sunglasses*. The setup isn't a threat of the order of, say, a charging mammoth, but any story generates a certain amount of suspense until it reaches its conclusion. The fact that you know how a joke works and expect a funny punch line increases this feeling of pleasant tension. The punch line works by resolving the suspense of the story in an unexpected way. Your brain responds to this tiny paradigm shift by making a conceptual leap that mirrors the jump from perceived threat to no threat, with the same result—laughter.

The pain-relieving ingredient, there's always got to be a lot of that. Nobody wants anything less than Extra-Strength. "Give me the maximum allowable human dosage. Figure out what will kill me, then back it off a little bit."—*Jerry Seinfeld*

If it's true that laughter originated as an expression of relief in response to a fearful situation that turned out to be harmless, it follows that the sensation of laughter is closely associated with pleasure—it's a release of tension. In fact, laughing is so pleasurable that we go to great lengths to recreate that sensation of release in completely artificial circumstances, by telling jokes. And it's still fun. There's no real threat in a joke, but we enjoy that slightly giddy shift of expectation nonetheless. Why is it so enjoyable to laugh? Especially considering that the best kind of laughter is the kind that starts to hurt; that takes our bodies over and sometimes even turns into tears. For years, scientists have been trying to determine the physical benefits of laughter. A recent study by Professor Robin Dunbar found that laughter raised people's pain thresholds. His explanation is that shared social laughter causes an endorphin rush and the release of oxytocin in the brain—the same chemical reactions that we have to human touch. Endorphins are natural opiates. They make us feel relaxed, encourage social and sexual interaction and increase our levels of trust.

Another study claimed to prove that people who laugh more have healthier immune systems. A third experiment appeared to show that the increase in heart rate produced by a good laugh had health benefits equivalent to fifteen minutes on an exercise bike. However, the doctors at the University of Maryland, whose research yielded the startling insight that people suffering from heart disease are precisely 40 percent less likely to see the funny side of life, were probably wasting their time, as well as ours.

Undaunted by the fact that not one of these studies

I'm addicted to placebos. I'd give them up, but it wouldn't make any difference.—*Jay Leno*

could be said to constitute compelling medical evidence, a whole industry has grown up around the notion that laughter isn't just enjoyable, but actively good for you. Which immediately makes it sound less fun, somehow, in the same way that the implicit imperative in "Fun Fair" guarantees anything but (£4 for a toffee apple, £5 for crippling nausea and no charge for the near certainty that your fourteen-year-old daughter will be pregnant by 9 P.M.). You can go on a Laughter Cruise, do Laughter Yoga and visit humor conferences to learn about pain management through giggling. In the mid-1960s a man called Norman Cousins was almost paralyzed by an agonizing and supposedly incurable degenerative disease called ankylosing spondylitis. He was so convinced of the benefits of laughter that he refused conventional treatment and cured himself with repeated viewings of the Marx Brothers movies. He later recovered from a massive heart attack using the same techniques, and finally died, peacefully and presumably chuckling away to himself, aged seventy-five. The books he wrote about his experiences coincided with a huge upsurge of interest in holistic healing and ensured that joking and laughter had a central place in the new movement.

The current poster boy for laughter as physical therapy is Dr. Hunter "Patch" Adams, immortalized by Robin Williams in a film so saccharine that, although we tried to watch it in the name of research, we had to switch it off halfway through because all our teeth were falling out. We have no idea how the film ends, but we do know that the real-life Adams recovered from a major breakdown in his early twenties by discovering his inner clown, and went on to found the Gesundheit Institute, a sort of comedy hospital staffed by clown-doctors that, despite more than thirty

What do you get if you divide the circumference of a pumpkin by its diameter?
Pumpkin pi.

years of planning and the revenues for the film rights to his life story, still exists more as an ideal than an actual health-care institution. Patch Adams has this to say about comedy:

> *Comic relief is a major way for happy folk to dissipate pain. In a healthier world, humor would be a way of life. People would be funny as a rule, not an exception. One of the best aids in the transition from a "heavy" to a "light" existence is to open up the comedian in oneself.*

Patch Adams has his detractors. As the old joke has it, "Laughter is the best medicine. Unless you've got VD, in which case I recommend penicillin." Certainly some of Adams's advice is not terribly practical: he advocates brightening up a depressing day by going to the grocery store with your underpants over your trousers, which is surely only a whisker away from what the rest of society likes to call mental illness. (In fact, why not try popping down to Kmart with your underpants on your *head*. Then they'll clearly see you're nuts.) But he also has thousands of supporters who testify to the therapeutic benefits of filling their lives with laughter and joking. In his defense, he puts forward the reasonable argument that "everyone who goes to a job he doesn't like is a lot weirder than I am."

On the other hand, we would like to call nineteenth-century novelist Anthony Trollope as a witness for the prosecution. We'd like to, but he's dead. The cause? Excessive laughter occasioned by readings from F. Anstey's comic novel *Vice Versa*. One of Trollope's biographers described the final curtain thus: "For a while, Uncle Tony roared as usual, then suddenly Tilley and Edith realized that as they

Two hydrogen atoms are talking. One says, "I think I've lost an electron." The other asks, "Are you sure?" The first replies, "Yes, I'm positive."

were laughing, he was silent." He had suffered a severe stroke; he never spoke again and died several weeks later. Doubtless it's what he would have wanted, although probably not as much as he would have wanted to *not die just yet. Vice Versa* is clearly a very dangerous book, which, incidentally, left a diabolic legacy. As the original identity-swap comedy, its many bastard progeny include *Freaky Friday* and *Big*, but as far as we know nobody has yet died laughing at either of them.

The demise of much-loved men of letters notwithstanding, it's clear that laughter can act as an intensely pleasurable physical release mechanism. It has even greater powers as a psychological pressure valve. According to anthropologist Terrence Deacon, laughter "is not just an expression of emotion. It is a public symptom of engaging in a kind of mental conflict resolution." When we first approached the question of jokes as therapy, we were, if we're honest, a little sneery about it. What changed our minds was the testimony of a depressed Welshwoman on the radio (*Woman's Hour*, BBC Radio 4—where else?). "My face didn't move for two years at first. Your face gets set, with the depression, doesn't it?" She is a member of a humor workshop led by Alice Hortop, an occupational therapist who first noticed the effects of laughter while fitting amputees with stump socks—a painful process that doesn't seem a terribly promising source of humor. But Alice found that telling jokes during the process reduced the patients' anxiety and helped them deal with the pain. Her anecdotal evidence is borne out by a number of studies (not least the recent one by Professor Dunbar, mentioned earlier) that suggest laughter raises our pain threshold. Hortop decided to apply her insights to psychological pain, with dramatic results.

A Canadian psychologist is selling a video that teaches you how to test your dog's IQ. Here's how it works: if you spend $12.99 for the video, your dog's smarter than you.—*Jay Leno*

The Swansea-based humor workshop group meets weekly to play games and tell jokes, under Alice Hortop's guidance. "It's not about orchestrated laughter in groups; we're trying to get genuine laughter." For many of them, even practicing a smile is a big step forward. Some weeks a participant is just too deeply depressed to even make it to the meeting. But little by little they start to take the laughter home with them. One woman talks about doing her homework—playing with her daughter, throwing M&Ms at each other and trying to catch them in their mouths. "It's nice for my daughter to see, because in the past she hasn't really seen her mum smiling or laughing."

It's rather moving. Hortop has created a very special space, a social arena where laughter and joking are celebrated. Some of us are lucky enough to live in this sort of environment all the time, taking it completely for granted, but for these people it's a rare opportunity to flex funny bones that have grown brittle through years of disuse. "We teach people how to be approachable, how to be witty, how to be confident—that's a big one. When you tell a joke and it goes flat, there's nothing worse. We teach people to find the right place to tell the joke, and we practice joke-telling in the group. Because we analyze our humor types at the workshop, people get an idea of what they're good at." For these depressed individuals, joking can unlock a childlike lightness of being that has been lost to their illness. This liberation comes first of all in the safe circle of the workshop, but with time and perseverance can spread throughout their lives. Every single person who has participated in the workshop has shown a reduction in symptoms of anxiety and depression, and a less tangible but far more important increase in general levels of happiness.

I've been smoking for thirty years now and there's nothing wrong with my lung.—*Freddie Starr*

The individuals in the laughter workshop are taking tentative steps toward being able to tell one joke, one day. At the other extreme, there are some people who joke compulsively—they just can't stop. In 2004, British comedian Tim Vine entered *Guinness World Records* for telling the highest number of jokes in an hour. It's an extraordinary feat of memory, and certainly represents outstanding value for money if you measure your stand-up comedy in terms of jokes per minute (approximately 8.3167 in this case, since you ask). Vine's jokes are also mini master classes in the art of the silly pun.

"I went to the butchers the other day and I bet him 50 quid that he couldn't reach the meat off the top shelf. And he said, 'No, the steaks are too high.'"

The press dubbed Vine "the Joke Machine Gun," perhaps because if you try to tell jokes that fast, the delivery is bound to get somewhat mechanical. And in fact the pun is the most mechanical of jokes, resting as it does on a relatively small number of linguistic rules. At any rate, "Comic sets new record" sounds like a challenge to us. So we decided to go looking for a new contender for Tim's record: a worthy adversary in the gags-per-minute game. Think Kasparov versus Deep Blue. What we need is an *actual* joke machine.

In 1957, Russian biochemist, science fiction writer and self-styled humor expert Isaac Asimov wrote a short story called "Jokester." It is set in the twenty-first century. In the story, a "ten mile long" computer named Multivac is tasked with explaining where all the jokes come from. It turns out that they are an experiment played on the human race by a

I don't believe in astrology. I'm a Sagittarian and we're skeptical.—*Arthur C. Clarke*

superior alien intelligence, and once this becomes known all the jokes vanish from the world. His inability to predict the size of twenty-first-century microprocessors notwithstanding, Asimov presents a terrifyingly convincing scenario.

Actually he doesn't; it's complete tosh. We found our joke machine much closer to home.

Ruli Manurung is indirectly responsible for writing tens of millions of jokes, but he's definitely not an extraterrestrial. Nor is he a comedian. He's a software engineer, and along with fellow academics Graeme Ritchie, Dave O'Mara and Helen Pain, he has created a computer program called STANDUP. We went to meet STANDUP at home in the Department of Informatics at Edinburgh University, and asked Ruli to put the joke machine through its paces. First of all he explained patiently that STANDUP isn't an actual machine, let alone a ten-mile-long one. It's a piece of software running on a normal PC. This was a bit of a letdown, but we did perk up considerably when we discovered that, despite his deceptively corporate laptop disguise, STANDUP can talk. In fact he does a mean impression of Professor Stephen Hawking (although it's definitely not as mean as Jimmy's).

STANDUP is based on a program developed ten years earlier by a young artificial intelligence researcher called Kim Binsted, who also happened to be an amateur improvisational comedian. As part of her Ph.D. thesis, Kim developed JAPE, the Joke Analysis and Production Engine, which was the first program capable of producing punning riddles using words from a general dictionary as its raw material. The best of the resulting riddles were blind-tested on schoolchildren alongside jokes from a standard kids' joke

I was high on life, but eventually I built up a tolerance.
—Arj Barker

book. Although the computer-generated jokes fared worse, on average, than those crafted by human beings, the overall top-rated joke came from JAPE, namely:

What's the difference between leaves and a car?
One you brush and rake, the other you rush and brake.

JAPE also came up with this subdued gem:

What do you call a depressed engine?
A low-comotive.

What Binsted proved was that simple puns can be created in a laboratory. Given a sophisticated electronic dictionary, a series of rules about the relation of words, and a great deal of trial and error, the computer occasionally throws out sentences that are recognizable as jokes.

The program can replicate some of the cognitive processes that Tim Vine applies when he writes a joke. STANDUP starts with the punch line, locating a word or phrase with a double meaning. Then it constructs a setup line that makes sense of both meanings. It has thirteen different joke formats—"what's the difference between a——and a———," for example—and a dictionary of around 200,000 words with which to fill in the blanks.

While there's no denying that STANDUP is an admirable academic achievement, Tim Vine's job is quite safe for the time being. We're still a long way off from creating a computer that knows what's funny: one that could actually entertain us on purpose.

What the computer program lacks, utterly and conclu-

Guns don't kill people, people kill people. And monkeys do too—if they have a gun.—*Eddie Izzard*

sively, is a sense of humor. A computer program has no worldview, no context for its jokes. Scientists cannot yet conceive of a computer that could contain all the information it would need to predict whether someone will find a joke funny. That means that STANDUP pours out its jokes in astonishing quantity—over ten million of the "brush and rake" type alone—but it does so completely indiscriminately. It is funny by accident, and one combs through screeds of nonsense to find something that even approximates a joke, like this:

What do you call a hip-hop tortilla?
A rap wrap.

STANDUP is funniest when it's rude. (That's a useful rule of thumb, but in this context we mean STANDUP the computer program, not stand-up comedy in general.) Our very favorite computer-generated joke is this one:

What's the difference between a man beard and a sexual excitement?
One is a buck fuzz, the other is a fuck buzz.

There's a sort of charming naïveté about STANDUP. Hearing these jokes, you could find yourself agreeing with Asimov, just for a moment, that jokes are written by aliens. Mind you, Ruli's going to have to remove some words from STANDUP's dictionary before it gets into the hands of its end-users. At this point we should reassure you that research funding isn't just allocated to projects like this in the interests of keeping academics amused with inadvertent double entendres—this project has a serious purpose.

I don't do drugs. If I want a rush, I get out of a chair when I'm not expecting it.—*Dylan Moran*

STANDUP stands for System To Augment Non-speakers' Dialogue Using Puns. The software is being developed so that speech-impaired children can tell jokes. The sort of language play that leads to puns is thought to serve an important function in the development of a child's language and communication skills. A child who suffers from, for example, cerebral palsy, may have very limited powers of speech and be unable to communicate except through a communication aid. These speech computers may give you a cool robot voice, but they don't offer much scope for creative use of language. The STANDUP program is intended to allow the child to experiment with language and try out humorous ideas by helping him or her to construct, evaluate and tell simple riddles.

Watching some of these children try out a prototype of the program, what's striking is how effortlessly they perform the one vital task that the computer can't. They distinguish instantly between jokes and not-jokes, and they are equally sure which jokes are funny and which aren't. What's more, their pleasure at hearing a successful joke—one that they find funny—seems to come from two distinct sources. They can appreciate the joke for itself and judge that one little word game is more satisfying than another; a particular pun or alliteration tickles them. But the greater source of pleasure seems to be the interaction with the carer or researcher—the actual telling of the joke. Jokes have this wonderful potential to create moments of social informality, a sort of leveling out of the teller's and hearer's sometimes very unequal roles. In this case, "telling" the joke through the voice synthesizer seems to make the children feel exhilarated at their new power to amuse their adult carer.

The Miss World Contest has always had its fair share of knockers.

This makes a lot of sense in the light of our earlier observation that laughter evolved as a noise to communicate emotion. For a joke to give pleasure, it needs to be shared. That's one of the reasons why human responses to particular jokes or even to humor in general are notoriously difficult to study in laboratory conditions. Robert Provine describes an abortive experiment to study laughter in individuals by playing them audio and video recordings of George Carlin, Joan Rivers, *Saturday Night Live* and so on. "Nothing seemed to work. My comic virtuosi elicited only a few grudging chuckles from the lab-bound subjects. . . . This was a humbling experience, for obtaining a sample of laughter does not qualify as what many people would consider rocket science." What this failed experiment taught Provine was fundamental. By their very inability or refusal to laugh, his subjects were telling us that laughter is social. Like misery, hilarity loves company.

Once Provine got out of the lab and into the field, examples of laughter were everywhere. Armed with little more than a pencil, a notebook and a false mustache, he and his students lurked inconspicuously on the fringes of ordinary conversations until they had collected twelve hundred "laugh episodes." They discovered that, in normal one-to-one conversations, the person who is speaking laughs 46 percent more, on average, than the person who is listening. They also found that less than 20 percent of the remarks that preceded laughter in these situations could be considered even remotely humorous. The ones that did resemble jokes or punch lines in the classic sense included "He didn't realize he was sitting in dog shit until he put his hand down to get up" (a classic slapstick premise, to be sure) and "Poor boy looks just like his father." The great

Cigarettes are a much cheaper and a more widely available alternative to nicotine patches.—*Bob Davies*

majority of the laughs they recorded were in response to remarks like "It was nice meeting you too" and "What is that supposed to mean?" All the people they listened to were using laughter as part of the rhythm, the ebb and flow of conversation and communication. They didn't need a finely honed punch line—the slightest chance remark would set them off. If laughter began as a way to communicate deferred threat, it surely endured as a group bonding exercise. It fizzes around our conversations like electricity, looking for a joke to earth it.

We began this chapter with a riddle: Why do human beings tell jokes? To make each other laugh. But like most riddles, this one has a twist in the tail. A joke is a highly sophisticated verbal flourish, a product of human culture and intellect and linguistic skill, which has so far defied science's efforts to reproduce it under laboratory conditions. Animals can't do it, and machines can't do it. Telling a joke is complex higher-order communication. But the way we enjoy the joke is totally primitive. Laughter—that's a guttural, an animal noise, a physical response halfway between fear and ecstasy that we share with the apes. It flies below our intellectual radar, at the level of instinct.

A joke has special powers to bridge the gap between the tickled chimp and the academic, to short-circuit our cultural trajectory and remind us how far we haven't come. The truth, it appears, is that we only invented jokes when it became socially unacceptable for grown-ups to tickle one another in public.

I slept like a baby. Every three hours I woke up looking for a bottle.—*Liam O'Reilly*

LET ME THROUGH—I'M CURIOUS

Here's a health warning: be suspicious of any doctor who tries to take your temperature with his finger.—*David Letterman*

First the doctor told me the good news—I was going to have a disease named after me.—*Steve Martin*

I tried to give blood the other day. But the blood bank wouldn't take it. They wanted to know where I got it from.—*Wally Wang*

I saw a woman wearing a sweatshirt with "Guess" on it. I said, "Thyroid problems?"—*Emo Philips*

When the doctor broke the news that I had cancer, I said, "Tell me straight, Doc, how long do I have?" He said, "Ten . . ." I said, "Ten what? Years, months, weeks?" He said, "Nine, eight, seven . . ."—*Bob Monkhouse*

—Doctor, doctor, my arm is broken in three places.
—Well, stay out of those places.—*Tommy Cooper*

I went to the dentist. He said, "Say, aaah." I said, "Why?" He said, "My dog's just died."

An apple a day keeps the doctor away, but in my experience so does an air rifle.—*Harry Hill*

What do you give a man who has everything?
Antibiotics.

A man walks into a doctor's. "Doctor, I'm suffering from silent gas emissions. All day at work, I have these silent gas emissions. Last night during a movie, I had ten silent gas emissions. On the way to your office I had five silent gas emissions. And while sitting in your waiting room I had three silent gas emissions. As a matter of fact, I've just had two more." The doctor replies, "Well, the first thing we're going to do is check your hearing."

A man goes to his doctor with a sprig of green sticking out of his bottom. "Doctor, I think I have a lettuce growing out of my backside," he says. The doctor examines the greenery and says, "I'm afraid I have bad news—it's only the tip of the iceberg."

A man walks into a doctor's. "Doctor, can you help me?" he says. "My penis has holes all up and down it. When I go to the toilet it sprays out in all directions." The doctor examines the organ and hands him a card with a name and address on it. "Is this the name of a specialist?" asks the man. "No," says the doctor. "He's a clarinet tutor. He'll teach you how to hold it."

A man walks into a crowded doctor's office and says to the receptionist, "There's something wrong with my dick." The receptionist looks up and says, "You shouldn't say things like that in a public area. Please leave, and when you come back, say there's something wrong with your ear, or something like that." The man walks out, then walks back and says, "There's something wrong with my ear." "And what's wrong with your ear?" says the receptionist. The man says, "It hurts when I piss out of it."

—"I tried to kill myself yesterday by taking a thousand asprin."
—"What happened?"
—"Oh, after the first two I felt better."

A man goes to a psychiatrist and says, "Doc, my brother's crazy, he thinks he's a chicken." The doctor says, "Why don't you turn him in?" The guy says, "We would. But we need the eggs."

CHAPTER THREE

Send in the Clowns

In which we trawl the annals in search of the joke's earliest antecedents, then run away screaming.

A child's laughter is pure until he first laughs at a clown.

BUFFO THE CLOWN IN ANGELA CARTER'S *NIGHTS AT THE CIRCUS*

Are you sitting down? We need to talk about clowns.

At first glance, clowns have very little to do with the sort of jokes that this book sets out to investigate. Most clowns are silent, save for the occasional pitiful honk of an old-fashioned car horn. Their jokes are of the more robust, practical variety. If you go to the circus, you can be fairly confident that sticks will be slapped. Custard pies will fly. All this may seem far removed from the sort of playful, allusive verbal fireworks that decorate these pages. But clowns are the precursors of modern-day stand-up comics, just as practical jokes are the ancient ancestors of the one-liner. It's not a straightforward lineage—the practical joke didn't die out once the verbal joke evolved. Think of it as more like the relationship between an alligator and a human being. We all crawled out of the same soup and some of us put in a bit of effort to make something of ourselves, what with fire, the wheel and so on. But like it or not, somewhere in the swampy depths of our DNA that dank, prehistoric throwback is still with us.

So let's relinquish for the moment the notion of the joke as a purely verbal construct. Forget punch lines. Forget

I have a stepladder. It's a very nice stepladder, but it's sad that I never knew my real ladder.

wordplay and linguistic dexterity, and the subtle buildup of narrative tension. What we're looking for here is something much, much older—perhaps even older than language itself. You could call it the spirit of the joke: the urge to turn things upside down and laugh at the results.

For as long as human thought and culture has existed, the comedian has existed too. The character of the joker or trickster is so consistent a part of every separate mythological system that pioneering psychoanalyst Carl Jung identified him as one of the archetypes, the central symbols of our collective unconscious. Jungian archetypes are images or patterns that are imprinted so deeply in the human psyche that they pop up wherever we do, as key elements of our shared species identity. They people our imaginations, finding expression in dreams, myths and fairy tales.

First to Africa, where it all started. It's largely accepted (pace Scientologists and creationists) that all humans are descended from a small population that emerged in Africa about sixty thousand years ago, so it's fitting that the oldest comedians should be found there too. The Yoruba people of what is now Nigeria have a mythical trickster deity called Elegba. He is a shape-shifter, the embodiment of contradiction, being neither large nor small, young nor old, but both at once. He has no home of his own, choosing to inhabit the marketplace, the crossroads and the thresholds of people's property, where boundaries are both negotiable and disputed; whenever a fight breaks out, Elegba is there.

Elegba is a vigorous practical joker, equally irreverent in his dealings with men and gods. A typical Elegba story

I bought an audio cleaning tape. I'm a big fan of theirs.
—Kevin Gildea

has him committing a crime—sometimes theft, sometimes murder—while wearing a special hat, which is made of two different-colored fabrics. Witnesses who saw the crime committed from the south swear that the criminal wore a red hat; those who looked on from the north insist that the hat was green. In the ensuing heated argument, Elegba takes the opportunity to kill, steal and generally create more confusion. He is also a highly sexualized figure, "always represented naked, seated with his hands on his knees, and with an immensely disproportionate phallus," according to A. B. Ellis's lip-smacking 1894 epic, *Yoruba-speaking Peoples of the Slave Coast of West Africa (Their religion, manners, customs, laws, language etc.)*.

So far, so funny?

Among the Native American tribes of the southwestern United States—the Hopi, Zuni and Anasazi—we find our proto-comedian once more, in fine priapic form. Kokopelli is a prehistoric deity with special responsibility for fertility, music and mischief. Legends of Kokopelli involve both lighthearted practical jokes and more sinister pranks. He is usually depicted in profile, a hunchbacked stick figure dancing along with a big sack of seeds on his back, a flute up his nose and a hearty erection. (Subsequent censorship by Catholic missionaries has deprived many of these images of at least one vital piece of equipment. At least poor Kokopelli usually got to keep his sack.)

The Winnebago tribe has its own version of this legendary trickster. He too has a huge, unruly phallus, with the additional unique advantage of detachability—he carries it around in a box. (One can only speculate why, when casting around for a brand name for their motor homes, the founders of Winnebago Industries found their eyes caught

In Vegas I got into a long argument with the man at the roulette wheel over what I considered to be an odd number. —*Steven Wright*

by a word that implies "a box with a prick in it.") One popular tale of the Winnebago trickster has him sending said organ to play with a chief's daughter who is swimming in a lake. His penis goes skimming merrily across the surface of the water like a little fleshy Jet Ski. "No, Little Brother! Come back! She'll be frightened if you rush up to her like that." And Trickster ties a stone to the penis and sends it forth again. This time, it sinks to the bottom. On the third attempt, he finds a stone of just the right weight and the pink torpedo stealthily approaches the chief's daughter and lodges firmly in her aft porthole. All laugh mightily, particularly on realizing that our collective unconscious also contains an archetype for the vibrator.

Mythological trickster figures tend to have three things in common: they are highly sexualized, expressing and acting out desires forbidden by society; they are ambivalent, being neither fully human nor fully divine, often acting as messengers between men and gods and living in some sort of no-man's-land; and, of course, they take delight in inverting the status quo, for no purpose other than mischief. In the ancient Greek tradition, the holy joker was represented by Hermes. As well as looking after mischief and trickery, he was responsible for medicine, music and (in his capacity as messenger to the gods) the Mount Olympus Post Office. Nice to see there's such an ancient precedent for people playing silly buggers with our mail. Hermes carried a staff, the caduceus, which has long been the chosen symbol of the Royal Society of Medicine but once upon a time was just a symbol of . . . well, if you are skeptical about the

Throwing acid is wrong, in some people's eyes.—*Jimmy Carr*

phallic significance of this staff, ponder on the fact that it is a big stick with two big snakes wrapped around it, and furthermore that statues representing the god Hermes, known as herms, consisted of a pillar with a head on top and a whacking great erect penis sticking out of the side. These statues were used as boundary markers at the edges of people's property. Like the African trickster Elegba, that homeless spirit who haunts doorways and crossroads, Hermes lived in the cracks between the spaces the Greeks inhabited, guarding the limits of their territories.

Hermes and Elegba were both represented as gatekeepers, monitoring the physical boundaries of the societies that conjured them into being. This literal guardianship reflects a more important metaphorical role, which they share with almost all trickster spirits, in policing society's moral and intellectual boundaries. The anarchy they represent, the unrestrained sexuality and the potential to turn orderly society upside down, means that they have to be pushed to the edge of things so as not to upset the main current of everyday life. But somehow their natural habitat—the tightrope edge of what's acceptable—turns them eventually into sentries, into guardians of the status quo. With these wild jokers at the gates, we feel safer; we are actually protected by their very existence from all the chaos they represent. They remind us where the edges are—of reason, of civilization, of normality. We shut our darkest fears outside, and they are filtered back to us through these comic watchers in the form of jokes.

So is the trickster god our enemy or our friend? There's nothing funny about a lot of the practical jokes he plays,

If you can keep your head when all about are losing theirs, you'll be taller than anybody else.—*Tim Brooke-Taylor*

which leave a trail of destruction and pain. In some mythologies, jokes themselves can have fatal consequences. A stock episode in Hawaiian legends is the *ho'opa'apa'a*, a riddling contest wherein the loser is generally killed and sometimes cooked and eaten too. These contests existed in real life and not just in stories, although there may well have been less emphasis on the cooking and eating. The rules of this comedy martial art are complex and prescribe arcane formulas for insults, conundrums and language play. Bets are placed, by both participants and spectators, on the outcome of each match. Puns in particular play an important part in Hawaiian jokes; after all, when your native alphabet makes do with only eight consonants and five vowels, the odds of finding one word that sort of sounds like another are pretty high.

A more famous killing joke was the legendary riddle of the Sphinx, which claimed the lives of countless travelers before Oedipus worked it out. Everyone who wanted to pass the Sphinx had first to answer her riddle correctly, or they were toast. (She was rather partial to toast.) Her joke went like this: What goes on four legs in the morning, two legs in the afternoon and three legs in the evening? The answer, of course, is Man, who in his lifetime first crawls, then walks, then uses a cane. It's not exactly a killer punch line, but then that's the whole point. When it comes to giant woman-headed lions, it's the killer setup you need to watch out for.

But for every episode of senseless destruction caused by tricksters and jokers, there are extraordinary creative acts too. Hermes gives knowledge of the healing arts and medicine to humankind. Kokopelli is responsible for the harvest. Another Native American trickster, Coyote, steals fire

Why do kamikaze pilots wear helmets? Smacks of indecision to me.—*Sean Meo*

from the gods and gives it to humans, as does Loki, the otherwise wholly sinister and horrible Norse god of mischief. And Anansi, the cheeky spider of Ashanti legend, is credited with making the very stuff out of which the first humans were fashioned, as well as giving mankind fire, grain and the tools of farming. These contradictory figures seem at once to embody chaos and to channel it, burning off its destructive forces and harnessing its power to create.

The trickster gods may be short on one-liners, but they give us important clues about the relationship between being funny and being human. For one thing, our ancestors seem to have been much more comfortable than we are with the interplay between the light and dark sides of joking behavior. They understood that, as well as providing light relief, the character who tells jokes and plays tricks is plugging in to a darker and more dangerous kind of energy, that clowning around always has the potential to tip over into violence. And that a little bit of pain just makes things funnier.

Alongside the stories that our ancestors told each other about tricksters and fools, they also brought these characters to life in ritual and celebration. During the Roman winter festival of Saturnalia, a man was chosen from among the ordinary people to be crowned as a Lord of Misrule. For the duration of this mock king's reign, he was expected to issue ludicrous commands and proclamations, which everyone had to obey. It's safe to assume many of these commands involved drinking and dancing. At any rate, Saturnalia gave everybody permission, at the turn of the year, to upend normal notions of custom and decency—the most striking

All those who believe in telekinesis, raise my hand.
—Emo Philips

example of this being that slaves were expected to sit at table, waited on by their masters. Our own April Fools' Day is probably a trace remnant of a similar turn-of-the-year festival, since New Year was once almost universally celebrated at the spring equinox—which falls at the end of March according to our modern calendar.

Pagan festivals—at least the ones that involve ordinary people eating, drinking, celebrating the harvest and so on—are extraordinarily tenacious. They tend to find a way to survive subsequent religious regulation. In medieval England, a Feast of Fools was observed by some churches on Twelfth Night. A choirboy was elected bishop, and everyone was allowed to mock the holy mysteries of the church. In France, where the custom was widespread, the higher church authorities tried for many years to suppress it. A regulation from 1444 stipulates, "At Vespers, not more than three buckets of water at most must be poured over the Precentor Stultorum [Bishop of Fools]."

By the end of the fifteenth century, the ecclesiastical Feast of Fools gradually began to decline, but the practice of setting aside a period of licence for chaotic or topsy-turvy behavior is still widespread to this day. In many predominantly Catholic countries it survives as Carnival, the crazy letting-off-steam before the sobriety of Lent. Its earliest origins probably lie in the discrepancies between the solar and the lunar calendar, and the fact that, however you measure your year, it won't end with solar and lunar phases drawing neatly to a close together—the solar year effectively has twelve months, while the lunar year has thirteen. This gives you some time to spare, which is boundary time, the very fringe of the year where things start to unravel if you're not careful. Trickster territory, if we're not very much mistaken.

An escalator can never break; it can only temporarily become stairs. You would never see an "Escalator Temporarily Out of Order" sign, just "Escalator Temporarily Stairs. Sorry for the Convenience."—*Mitch Hedberg*

The notion of turning a fool into a king for a spell suits the mood of these unreal days at the dark turn of the year. The tiniest trace of the notion survives in our own leap year reversal of normal wooing conventions. Dare we suggest that the UK custom of allowing a woman to ask a man to marry her on April 1 has its roots in human sacrifice? Because here's the thing: the original fool kings of Saturnalia were killed at the end of their reign. We know that this practice continued until at least A.D. 303, when the garrison of Roman soldiers at Durostorum (on the Danube in what is now Bulgaria) picked as their Saturnalia king a Christian soldier named Dasius. He was expected to reign for thirty days, playing the part of the god Saturn and indulging in every imaginable earthly pleasure, aided and abetted by his fellow soldiers, before slitting his own throat on the altar of Saturn. When Dasius refused to take part in this heathen ritual, they beheaded him anyway for spoiling their fun. Thus martyred, he became St. Dasius, patron saint of party poopers.

The sacrifice of a temporary king has been practiced at some point in a great many cultures, notably by the Aztecs but also among the Celts and the Vikings. The Saturnalia kings were killed to appease the gods, and their sacrifice drew the festivities to an end, putting the topsy-turvy world back on its feet again. As much as human beings need the release of a chaotic period of clowning and moral licence, it seems our sense of balance can only be restored if someone pays the price for our transgressions.

Of course, it's been a long time since we cut the throats of any of our clowns. But our enjoyment of a joke still seems

I keep a lighter in my pocket at all times. I'm not a smoker, I just really love certain songs.—*Demetri Martin*

to be deepened by suffering—anyone's suffering but our own. This is the saddest story about comedy ever told. A man comes into a psychiatrist's office in Hamburg in 1950. He's in miserable shape. "Doctor, I just don't think I can go on. Life has no meaning for me. Everywhere I look I see nothing but misery and sadness." The psychiatrist replies, "What you need to do is lighten your heart. Learn to laugh. I know just the thing—the greatest clown in Europe is performing in Hamburg this week with his circus. His name is Grock. See him and you'll be sure to forget your troubles." The man just shakes his head. "Doctor," he replies, "I am Grock."

The story is almost certainly apocryphal, but Grock the clown really did exist. He was the creation of one Karl Adrien Wettach, who was born in Switzerland in 1880 and gave his farewell performance in 1954. At the height of his fame he was said to be Europe's highest-paid entertainer. Despite the anecdote quoted above, Herr Wettach seems to have been rather a contented man. In his autobiography he wrote (while sitting in the fifty-room villa on the Italian Riviera which Grock's antics built for him), "I am a lucky man, a very lucky man. . . . I am at peace within myself." But this won't really do for us. We don't want our clowns to be happy; the stereotype of the entertainer with a big greasepaint smile who's crying on the inside is a powerful one. We find something inherently suspicious about a person who keeps up a front of relentless cheerfulness. And in recent years the steady trickle of famous comedians who've come to a genuinely sad end does little to dispel the persistent belief that men and women who are comic in public must be tragic behind closed doors.

Let's cheer ourselves up, then, with a list of modern-day

When people ask me how I'm getting to the airport I say, "Well, I'm flying to one of them."—*Steven Wright*

comedians who are popularly supposed to fit the sad-clown stereotype. There are the depressives: Kenneth Williams, Woody Allen, Roseanne Barr, Benny Hill, John Cleese, Les Dawson. Then there are the addicts: Buster Keaton, Jackie Gleason, Richard Pryor, Robin Williams, Eddie Murphy. Finally, the self-destructors and suicides: Tony Hancock, Lenny Bruce, John Belushi. Sad and long though the list is, it proves very little. A 1992 study conducted by psychologist James Rotton found that comedians were actually no more prone to suicidal depression than any other group.

Other surveys would have us believe that dentistry is the most suicidal profession, or that poets have the lowest life expectancy (although the First World War skews those statistics—a little less focus on scansion and a little more on rifle drill would surely have made all the difference). And during the course of our research for this book, we have talked to dozens of comedians and comedy fans who have their own explanation for the sad-clown myth. "Of course, you know that an incredibly high proportion of comedians are adopted/from broken homes/dyslexic/from small dead-end towns/victims of childhood abuse," run the received wisdoms, although the facts are generally pretty hazy; no one seems quite sure what constitutes a statistically significant number of fucked-up comics.

Assuming we buy the line that childhood trauma or hardship can, in some cases, spur individuals on to high-profile achievements, it's not surprising at all that many successful and famous jokers have less than Walton-esque family backgrounds. But would you find any fewer damaged individuals if you were to look at rock musicians, or actors, or any other deeply competitive profession where the

Everywhere is within walking distance if you have the time.
—Steven Wright

stakes are high, your personality is exposed to harsh public criticism and you have a bit too much time on your hands? Would you expect any fewer incidences of drink and drug dependence among DJs, traveling salesmen or anyone else who schleps around the country, staying in bleak bed-and-breakfasts, in pursuit of a barely living wage? The Rotton study also compared the longevity of comedians with that of other entertainers and non-entertainers. Sure enough, the entertainers (including comedians) died younger, on average, than the general population, but there was no difference between the life expectancy of a comedian and any other sort of entertainer.

To counterbalance the early drug-related deaths of Lenny Bruce (at forty) or John Belushi (thirty-three), we can readily point to George Burns or Bob Hope (both one hundred when they died). For every tortured genius, there's an averagely happy family man who doesn't get the press. It's the sheer irony of the notion we can't resist. We are fascinated by the idea that a funny man who makes himself a fool for our enjoyment is in fact constructing a makeshift comedy trapdoor over an existential void. Some of us suspect that any kind of joke is a telltale marker for hidden pain.

Others persist in seeing only the clown's smile. And they're wrong too.

For these giddy optimists, deaf to the joker's cries for help, clowns symbolize a sort of childlike joy and happiness. Why else would the McDonald's corporation enlist the services of Ronald the clown to sell Happy Meals to our children? Although perhaps it reveals more than they intended about their high regard for the consumer: they appear to believe McDonald's customers will most easily

I bought a packet of Animal Crackers and it said on it, "Do not eat if seal is broken." So I opened it up, and sure enough . . .
—Brian Kiley

relate to a grinning, voiceless imbecile in outsize slacks. A substantial society of committed Christian clowns applies a similar principle to church congregations, using clownish skits to preach the gospel. The theory is that dressing up as a clown allows an adult to reveal solemn truths with child-like innocence and playfulness. Yet it was with heavy hearts and a certain biting of knuckles that we investigated "Clown Skit for Easter Day." Would it help you to understand the solemn mystery of the crucifixion and resurrection of Christ, do you think, if you were to go to church on Easter Sunday only to witness three clowns attempting to balance eggs on a big wooden cross, with hilarious egg-smashing consequences? Clowns for Christ certainly think it would; good luck to them.

Then there's a certain type of woman who collects clown dolls: sad-eyed china Pierrots, Harlequins in satin pantaloons, and shock-haired, red-nosed Augusts. Unfortunately there's a high statistical probability that this woman also runs a bed-and-breakfast. It's an experience you won't forget in a hurry; shelves of dead-eyed clowns, goggling at you over your eggs and fried slice, dredging up deeply buried race memories of capering demons and human sacrifice. Lucy has been through this experience on three separate occasions, the most recent and fearsome being in a remote roadside motel in Arizona. In a hideous refinement of the phenomenon, this landlady had augmented her collection of clown dolls with about fifty novelty German nutcrackers shaped like little men—row upon row of grinning wooden mannequins with BIG SNAPPY JAWS. She told us her husband had been killed in action in 'Nam and her three sons were serving in Afghanistan with U.S. Special Forces. It sounded like a cover story, frankly. It seems much

I don't kill flies but I like to mess with their minds. I hold them above globes. They freak out and yell, "Whoa, I'm way too high!"—*Bruce Baum*

more likely that it was the clowns that drove them out; wherever her menfolk are, they are probably still running.

We can't help feeling that these clown fellows love a captive audience. The fact is that many professional clowns specialize in spreading joy (with extreme force) among the most vulnerable members of society: the young, the sick and the old. Children's parties, retirement homes, hospital wards—not much chance of walkouts. Every children's hospital in America appears to have an on-call clown, and it would be churlish of us to raise objections—after all, only a small proportion of those children will have nightmares for the rest of their lives. Fear of clowns has a proper Latin name—coulrophobia—and an online community (at *www.ihateclowns.com*, among others) which is only half joking about its loathing of "the grease-painted ones." Reading the testimonies of contributors to the site, it's clear that the phobia is usually rooted in a childhood encounter. One particularly harrowing tale describes the horror of seeing the startling contrast between the clown's flesh-colored clown makeup and his flesh-colored . . . well, flesh, around the edges of his frilly collar.

The tension between the outer appearance of the clown, his aggressive bonhomie, and what humanity we assume to be concealed beneath it is at the root of this second popular stereotype: that clowns are not only sad but downright sinister. And when you really examine the roots of clown character, costume and makeup, it becomes harder and harder to see them as cute children's entertainers. Clowns started out as stock characters in street theater,

I hated my last boss. He asked, "Why are you two hours late?" I said, "I fell downstairs." He said, "That doesn't take two hours."—*Johnny Carson*

bawdy and satirical and certainly aimed at an adult audience. The sad Pierrots or capering Harlequins were stereotypes of the stupid man who thinks he's clever, and the clever man for whom things still go wrong because he isn't quite so clever as he thinks. These classic comic stereotypes are perennial, getting a fresh lease of life in the forms of Inspector Clouseau, Basil Fawlty, David Brent and Mr. Bean.

The archetypal circus clown—red-nosed, baldpated, baggy-trousered, with a white face and wide red grin—is called the August, and is actually a relatively modern development. This costume came about in the second half of the nineteenth century, and the invention of the red nose that's come to symbolize clowning is credited to Albert Fratellini (1886–1961). It was at about the same time that the big top circus came to be seen as "family entertainment" that clowns really began to turn nasty. Of particular note is the story of the clown Pagliacci who, in Leoncavallo's 1892 opera of the same name, murders his wife and her lover to poignant effect, but sadly not with a custard pie.

Parents: forget clowns; why not save money by inviting a homeless person to entertain the guests at your child's next birthday party? In the twentieth century, clowns began to offer even more pointed caricatures of society's most unfortunate members. As that masterful cinema clown Jerry Lewis pointed out, "The premise of all comedy is a man in trouble." The bumbling, drunken yokel inspired the August costume, with its red nose and baldpate. This pathetic character, a down-and-out no-hoper, is made even more explicit by the hobo type of clown costume, which originated in America during the 1920s as a hilarious caricature of the down-and-outs made homeless by the early years of the Great Depression. The hobo clown's makeup

The hardest part about being a clown, it seems to me, would be that you're constantly referred to as a clown. "Who was that clown?" "I'm not working with that clown. Did you hire that clown?" "The guy's a clown!"—*Jerry Seinfeld*

mimics the bulbous nose of the alcoholic and the smut-blackened face of the railroad rider. The patched, sorry clothes, the unkempt hair, the drunken clumsiness—this is vicious satire resold as children's entertainment.

The original comedy down-and-out was Weary Willie, the alter ego of Kansas-born clown Emmett Kelly. Weary Willie, a strong influence on Charlie Chaplin's Tramp, helped Prohibition-era Americans to laugh in the face of the grim reality that, as if not being able to buy a drink wasn't bad enough, the agricultural heartland of their nation was about to turn into a gigantic dust bowl. "I am a sad, ragged little guy who is very serious about everything he attempts to do—no matter how futile or how foolish it appears to be," said Kelly of his creation. "I am the hobo who found out the hard way that the deck is stacked, the dice 'frozen,' the race fixed and the wheel crooked, but there is always present that one tiny, forlorn spark of hope still glimmering in his soul, which makes him keep trying." When Kelly died, the persona of Weary Willie was passed on to his son, Emmett Kelly Jr., who continued to entertain a new generation with his adorable (unwashed, penniless, meths-drinking) antics. The trouble really started in the 1970s, when Emmett Jr.'s estranged, one-legged, bipolar son, Paul, decided that he was the "real" Weary Willie.

Paul lived in a two-bedroom flat ("one for me and one for Willie") in Oceanside, California. According to a contemporary account, Paul Kelly "introduced Willie to the local gay scene." We suspect that went down pretty well. In November 1979, he attended a Halloween costume party as Weary Willie, winning first prize. Second prize went to a man dressed as Charlie Chaplin. The two pantomime tramps hit it off, but "Charlie's" body was found in an aban-

Reality is just a crutch for people who can't cope with drugs.
—Robin Williams

doned car the following day sans costume and, regrettably, sans life. We would love to believe the story that the body was found by two *genuine* tramps, but it seems just a bit too creepily symmetrical to be true. Less than two weeks later, a sixty-seven-year-old Presbyterian minister met Kelly in a local pick-up joint, and was battered to death in his bedroom later that night. Paul Kelly was sentenced to life for both murders. His defense? The clown did it. Kelly claimed that he had only hit the minister once, but Weary Willie had hit him fifteen more times.

Stories like this, and that of John Wayne Gacy, serial murderer of thirty-three young boys and part-time clown, give rise to the persistent urban myth of the Killer Clown. Evil clowns appear in several films of the 1970s, but it wasn't until after the Gacy case hit the headlines that homicidal maniacs in greasepaint became a cinema staple. In fact, Gacy's interest in the circus arts was quite divorced from his murdering—he dressed as Pogo the Clown and entertained children as part of his outwardly respectable everyday life, rather than stalking the midnight streets of Norwood Park, Illinois, in oversized shoes and a red nose. Stephen King's novel *It* created a much more cinematic spectacle in sewer-dwelling supernatural clown killer Pennywise. The notion of pure evil thinly disguised as children's entertainer is irresistibly frightening. The flimsy brightness of a clown suit so horribly out of place is summed up in a quote often attributed to Lon Chaney, star of countless scary silent movies: "The essence of horror is a clown at midnight."

Before we leave this subject, let's be clear that, apart from the first Paul Kelly murder, we have not been able to find a single verifiable account of a crime committed in full

Two cannibals eating a clown. One says to the other, "Does this taste funny to you?"—*Tommy Cooper*

clown makeup. In real life a red fright wig and huge bow tie would strike even the most backward criminal as attention-grabbing attire, likely to be remarked on and remembered by passersby (later known as "witnesses"). Tip number one in Crime for Dummies is surely "Hooded tops are hated by policemen for a reason. When engaged in criminal activity, wear anonymous sportswear that disguises your physique and obscures your face," and not "When selecting the get-away vehicle, it's important to ensure that all four wheels fall off simultaneously as soon as the engine is started." The closest we could find to a proper, red-nosed Killer Clown that's still at large is a fiberglass Ronald McDonald statue at a certain fast-food franchise in Indiana. In 1992 Ronald fell on a six-year-old girl, who subsequently won $41,400 in damages for suffering a "malformed fingernail." That's what we call a Happy Meal.

Despite the dearth of evidence, the Killer Clown, like the Sad Clown, is an enduring myth. It's just another gig for the Trickster, who pops up again and again throughout history, his face painted in a thousand different guises. Societies develop their own clown rituals, both to contain the anarchy of the trickster spirits and to give their obscenity a safe outlet. Saturnalia gives way to Carnival and the Feast of Fools, Commedia dell'arte, and Punch and Judy. These days we keep our clowns in a sawdust circus ring, and arm them with nothing more dangerous than a squirty flower, a precariously balanced bucket of water and a banana skin. The Pueblo Indians of the American Southwest go in for a more organic approach, chucking buckets of urine over each other during their clowning ceremonies and pretending to eat feces. By all accounts, they are rather serious people most of the time, with a strict sense of their roles and

In spite of the cost of living, it's still popular.
—Kathleen Norris

responsibilities within the community. But on certain feast days, the clowns take over the pueblo and turn it upside down. Contravention of the everyday laws of purity and propriety is part and parcel of the clown's job; whitewash and custard pies may have replaced somewhat fouler missiles, but the principle of matter out of place and the sense of release from restrictive social rules are the same, whether we're in the plaza of a Zuni pueblo or the big top of Zippo's circus. Or, for that matter, at the studio recording of a Saturday morning kids' TV show, where hosts and pop stars splatter each other with gloop or climb into the punitive "gunk tank."

So why do we take our children to circuses and pantomimes, "family shows" that tap straight into our visceral responses to excretion, contamination and transgression? Because, until they get too self-aware, kids absolutely love it. They understand, in a way that we as adults only vaguely remember, that clowns are horrifying and hysterical in equal measure. We say, "I think clowns are really creepy/scary/sad; they're not cute/harmless/funny at all," as though we've discovered some startling hidden side that the clowns have inadvertently revealed. The truth is that clowns are supposed to be scary. They are dark and satirical and mischievous, just like the legendary trickster figures that spawned them. Wherever scary and funny collide, you can be sure to find the spirit of the joke.

There's a store in my neighborhood called Futon World. I love that name. It makes me think of a magical place . . . that gets less comfortable over time.—*Demetri Martin*

COMEDY BEGINS AT HOME

Tragically I was an only twin.—*Peter Cook*

You know when you're young, you think your dad is Superman. Then you grow up and you realize he's just a regular guy who wears a cape.—*Dave Attell*

I won't say ours was a tough school, but we had our own coroner. We used to write essays like "What I'm going to be if I grow up."—*Lenny Bruce*

Sex education at my school was a muttered warning about the janitor.—*Frankie Boyle*

The one thing I remember about Christmas was that my father used to take me out in a boat about ten miles offshore on Christmas Day, and I used to have to swim back. Extraordinary. It was a ritual. Mind you, that wasn't the hard part. The difficult bit was getting out of the sack.—*John Cleese*

Basically my wife is very immature. I'd be at home taking a bath and she'd come in and sink my boats.—*Woody Allen*

Somewhere on this globe, every ten seconds, there is a woman giving birth to a child. She must be found and stopped.
—*Sam Levenson*

I was asking a friend who has children, "What if I have a baby and I dedicate my life to it and it grows up to hate me, and it blames everything wrong with its life on me?" And she said, "What do you mean, if?"—*Rita Rudner*

By far the most common craving of pregnant women is not to be pregnant.—*Phyllis Diller*

I felt like a man trapped in a woman's body. Then I was born.
—*Chris Bliss*

I was raised by just my mom. See, my father died when I was eight years old. At least, that's what he told us in the letter.
—*Drew Carey*

Kids? It's like living with homeless people. They're cute but they just chase you around all day going, "Can I have a dollar? I'm missing a shoe! I need a ride!"—*Kathleen Madigan*

A Jewish grandmother is watching her grandchild playing on the beach when a huge wave comes and takes him out to sea. She pleads, "Please God, save my only grandson. I beg of you, bring him back." And a big wave comes and washes the boy back onto the beach, good as new. She looks up to heaven and says: "He had a hat!"

A woman gets on a bus with her baby. The bus driver says: "Ugh! That's the ugliest baby that I've ever seen."

The woman goes to the rear of the bus and sits down, fuming. She says to a man next to her: "The driver just insulted me!"

The man says: "You go right up there and tell him off. . . . Go ahead, I'll hold your monkey for you."

A small boy holds up an ice cream van. He says, "Give me everything you've got."

The woman says, "Do you want crushed nuts?" And the boy says, "Do you want your tits blown off?"
—*Tommy Cooper*

My dad was the town drunk. A lot of times that's not so bad, but New York City?—*Henny Youngman*

It's nonsense to say that children are affected by playing computer games. If Pac-Man had affected us as kids, we'd be running around in dark rooms, munching pills and listening to repetitive music.—*Marcus Brigstocke*

Mother always said, "If you haven't got anything nice to say, then fuck off."—*Jimmy Carr*

My grandfather started walking five miles a day when he was sixty. Now he's eighty-five and we don't know where the hell he is.—*Ellen DeGeneres*

CHAPTER FOUR

Only Kidding

In which we are intimidated by tiny children and their potty-mouthed joking antics, but survive to learn some universal truths.

When I was a kid I told my mother I wanted to grow up and be a comedian. She said, "You can't do both."

It's 3 P.M. on a sunny Sunday afternoon in Southwark, and the world's strangest comedy club is about to open. Tiny people hurtle around the bar like pinballs, shouting at each other to be heard above the din of ringtones being downloaded. Inside the theater, the crowd goes wild(er) as the host, a rakish, elastic-limbed man in his early thirties, bounds onto the stage. "Hello and welcome to the show. My name's James Campbell, and this is Comedy 4 Kids."

Like many childless, thirty-ish Londoners, we live our lives largely untroubled by people under four foot six. Venturing into this club makes us feel like anthropologists surrounded by a hostile tribe of pygmy bushmen. Despite our fear, we are determined to observe them objectively. The atmosphere is charged with energy: a potent cocktail of excitement, hilarity and the continual threat of low-grade physical violence. Where does all this energy come from? Well, it's not reassuring to note that many of the little darlings are hopped up on Diet Coke and cheesy crisps. We blame the parents, most of whom have discreetly chosen seats far enough away from their own children to be able to

Where would you weigh a whale?
At the whale-weigh station.

disclaim responsibility. We huddle a little closer together and contemplate moving to seats nearer the exit. We've read *Lord of the Flies;* we know what happens next. . . .

Miraculously, the next two hours pass off without major incident. Sure, it's anarchy, but Campbell is an old hand, tossing out half-formed jokes and riding the great waves of raw imagination that his young audience flings back at him. Two other professional comics, clearly terrified, present adapted versions of their adult sets. Both manage admirably, although at least one "Christ almighty!" does slip out in an unguarded moment. There's even the occasional piece of innuendo that whizzes over the children's heads and keeps us grown-ups happy. But the star of the show is Luca. He's nine years old and a graduate of Campbell's Comedy Academy, a weekly class for seven- to fifteen-year-olds. His mic technique and timing are excellent, and he has a nice riff about hamsters. He drops in a couple of classics with some insouciance. What do you call a woman with one leg? Eileen! What do you call a man with no shins? Tony!

Critics of the noble art of joking tend to dismiss it as a regressive tendency, something inherently childish. The Americans even gave us a new word for it—kidding—that places it explicitly in the playground. A kinder observer might counter that joking in adulthood allows us to access our elusive inner child, and thus recapture some of the exuberant anarchy of youth. But this would be to oversimplify the very serious function of jokes in children's lives—a seriousness which we play down and then suppress altogether

What's short, green and goes camping?
A Boy Sprout.

as we grow up. Learning to joke adds to our social skills, for sure. But it seems to do more than that. Watching the Comedy 4 Kids show, you don't just get a sense of the next generation of stand-ups and comedy fans beginning to take shape. You can also see the workings: watch consciousness and cognitive skills develop before your eyes. You can discern, in the raw expression of these children's jokes and responses, the outline of some of the vital cogs in our psychic machinery.

Almost as soon as they begin to learn language, children begin to play with words. Russian educationist Kornei Chukovsky was particularly struck by very young children's instinctive attraction to the nonsensical. He writes about "the inexhaustible need of every healthy child of every era and every nation to introduce nonsense into his small but ordered world, with which he has only recently become acquainted. Hardly has the child comprehended with certainty which objects go together and which do not, when he begins to listen happily to verses of absurdity. For some mysterious reason the child is attracted to that topsy-turvy world where legless men run, horses gallop astride their riders and cows nibble peas on top of birch trees." Which implies that we are hardwired from birth to enjoy the comedy of Dr. Seuss, Spike Milligan and Eddie Izzard.

Between the ages of about three and six, children laugh abundantly at their own and others' funny stories and surreal imaginings. The earliest verbal "jokes" that children tell are often to do with the deliberate misuse or misapprehension of names. Three- and four-year-olds find exchanging names, and especially exchanging genders, extremely amusing. Simply saying to your little classmate Peter, "You're Jane!" or telling Miss Jones, "You're a boy!" is considered the

What's big, red and eats rocks?
A big, red rock eater.

height of playgroup wit. Since the notion of novelty in a joke as a prerequisite for laughter is not yet established, this kind of thing can continue at great length. However, Miss Jones can comfort herself with the knowledge that this playful exploration of the flexibility of identities and descriptions helps children to grasp the notion that the name of the thing is not the thing itself, and that divorcing the two produces a startling effect. And they'll grow out of it at some point.

Once the process of institutionalization represented by formal education is properly under way, children begin to distance themselves a little from their earlier love of nonsense. The fetters of academic ambition tighten around their imaginations. By the time they reach the age of six or seven, children are more likely to dismiss nonsensical joking as "childish" or "silly." However, at around the same time they start to develop an interest in formal joking riddles, of the sort you used to find on Bazooka Joe wrappers. Why did the chicken cross the road? How can you tell if an elephant's hiding in your fridge? What do you get if you cross a sheep with a kangaroo? The crucial difference between this sort of joke and a younger child's funny story is that, although the answers to these riddles are also surreal, they have an internal logic and a single, inevitable answer. By the age of six, most schoolchildren are preoccupied with knowing the right answer to things. The scale of the task of learning that lies before them is just starting to become apparent, and this makes them anxious. A riddle gives them a double whammy: it's a question that you can easily learn the answer to, *and* you can get one over on your classmates because the answer seems impossible to guess. You, and you alone, possess the knowledge that it was (of course) to get

What happened to the cat who swallowed a ball of wool?
She had mittens.

to the other side, by the footprints in the butter and a woolly jumper. You also begin to understand that a joke is only funny the first time you hear it, because after that, you know the answer.

However many riddles we may learn at primary school, our understanding of the ground rules of joking is slower to develop. We know when a joke is funny, but we don't quite know how to explain, let alone replicate it. Many years ago, as a reluctant babysitter, Lucy was required to laugh loudly at the following effort, told by a seven-year-old with the characteristic intensity that children bring to the task of joking:

> Knock knock.
> *Who's there?*
> Maggie.
> *Maggie who?*
> Maggie Thatcher.

It may have been an early stab at political satire, but it's not exactly a joke.

Being a child is a deeply and continually frustrating predicament. You're always too little to do the things that bigger, more powerful adults—and even your only slightly bigger older brother—can do. You have an inadequate frame of reference for many of the events that make you anxious; most of them are hitting you for the very first time. As Jerry Seinfeld puts it, "When you're little, your life is up. Everything you want is up. 'Wait up! Hold up! Shut up! Mama, clean this up! Let me stay up!' With parents, of course, it's just the opposite. Everything is down: 'Just calm down! Slow down! Come down here! Sit down! Put that down!'"

How do you kill a circus?
Go for the juggler.

Jokes are one way for children to regain control of their surroundings, or at least to alleviate their sense of frustration and impotence. Jokes can help children to turn pain into laughter, make light of mistakes and ridicule the grown-ups whose powers they envy. A great many jokes that children enjoy play with the contrasts between big and little, child and adult. They feature impossible contradictions of scale, like elephants hiding in the fridge or in your pajamas. Or they show children getting one over on their teacher or parent, not by cleverness but by a certain deliberate naïveté, bordering on insolence:

> Teacher: *If you had a quarter, and you asked your dad for another quarter, how much would you have?*
> Boy: *Er . . . a quarter, sir.*
> Teacher: *You don't know your arithmetic, boy!*
> Boy: *You don't know my dad, sir.*

Joking is a particularly good device for deflecting the strictures of those in authority; this is true throughout our lives, but we learn the trick as children. Deliberately misunderstanding a parent or teacher probably supplies our first taste of the subversive joy that can be had through joking. "Put that away in the bottom drawer, Timothy!" "Mum! You said BOTTOM!" Jokes as weapons are useful in the playground too. All of us, particularly if we had (or were) a smart-arsed older sibling, must have heard this one, or something like it:

> What's frozen water?
> *Ice.*
> What's frozen cream?

They say cheese gives you nightmares. Ridiculous! I'm not scared of cheese.—*Ross Noble*

Ice cream.
What's frozen tea?
Iced tea.
What's frozen ink?
Iced ink.
Then take a bath!

This kind of joke sanctions our violent impulses by getting the victim to give us permission to hurt them, so that the wound is in effect self-inflicted. We can see a similar process in jokes where the victim is compelled to humiliate himself in some way, the simplest being, "How do you confuse a moron?" to which the answer is, "Thirty-two." The best playground jokes introduce an element of public humiliation too, by drawing loud attention to the victim. This is our favorite:

A: "*Are you a bummer tied to a tree?*"
B: "*No.*"
A *(shouts)*: "*BUMMER ON THE LOOSE! BUMMER ON THE LOOSE!*"

At the same time as our ear for humiliating language play is becoming attuned, we also start to develop our eye for physical comedy, or as it's otherwise known, extreme violence. By the time children reach the age of four, their taste for tickling and peek-a-boo games is usually superseded by a tendency to find sudden, extreme violence hilariously funny. They laugh, a lot, at people falling over. They even learn to laugh at themselves; having fallen over accidentally, but not

What's ET short for?
Because he's got little legs.

too seriously, they will often follow up with a deliberate pratfall in order to turn the unpleasant surprise of falling into something funny. That this link between violence and humor persists through our childhood—and indeed beyond—is confirmed by the young audience at James Campbell's show. At one point he asks, darkly, "You know what keeps me awake at night? Unanswered questions. Like, how much of yourself could you eat before you died?" Thanks, James. Now it's keeping us awake at night too. But the kids ooh and aah and guffaw. At the show's climax, a ten-year-old boy is up on stage helping to tie up a sword-swallowing lady escapologist named Miss Behave. (Just take our word for it—we'll explain later.) His gaggle of friends, mostly female, shouts from the back of the room in an orgy of aggression: "Yank it!" (of the chain around Miss Behave's neck), "Bash her head in!" and, most worryingly given that young Ryan is holding a sword, "Stick it in her!"

Which brings us neatly on to the second major thematic preoccupation (allegedly) of children's humor: sex. One of the less predictable problems with reading up on child psychology in the interests of researching a light-hearted romp through the world of the joke is that you end up wading through a lot of sticky Freudianism. According to Freud and his disciples, sexual curiosity, and frustration at not getting the whole story from Mum and Dad, are major driving forces in our childhood development, and the root cause of many if not all of our later neuroses. And as far as Freud is concerned, you may as well substitute the word "jokes" for the word "neuroses" there, because jokes are no more or less than symbolic representations of our darkest sexual fears. Among the many, many familiar objects that Freudians believe disguise a darker sexual meaning when

What do Alexander the Great and Winnie the Pooh have in common?
Same middle name.

they appear in a joke are houses, windows, hats, pets and falling over. One child psychologist particularly influenced by Freud's ideas was Martha Wolfenstein, an insightful and generally sensible observer of childhood joking. However, she's given to somewhat far-fetched interpretations of playground riddles: one of the most extreme involves the joke "What's black and white and re(a)d all over?" She claims that children are interested in this joke because, on the unconscious level, "black and white" represents a naked human body (white skin and black hair) and "red all over" represents blushing in shame at the exposure of nakedness. We can't help feeling the punch line she's really looking for is not the one she gives us—the children's choice of a harmless pun, "a newspaper"—but rather the adult version: What's black and white and red all over? A pregnant nun in the confessional.

The trouble is, once you're primed to seek phallic and vaginal symbols everywhere, you tend to find them. Even in a comedy show for kids. There's the bit where James rummages in the moist, forbidden folds of a lady's pink handbag—we exchange meaningful looks. A precocious twelve-year-old heckles, "You can't do that, it's a violation of human rights!" The air is suddenly thick with symbolism and the merest ghostly whiff of pipe tobacco. "Despite her imperfect grasp of the European Convention, she has inadvertently drawn attention to zis symbolic act of rape," whispers the spectral voice of Vienna's most famous son, who seems to have decided to haunt us for the afternoon. Then a child in the audience asks comic Matt Kirshen, "Why are you strangling the microphone like that?" Kirshen is indeed gripping the mic as though his life depended on it. "Because he is insecure about ze size of his penis,"

Knock knock
Who's there?
Interrupting sheep.
Interrupting sheep wh—
BAAAAAAA!

Freud helpfully bellows. And finally, the climax of the show features strapping, tattooed Miss Behave *swallowing a twelve-inch sword.* "Now zey are taking ze piss!" stammers the awestruck ghost, disappearing in a puff of innuendo.

We're on safer ground with pee and poo, which are perennial favorite joke topics for primary school children. Jokes about sex and bodily functions provide a way to say the unsayable. Children learn very early on to joke and laugh about these taboo topics, and from the evidence of the audience at Campbell's show, these jokes provide a necessary safety valve for all that roiling prepubescent energy. Any sort of mess and dirt—matter out of place—is a potential source of humor for children. As they learn that "making a mess" is wicked, they also learn to deal with this transgression safely within a world of jokes. Playful treatment of dirt is apparent in the practical-joking zone of mud pies and plastic doggie-do. It's the key to the appeal of the circus custard pie and the TV gunk tank, as we've already mentioned. But children are plenty mucky in their verbal jokes too. The "jokes" they make up themselves are often highly scatological; and of those adult-sanctioned jokes that kids enjoy, many of the most popular have muck concealed about their person somewhere. The old classic "What's brown and sticky? A stick" is a favorite mainly because the unspoken—unspeakable—punch line is a resounding cry of "Poooooo!"

From as early as three, children show a gleeful awareness of the shock value of rude words. At least that's what the books say, but we think it starts even earlier than that. Lucy was horrified when her two-year-old nephew began to

Knock knock!
Who's there?
Little old lady.
Little old lady who?
I didn't know you could yodel.

listen in to her conversations with his mother and single out, with unerring accuracy, the one careless word that would least stand up to public repetition. The dear little mite drew attention—quite effectively, it must be said—to his newfound skill at bathtime one night by shouting "SKANKY! SKANKY! SKANKY!" at the top of his lungs, while his mother and the World's Least Responsible Aunt frantically flushed toilets and ran taps in an effort to keep his grandmother in the dark about his rapidly expanding vocabulary. In fact, the innocently knowing child is a stock joke character in its own right. For example, there's the little boy who answers the door to a traveling salesman. The boy is wearing a smoking jacket and holding a glass of brandy in one hand and a fat cigar in the other. "Hello, son, are your parents in?" asks the salesman. "What the fuck do you think?" the boy replies jadedly.

Certainly much of the joy of watching a comedy show for kids, as an adult, is wrapped up in the smaller audience members' responses. Their imperfect grasp of the full comic potential of their own comments is funny in itself. By this point you will have realized that the Comedy 4 Kids show involves a fair degree of audience participation. In fact this is the most striking point of difference from a mainstream adult comedy club. Contrary to popular opinion, regular comedy clubs (with a couple of notable and notorious exceptions) are actually incredibly orderly places, governed by a very strict set of social rules. Just listen to the tutting when a drunk tries one heckle too many. But here among the hostile pygmies, any social constraints that are in operation are only dimly apparent. You can sit upside down in your chair, pull your dress up over your face, shout out whatever comes into your head, wave your arms around in

I was walking down the street and I saw a dead baby ghost in the road.
On reflection, it might have been a handkerchief.
—Milton Jones

front of the comedian's face in a transparent bid to draw attention to yourself. When, in a routine about Spider-Man, James asks his audience, "Has anybody here been bitten by anything on a school trip?" *every single* small hand in the audience goes up. "Really?" he says. "You've *all* been bitten on a school trip? What were you bitten by?" Most of the hands go down at this point, but some more enterprising ones shoot up again. "A ROCK!" roars one gleeful girl. "I was bitten by a rock and my special power is standing still!" "Aha, Rock Girl, mortal enemy of Scissors Man!" ad-libs Kirshen. It's a room full of hecklers, and hecklers unfettered by any but the lightest bonds of logic.

It's also striking that although these children are mostly old enough to "get" joking, the pleasure they derive from it seems far from simple. They don't respond to every half-decent punch line with a shout of laughter, in the way that adults in a similar situation would. They haven't yet learned that their response to a joke is a social signal, so in some ways their laughter, when it does come, is purer and less qualified. But a lot of the time they seem rather solemn, particularly when they watch little Luca perform. In fact, it's very much like sitting in a room full of stand-up comics; rather than laughing, they greet each joke with a grudging acknowledgment as they try to commit it to memory, and they visibly yearn to try to cap it with one of their own. This undoubtedly says more about stand-up comics than about seven-year-olds.

The textbook preoccupations of children's jokes are little different from their adult counterparts: playful violence,

What's orange and sounds like a parrot?
A carrot.

sexual curiosity, anxiety about physical shortcomings, frustration and impotence in the face of an unfair world. A great many stand-up comedians, like a lot of people who are funny in private, get their start in the playground. The smart-mouthed misfit is likely to learn very early on that if you can make your peers laugh, attention and status will follow. There does seem to be a certain type of contrary child who is drawn to comedic behavior. James Campbell explains, "In most schoolrooms, you have perhaps one class clown, the child who answers back. . . . My problem is I have to teach a whole class of those kids."

Psychologist Oliver James wrote recently, "It's very hard to be adult in a developed nation and retain the spontaneity and inventiveness found in three-year-olds without being mad, personality disordered or employed as an artist." But, claims James, "these childlike attributes are the cornerstone of mental well-being." What society chooses to call "mad" is sometimes just creativity out of context. An ability to sit loose in the saddle, to take a flexible approach to the conventionally assigned meanings of things, comes naturally to children and crazy people. It's an essential skill for a good comedian too. Deadpan Boston existentialist Steven Wright once analyzed his comedy as "the thoughts of a child, with an adult voice." He asks all the "Why?" questions that an intelligent eight-year-old might. "Kids haven't been brainwashed yet. You tell a kid the line's busy, he might want to know what it's doing."

As the connections we make between objects, their names and their functions become ossified, and our obedience to social rules becomes absolute, we unwittingly restrict our creative options. Mel Brooks says that the best comedians have managed to hang on to a childlike quality,

What do you call cheese that isn't yours?
Nacho Cheese.

despite all this. "All of us have the heartache of lost innocence, of innocence betrayed by reality. The great comics—their cry is . . . what happened to the joy of just being alive?" All the hard lessons of adolescence and adulthood are apt to suppress the delight in free association that we experienced as children. Luckily, a good joke can offer even the stuffiest of adults the opportunity to throw open an internal window onto the fresh, freewheeling creativity of childish imagination.

What do you call a fish with no eyes?
A fsh.

EAT, DRINK AND BE MERRY

I went to a restaurant that serves "breakfast at any time." So I ordered French toast during the Renaissance.—*Steven Wright*

If you eat a lot of spicy food, you can damage your sense of taste. When I was in India last year I was listening to a lot of Michael Bolton.—*Jimmy Carr*

I can't cook. I use a smoke alarm as a timer.—*Carol Siskind*

Give a man a fish and he eats for the day. Teach him to how to fish and you get rid of him for the whole weekend. —*Zenna Schaffer*

Build a man a fire and he'll be warm for a day. Set a man on fire and he'll be warm for the rest of his life.—*Terry Pratchett*

Old Jewish lady to her friend: "The food in this restaurant is terrible."

"Yes, and such small portions!"

A man goes into a restaurant and says, "How do you prepare the chicken?" "We don't," replies the waiter. "We just tell it straight that it's going to die."

A man orders a pizza and the clerk asks if he should cut it into six pieces or twelve. "Make it six," says the man. "I could never eat twelve."

A sandwich walks into a bar. The barman says, "Sorry, we don't serve food in here."

Two muffins are in the grill. The first muffin says, "Boy, it's hot in here." The second muffin says, "I don't believe it! A talking muffin!"

People say, "Now you've given up booze at least you can remember what you did last night." I say, "Yeah, nothing." —*Frank Skinner*

A man walks into a bar carrying an alligator. He says to the patrons, "Here's the deal. I'll open this alligator's mouth and place my genitals inside. The alligator will close his mouth for one minute, then open it, and I'll remove my unit unscathed. If it works, everyone buys me drinks." The crowd agrees. The man drops his pants and puts his privates in the alligator's mouth. The alligator closes its mouth. After a minute, the man grabs a beer bottle and bangs the alligator on the top of its head. The alligator opens wide, and he removes his genitals unscathed. Everyone buys him drinks. Then he says: "I'll pay anyone $100 who's willing to give it a try." After a while, a hand goes up in the back of the bar. It's a woman. "I'll give it a try," she says, "but you have to promise not to hit me on the head with the beer bottle."

A priest, a rabbi and a vicar walk into a bar. The barman says, "Is this some kind of joke?"

A woman walks into a bar and asks for a double entendre—so the barman gives her one.

A guy meets a hooker in a bar. She says, "This is your lucky night. I've got a special game for you. I'll do absolutely anything you want for $300, as long as you can say it in three words." The guy replies, "Hey, why not?" He pulls his wallet out of his pocket, and one at a time lays three hundred-dollar bills on the bar, and says, slowly: "Paint . . . my . . . house."

It's night and a drunk is crawling along the pavement looking for something. A passerby offers to help and asks what's missing. The drunk replies that he's lost his watch. "And whereabouts did you lose it?" asks the passerby. "About half a mile up the road," replies the drunk. "So what are you doing down here?" asks the passerby. The drunk replies, "Down here the lighting is better."

Two drunks are walking down the street when they come across a dog, sitting on the curb, licking its privates. They watch for a while before one of them says, "I sure wish I could do that!" The other looks at him and says, "Wouldn't you like to make friends with him first?"

CHAPTER FIVE

Nuts, Bolts and Hydraulic Brains

In which we unpick some philosophical arguments about humor, and try not to spoil everyone's fun.

Analyzing humor is like dissecting a frog. Few people are interested, and the frog dies.

E. B. WHITE

In 1937, Max Eastman wrote a book called *Enjoyment of Laughter*. As it turns out, the title is somewhat misleading. The introduction explains, with lugubrious irony:

> *I must warn you, reader, that it is not the purpose of this book to make you laugh. As you know, nothing kills the laugh quicker than to explain a joke. I intend to explain all jokes, and the proper and logical outcome will be, not only that you will not laugh now, but that you will never laugh again. So prepare for the descending gloom.*

It is fortunate for Mr. Eastman's sales, though not for his misled readers, that this quote did not appear on the book's jacket. But he has a point—as soon as a joke needs to be explained, it ceases to make us laugh. There's no sadder predicament than an academic sense of humor that recognizes certain jokes as funny but cannot release a spontaneous laugh. In the main, the body of scholarship on the subject of humor is stubbornly unfunny. This is probably

You are never going to fail unless you try.

because the academics who study humor are fed up with being ridiculed by colleagues who are researching "proper" subjects, and sick of being asked to say something funny at conferences. Or it could be that the field attracts mainly those individuals who, lacking a sense of humor themselves, seek an explanation for this dangerous and alien condition. They therefore approach the subject much as a microbiologist might approach a virus. The unpalatable alternative explanation is that studying jokes actually eats away at your ability to find them funny, leaving you permanently humor-impaired—a fate too horrible to contemplate.

But do take heed: even for the casual reader, joke overdose is a very real risk. Jokes, like martinis, are not designed to be consumed in private in enormous quantities. They live out loud, in a social context. Take us, for example: in the process of researching this book we must have sifted through over twenty thousand jokes, mostly in solitary silence. About halfway through the process Lucy went temporarily "joke-blind"—an affliction that renders the sufferer incapable of distinguishing a funny joke from a hopeless one. Jimmy, already acclimatized to the strange and rarefied air of the high joke country, was completely unaffected. The antidote, by the way, is a quick dose of misery: a walk in the drizzling rain, a touch of Sylvia Plath or a few bars of Leonard Cohen are usually enough to reinvigorate one's appetite for the lighter side of life.

Humor scholarship—sense of humor optional—is not a modern invention. Joking and laughter have fascinated philosophers for more than two millennia. We promised, at the start of this book, that we wouldn't weigh you down with theories of comedy. And we tried, we really did. Sev-

Tragedy is when I cut my finger. Comedy is when you fall into an open sewer and die.—*Mel Brooks*

eral whole chapters went past, breezy, buoyant and very nearly theory-free. We stuck to simple observations and funny stories about monkeys. We didn't get too metaphysical on yo' ass. So as we gaze navel-ward and contemplate the forthcoming onslaught of theorizing, we could be forgiven for feeling some trepidation: Can we explain a little about how jokes work without ruining them for everyone? Can we keep that poor dissected frog on life support? Nothing ventured, nothing gained. . . .

We tried to count all the different theories of humor we came across, but gave up somewhere north of a hundred. That's when we realized, to our great relief, that there are really only four main principles that help to explain what's going on when you tell a joke. So here they are.

SUPERIORITY

The Superiority Theory implies that the point of joking is to feel better about our sorry selves by mocking people or situations that we find ridiculous. This is probably the oldest attempt to explain what's going on when we tell jokes, dating back at least as far as Aristotle, who called humor "educated insolence." Seventeenth-century stand-up Thomas Hobbes thought that laughter was "nothing else but a sudden glory arising from some sudden conception of some eminency in ourselves, by comparison with the infirmity of others." Later refinements of the theory suggest that we also gain some psychological comfort from laughing at people who we purport to find ridiculous, but secretly hate and fear. The superiority idea was revisited by Henri Bergson in his famous 1900 essay "Laughter and the

I used to think that the brain was the greatest organ in the human body, then I realized, "Hey! Look what's telling me that!"—*Emo Philips*

Meaning of the Comic." He thought that in making a joke or in laughing at one we are experiencing a spontaneous failure of empathy, and the situations that strike us as comic are those that enable us to see a human being as somehow mechanical, as less than human. For Bergson, joking had a social purpose: to ridicule eccentricity, thus brushing aside any untidy idiosyncrasies and weaknesses that might otherwise constitute trip-hazards on the pathway of society.

More recently, Charles R. Gruner has developed a new Superiority Theory that reads joking as a playful game, but one with clear winners and losers. Finding the winner and loser isn't always simple. Often, the joke-teller "wins" and the audience "loses"; for example, in the case of a riddle where the teller's intention is to leave an audience stumped. Even simple puns can be seen as expressions of superiority according to this reading, since the punner intends to prove himself intellectually superior to his audience. Other jokes have a clearer butt—an Irishman, a lawyer or some other hapless (deserving?) victim—and joke-teller and audience both "win" at the expense of the character in the joke. Clearly this will to win is the motivation behind a lot of humor, and a useful explanation of our response to certain jokes. We've surely all come across an individual in our own social circle who uses jokes to score points, usually at the expense of actual humor.

To illustrate the Superiority Theory, Jimmy has reluctantly decided to sacrifice one of his own jokes as a specimen for dissection. He's fished out one of the weaker ones from the shallow end of the pond and pegged it out, ready for the scalpel. Like Abraham leading Isaac to the rock, he proffers it with a heavy heart but in the knowledge that

You cannot have everything. I mean where would you put it?
—Steven Wright

duty must be done. Good-bye, old friend. After this, you'll never be funny again. . . .

> *I'm not gay. Unless you're from Newcastle, and by "gay" you mean "owns a coat."*

This joke does not exist in a vacuum. In its natural habitat, it's told by an extremely smartly dressed, well-spoken man in his early thirties. A casual British observer tends immediately to assume that he: (a) hails from the moneyed middle classes of the Home Counties, (b) received an expensive public school education, and (c) does not like football. In actual fact, only one of these things is true. And even football's OK in small doses. But Jimmy's stage persona is posh, highly educated, slightly fastidious. So superficially, this joke may seem a straightforward expression of superiority over those tough Northern working-class lads who proverbially go about the "toon" in their shirtsleeves even in the dead of winter. For Bergson, this joke would read as an attempt by a man of a certain class in a particular region to assert both his masculinity and his heterosexuality by excluding and ridiculing another regional type, whose aggressive masculinity implies a threat to his own identity.

You could choose to regard the joke as a straightforward assertion of superiority on Jimmy's part, but that doesn't explain everything that's going on. For example, while it undoubtedly mocks the menfolk of Newcastle, at least part of the mockery rebounds back onto the comic's stage persona, as the audience gets a laugh from his supercilious air and his apparent defensiveness at the suggestion that you might think he was homosexual. According to

These are my principles. If you don't like them, I have others.—*Groucho Marx*

superiority theorists, joking is a multifaceted power game in which the joke-teller and his audience play with ideas of who's superior to whom.

The Superiority Theory requires us to see *all* jokes as acts of playful aggression, the verbal equivalent of a tickling attack. The joke is a power struggle played out for our entertainment. It's easy to see the aggression in jokes like this:

> *Men are like carpet tiles. Lay them right and you can walk all over them for the next thirty years.*

The female teller and the female half of the audience supposedly "win," while the thinly sliced men "lose." (Although there's a powerful whiff of self-hatred about the joke as well, so perhaps we're all losers.) If you're determined to find it, you can locate aggression in every joke, however innocent it might at first appear. But it's apparent to us that it will take more than one theory to explain how *all* jokes work. Eddie Izzard once told a joke that went something like this:

> *The other night I went to a bar, had a few jars. Then I went to another bar . . . had another couple of jars. Then I met some friends and we went to a nightclub, and I had a few jars. . . . That was enough jam for me.*

Well, you can award the medal and the wooden spoon to this particular joker and his audience in any way you will. You can have it both ways, implying either that we're winning by laughing at Izzard's stupidity and/or that he's got one over on us by leading us up the garden path. But it's

Sincerity is everything. If you can fake that, you've got it made.—*George Burns*

just not as simple as laughter = winning. For one thing, if we accept the winner/loser model where the joke-teller "wins" on account of his cleverness, then it's normally the loser (audience) who's rewarded with the pleasure of laughter. And a clever joke that is too clever for the audience to "get" is mortifying for the joke-teller—he has failed, not his audience. The competitive aspect of joking is always there (if you look for it), but it's not the only, or even the primary, catalyst for laughter. Groucho Marx said that this is why good comedy is so much harder to pull off than tragedy, because "people laugh in many different ways, but they cry in only one."

INCONGRUITY

The Incongruity Theory was described badly by Immanuel Kant in 1790 when he said that laughter "is an affectation arising from the sudden transformation of strained expectation into nothing." Even allowing for a certain amount of style being lost in translation, that still sounds more like a wet fart than a laugh. His grouchy compatriot Schopenhauer later elaborated on this, defining humor as "the incongruity between a concept and the real object to which it was designed to relate." And what hilarious gag did Arthur Schopenhauer put forward to support his theory? "For example, the amusing look of the angle formed by the meeting of the tangent and the curve of the circle." Yes, Frankfurt positively rocked with laughter in the 1840s—the golden age of German comedy.

This theory essentially explains the classic joke structure we discussed in the last chapter. The setup of a joke

Cleanliness is next to impossible.—*Audrey Austin*

creates a scenario with an assumed conclusion; the punch line provides a quite different conclusion, which subverts your previously held assumptions about the joke scenario. The way this is done often exploits some ambiguity in the language of the joke, as well as inverting certain conventions of social behavior. For example:

How do you make a dog drink?
Put him in a blender.

The English language is particularly rich in homophones (words that sound the same but differ in meaning) and homonyms (words that sound the same and are spelled identically, but differ in meaning). It therefore lends itself very well to precisely this sort of wordplay. In the joke above, for example, the two implied meanings of the word "drink" are homonyms: a verb (meaning imbibe) and a noun (meaning beverage). This last paragraph is also a perfect example of how to ruin a joke by subjecting it to linguistic analysis. Just so you know.

It's not just the words that make a joke work. The best jokes use language with skill and economy to conjure up mental pictures that are hilarious by virtue of their incongruity, shock value or just sheer silliness. Here's a lovely one:

Two monkeys are having a bath.
One turns to the other and says, "Oo oo ah ah!"
The other replies, "Well, put the cold tap on then."

This joke presents a funny picture to start with—who wouldn't laugh at two monkeys in a bath? Then the teller does a monkey impression, making the mental picture even

I ordered a wake-up call the other day. The phone rang and a woman's voice said, "What the hell are you doing with your life?"—*Demetri Martin*

more vivid. Finally, the punch line applies a dizzy little twist to the image, when the second monkey turns out to be a fully developed character—a sort of exasperated older brother whom some of us might well recognize from joint bathing experiences of our own childhood.

It's clear that even the simplest one-liner can be prodded and poked and analyzed within an inch of its life using a combination of the Superiority and Incongruity models. But wait—there's more.

AMBIVALENCE

According to this concept of humor, our laughter is the symptom of an internal battle between opposing emotions. In 1653 Louis Joubert sowed the seeds of this theory when he proposed that comic laughter is an emotion located in the heart. When we experience a conflict between joy and sadness, the heart shakes the diaphragm, resulting in laughter. A century or so later James Beattie wrote that laughter is evoked by "an opposition of suitableness and unsuitableness." William Hazlitt also contributed to this school of thought, noting in 1819 that "the jostling of one feeling against another" was an essential element of the comical. In recent years the platform for this debate has been increasingly philosophical rather than physiological—less emphasis on shaky diaphragms and even shakier anatomical knowledge—but for all these theorists, laughter is an outward sign of inward conflict. Psychologist J. Y. T. Greig asserts that all humor is based on a conflict between love and fear, while George Milner suggests that the clash between culture and nature is to blame.

People often say to me, "What are you doing in my garden?"
—Michael Redmond

Let's go back to the gay/owns a coat joke. (It's twitching feebly on the dissection table, but we think it's good for one more lesson.) According to the Ambivalence Theory, we might speculate that we respond to this joke because it juxtaposes the two essentially conflicting notions of short-sleeved Geordie lads (excessively macho) and velvet-coated homosexuals (excessively feminine), and establishes normality as a point somewhere between the two. Or that we love the Southern dandy and fear the rough Northerner. Or that the coatless individual represents nature in all her raw, untrammeled power, and the bejacketed fop (J. Carr Esq.) is the epitome of civilized (emasculated, self-indulgent) culture. Or, with Joubert, that we laugh because we are unsure whether to feel happy for the man with a coat or sad for the man who has none. According to ambivalence theorists, laughter is essentially a wobble of uncertainty—even, perhaps, a snort of embarrassment, of not knowing how to react.

It's a nice theory, but it's a bit sweeping. For a start, not every "jostling of one feeling against another" results in humor—far from it. Ambivalence about such existential oppositions as love and fear is more likely to result in uncertainty, brow-furrowing and panic attacks, even though joking about it might help to diminish the angst. You could also argue that the tension between nature and culture defines the human condition, not just the psychology of humor. As human beings, we are also apes aspiring to the condition of angels. The results of this struggle seldom rise above the farcical. So in effect, all the Ambivalence Theory of humor tells us is that we think, therefore we laugh.

People come up to me and say, "Emo, do people really come up to you?"—*Emo Philips*

The Release Theory sees jokes as a sort of pressure valve: a socially sanctioned way of letting out taboo thoughts and feelings. Like the Superiority Theory, it assumes that the joke is an aggressive social act, but crucially that it is also a subversive act, a rebellion against the constraints of rational adult behavior. It can be a useful way to understand people's penchant for off-color jokes, and the frequency with which humor is used to mask hostility or fear. It's also a good way to explain the popularity of comedy clubs, where people go to "let off steam" by laughing.

Sigmund Freud had a lifelong fascination with jokes, and wrote a book, *The Joke and Its Relation to the Unconscious*, that attempts to shoehorn his ideas about joking into his life's work of psychoanalysis. It seems that in the course of his more famous research on the interpretation of dreams, Freud was struck by the similarities between the topsy-turvy logic of the dream world and that of the joke world. Dreams and jokes seemed to him to be parallel universes where reason does not rebel against absurd premises, such as "A horse walked into a bar . . ."[1] Or "Doctor, Doctor, I think I'm a pair of curtains."[2]

Taking the argument in huge illogical strides, Freud reasoned that if dreams are the spontaneous nocturnal emissions of the psyche, a way of processing information that is not available to or is suppressed by the patient's conscious mind, perhaps jokes serve a similar function during our waking hours. He argued that a joke, like a dream, comes from beyond or beneath the conscious mind and that the jokes we tell reveal our hidden neuroses even as they relieve them. The pleasure that we get from telling a

[1] *The barman said, "Why the long face?"*

[2] *"For goodness' sake, pull yourself together!"*

I've been married seven times—all to women named Brenda. It's just a coincidence. The psychiatrists can make anything they like of that, but as my mom, Brenda, used to say . . .
—Rich Hall (as Otis Lee Crenshaw)

joke, or from laughing at it, comes from satisfying some element of our libido that we can't openly reveal, because our culture and society forbids us to do so. Freud did at least concede that some witticisms are harmless, satisfying merely our appetite for nonsense. But he didn't find these funny; he was far more interested in "tendentious" jokes—that is, the dirty ones. Every joke that really makes you laugh, according to this reading, is either an act of veiled sexual aggression or a cry for help stemming from some childhood sexual trauma. On a brighter note, the very act of telling the joke is a sort of pressure valve that relieves some of the built-up libidinal steam we're all repressing.

Freud's attempts to turn psychoanalysis into a science were influenced by earlier theories that explained the workings of the brain in terms of hydraulics. Yes, that's right. The brain pumps some sort of sticky psychic liquid around your system, and various actions and reactions, both mechanical and emotional, result. Oh, come on, cut them a little slack, you sneering space-age skeptics. After all, nowadays we still discuss the human body in technological terms—think of "genetic engineering"—and doubtless the next great scientific advance will give us a new model. Hydraulics was the best technological model available at the time. In 1860 Herbert Spencer published an essay, "The Physiology of Laughter," that asserted that certain spectacles or statements caused a buildup of psychic energy in the brain, which then overflowed suddenly, making the noise of laughter. Specifically he thought laughter resulted when a person's expectation of a momentous event was undermined by the occurrence of an inconsequential event—a refinement of the Incongruity Theory we discussed above.

I had dinner with my father last night, and made a classic Freudian slip. I meant to say, "Please pass the salt," but it came out, "You prick, you ruined my childhood."—*Jonathan Katz*

Spencer's theories were further developed by Freud's contemporary and fellow psychoanalyst Theodor Lipps. Herr Lipps[3] reasoned that the conscious mind represents the uppermost pond of a series of reservoirs, and that raising a thought into the conscious mind requires an expenditure of energy: Thinking is like pushing water uphill. It takes great effort to push weighty thoughts up into the reservoir of consciousness—thoughts about our own unavoidable mortality, perhaps, or why popular brands of candy seem smaller than they did when we were children. If we suddenly have to make this effort with no warning, we are unprepared and it's especially hard. If, on the other hand, we are all ready to tackle a question of life and death and it turns out to be nothing of the sort, all that pent-up energy we've prepared comes whooshing back down in a waterfall of laughter. Laughter is the pleasurable result of the psychic energy we save when our expectations of something effortful are rewarded with a feeling of effortlessness.

[3]Sometimes the jokes just write themselves.

The cardinal error that Spencer and Lipps made was to mistake an elegant metaphor for a scientifically observable model, and it's a trap that Freud too fails to sidestep. Perhaps he was seduced by the almost poetic parallel between his own theories of the subconscious libido and the notion of those internal lakes of bubbling liquid energy. The trouble is that Sigmund was never one to let the facts get in the way of a good theory, and his theory demands that pretty much every single human action is motivated solely by the surging tides of sexual appetite. One of his footnotes explains, quite erroneously, that a baby first laughs when "the satisfied and satiated nursling . . . drowsily quits the breasts." This un-fact he sees as proof that laughter denotes

Imagine if there were no hypothetical situations.

the satisfaction of a deep libidinal urge. A Freudian slip: to say one thing while thinking about a mother.

But Freud was right about jokes in at least one important way. Dirty jokes often are more laugh-provoking and more liberating than clean ones. Compare, for example, the following:

How do you make a dog drink?
Put him in a blender.

How do you stop a dog from humping your leg?
Pick him up and suck his cock.

The second joke takes the first as a model and subverts it, relying for its humor not just on the incongruity of the notion that you can avert the social embarrassment experienced when a dog attempts to mate with your leg by indulging in a spot of canine fellatio, but on the taboo nature of the image. No doubt Freud would go further, and tell us that our enjoyment of the joke reveals a suppressed interest in bestiality.

Freud's theory is best applied as a sort of creative practical criticism, in that you can take the text of any joke and impute a hidden sexual motive to it, if that's what turns you on. Freud's followers continue, to this day, to come up with truly ingenious ways of finding libidinal subtexts wherever they look. And not just in the obviously "dirty" jokes. Any hollow object in a joke—a door, a cup, a hat—represents the female sex organ. Any juxtaposition of great and small—a mouse and an elephant, an adult and a child—represents anxiety over penis size. It's a great game, but ultimately fails to explain the psychology of jokes to anybody's great satisfaction. Perhaps this is because it says more about

According to Freud, what comes between fear and sex?
Fünf.

the person who's analyzing the joke than about the original joke-teller and tellee. If you go looking for concealed sexual motives in the text of a particular joke, it's like scattering coins with one hand while wielding the metal detector with the other.

Usually the narrative of a particular joke—however many hats or elephants it involves—is far less deserving of psychological analysis than how, where and to whom it is told. Most hostilities and neuroses are exposed by the joke's surface details rather than hidden within the narrative it describes. For example, there's a typically unedifying Bernard Manning joke about "a Paki in Yorkshire who wants converting. So they take him to Headingley and boot him over the crossbar." Manning "adapted" this from an older joke concerning an atheist who goes to a Welsh Methodist chapel and asks to be converted. The congregation takes him to the village rugby pitch and boots him, etc., etc. It's a joke about the twin Welsh passions for Methodism and rugby, which Manning has converted into a conscious expression of racial hatred. By twisting the original joke to fit his own agenda, Manning moves the goalposts and makes it a specific racial attack; no need to look for hidden meanings here. Manning's bigotry, fear of difference and desperate need to cling to a macho world of violence and intimidation are hardly buried in his subconscious. He wears his colors proudly on his sleeve, except he calls them "common sense." Equally, these dark squirmings of the id are pretty much absent from the Welsh version of the joke, even though it is structurally almost identical. A man still gets kicked over a rugby goal, but somehow it's *nothing personal.*

Sigmund Freud labored under a great need to be right about everything, to explain or expose to people things that

Before you criticize someone, you should walk a mile in their shoes. That way, when you criticize them, you're a mile away and you have their shoes.—*Jack Handey*

they themselves did not know. Lucy thinks it's because he was a Taurean and they are very stubborn. Jimmy thinks it's because he was a man. Whatever the reason, this tendency might also explain his fascination with jokes. Jokes confer a certain power on the teller in that they contain a story in which the hearer is very unlikely to be able to guess what happens next by applying conventional logic. They are ambivalent, and only the joke-teller is allowed to pick the "right" answer. So Freud insists on everyone else being very much less perceptive than he, both in his treatment of dreams and his treatment of jokes. And, it could be argued, in his treatment of his patients. He would like you to believe that you, the patient, cannot satisfactorily explain why you like to tell or laugh at a certain joke; only Dr. Freud can do that for you. Your motives are hidden even from yourself. In fact, the truth is that every dream and every joke is open to a very great many different possible explanations, and not all of them involve our neuroses and phobias.

Like any other theory of the psychology of humor, Freud's works adequately in library conditions but tends to fall apart in a real joke-telling situation. We'll leave the last word on the matter to Ken Dodd: "Freud's theory was that when a joke opens a window and all those bats and bogeymen fly out, you get a marvelous feeling of relief and elation. The trouble with Freud is that he never had to play the old Glasgow Empire on a Saturday night after Rangers and Celtic had both lost."

So there you have it: four schools of thought, each of which is passionately defended by its devotees. Each of the

Nostalgia just ain't what it used to be.

theories is useful, but it's crazy to attempt to analyze all jokes using just one of them. The Superiority Theory makes jokes a product of pure emotion and instinct: aggressive, masculine, competitive. The Incongruity and Ambivalence theories see jokes as products of reason, crediting us all with perhaps too much cognitive clarity. And the Release Theory tries to mirror the physical pleasure of laughter with a similar psychological response.

As we've seen, Freud believed that the jokes you enjoy are highly psychologically revealing. We'd like to suggest that it's the *theory* of humor that most appeals to you that provides a more accurate personality test. The truth is that you can't help but invest jokes with something of your own character. Take, for example, the academic Charles R. Gruner, passionate advocate of the Superiority Theory of humor. He makes clever and persuasive arguments for jokes as a competitive social behavior. Every joke, to Gruner, has a winner and a loser—however innocent it may initially seem. Imagine our surprise when Gruner reveals himself to be perhaps the most competitive man ever in the whole gory history of academic one-upmanship. In his 1997 book, *The Game of Humor*, he reaffirms his long-running challenge to his academic peers to produce one single joke that he can't prove has a winner and a loser, and devotes the entire last chapter to updating us on the scalps he's collected so far.

Another case in point is Gershon Legman,[4] arch-Freudian and self-styled erotic humor expert. Although clearly drawn to certain macho aspects of the Superiority Theory, he's a Release man through and through. Legman collected dirty jokes compulsively for fifty years, but didn't find them at all funny. In fact he was pretty disgusted by the practice of joking. "Under the mask of humor, our society

[4] *Honestly, we're not making up these names.*

I have kleptomania. But when it gets bad, I take something for it.—*Ken Dodd*

allows infinite aggressions, by everyone and against everyone." In this reading, every joke is an aggressive attempt by the teller to "slough off" his own hang-up by passing it on to the tellee. In doing so, the joker strips the audience naked by drawing attention to sexual or otherwise taboo attributes, normally left concealed by tacit agreement. Legman classifies sexual jokes as "verbal rape," and believes that a person's favorite joke is deeply revealing of the person's own neuroses.

His most famous book, *No Laughing Matter: The Rationale of the Dirty Joke*, was published in 1968. The book enumerates and analyzes over two thousand jokes, categorizing them according to which particular hang-up they expose. Topics include incest, bestiality, pedophilia and, perhaps most horrifying of all, marriage. Legman suggests that the proliferation of jokes about wives can lead us to the conclusion that "monogamic marriage, as practiced in the West, is actually the principle focus of male sexual anxiety." Well, it certainly seems to be the principle focus of Legman's anxiety: not a notable monogamist, he was married four times—once bigamously and twice to the same woman (she took him back after the bigamy escapade). During his short-lived tenure at San Diego University in the early sixties (he was banned from teaching after just one semester) and while his first wife, Beverley, was dying of lung cancer in their home in France, he boasted that "as a single man in a college town full of father-complex kids. . . . I had a wall-to-wall freshman girl carpet, and it nearly killed me." That's the trouble with being a Freudian—you just can't help but be hoist with your own phallic petard.

While he was undoubtedly a fearless seeker of truth, Legman's analysis of the world of jokes is not without bias.

Life doesn't imitate art—it imitates bad television.
—Woody Allen

Eagle-eyed readers may discern in him a certain predisposition to see the smutty side of things. Let's examine the evidence: His first book, published under a pseudonym in 1939, was a practical manual named *Oragenitalism*, dealing earnestly with "Oral Techniques in Genital Excitation for Gentlemen." In later life his prowess in the field of erotic origami was much admired; he designed the definitive folded-paper genitals (both male and female) but fell out with the United States Origami Association in a dispute over a badly bent corner. He worked for a while as a researcher for the daddy of all sexologists, Alfred Kinsey, occupying himself with an ultimately unsuccessful attempt to establish the average length of the American male member. He also claimed to have invented the "vibrating dildo." Reading about Legman's life, it's tempting to cast him as another reincarnation of the mythic trickster figure: sexually prolific, a compulsive agitator, living on the boundaries of the acceptable, brandishing his vibrator at the shocked matron of academia. The man himself acknowledged that even his own name was a sort of dirty joke—although it turns out he was actually a breast man.

A joke on paper is a pale and inadequate one-dimensional reproduction of itself. It scarcely exists until someone has told it and someone else has laughed—or not. The who, where, when, what and why of its telling can be more significant than the topic or implication of the joke itself. Context is everything. That's why it's so hard to argue, on paper, for one single underlying philosophy to explain how jokes work. None of the four theories we've discussed here

Go ahead and play the blues if it'll make you happy.
—Homer Simpson

will explain every joke or every response to that joke, although each of them will work some of the time.

Jokes are a bit like fairground mirrors. We can't help but see our gruesome reflections winking back at us from the jokes we enjoy. If you are a heartily competitive individual, like Dr. Gruner, you probably do use humor as a weapon, if you use it at all. You are drawn to the kind of jokes that help you to win. If you are as mucky-minded as Gershon Legman, you see innuendo everywhere and use jokes to express or to disguise your sexual urges. And if you're an averagely well-balanced individual, you can probably enjoy almost all the same jokes on different days, for different reasons, but mainly for the little holidays that they give you from taking everything too seriously.

Don't bother discussing sex with small children. They rarely have anything to add.—*Fran Lebowitz*

HE'S NOT ALLOWED ON THE COUCH

A rabbit comes into a butcher's shop and asks, "Got any lettuce?"

The butcher replies, "We don't sell lettuce here. You need the greengrocer across the road." The next day, the rabbit comes back into the shop and asks, "Got any lettuce?" The butcher says, "Look, I told you yesterday. We don't sell lettuce. This is a butcher's shop. You need a greengrocer." When the rabbit comes into the shop the following day and asks, "Got any lettuce?" the butcher goes crazy. "Look, I'm sick of this. If you come in here one more time asking for lettuce I'm going to nail your stupid ears to the floor."

The next day, the rabbit is back. He asks the butcher, "Got any nails?" "Nails? *No.*" "Right, then," says the rabbit. "Got any lettuce?"

An elephant and a mouse are talking philosophy. "Why is it," says the elephant, "that although we are both God's creatures, with souls of equal worth, I am so huge and strong and magnificent, yet you are so tiny, puny and gray?"

"Well," says the mouse, "I've been ill, haven't I?"

A man is sitting at home when he hears a knock at the door. He opens the door and sees a snail on the porch. He picks up the snail and throws it as far as he can. Three years later, there's a knock on the door. He opens it and sees the same snail. The snail says, "What the hell was that all about?"

You can lead a cow upstairs but not down. It's the way their joints don't oppose. But I feel sorry for the poor person who found that out the hard way. "Come on, Daisy, down you go."

"I can't go downstairs, it's the way my joints are."

"I don't care about your joints. My wife's coming home in five minutes. Get down the stairs."—*Ricky Gervais*

NOT SO SHAGGY AS THAT, SIR!

On his first night in prison, a convict is glumly eating his dinner when another convict leaps to his feet, shouts "Thirty-seven" and all the other inmates laugh hysterically. Later another shouts, "Four hundred and twenty" with exactly the same result.

"What's going on?" says the convict to his cellmate, sitting next to him.

"It's like this: We only have one joke book in prison and everyone knows all the jokes off by heart. So instead of telling the whole joke, we just stand up and shout a number."

A few days later, the new convict decides that it's time to try it out for himself. So he stands up and shouts, "Fourteen."

Silence.

Turning to his cellmate, he asks, "What went wrong?"

"It's the way you tell them."

I was sitting at the bottom of the garden a week ago, smoking a reflective cheroot, thinking about this and that—mostly that—and I just happened to glance up at the night sky and I marveled at the millions of stars, glistening like quicksilver thrown carelessly onto black velvet. In awe I watched the waxen moon ride across the zenith of the heavens like an amber chariot toward the void of infinite space within which the tethered bolts of Jupiter and Mars hang forever in their orbital majesty, and as I looked at this, I thought, "I must put a roof on this lavatory."—*Les Dawson*

CHAPTER SIX

No Way to Make a Living

In which we scrutinize professional joke-tellers, wonder where jokes come from and ask, is it really all in the way you tell them?

**They all laughed when I said
I wanted to be a comedian.
They're not laughing now.**

BOB MONKHOUSE

Stand-up comedy is a peculiar performance art form. In a room filled with people, the comedian is the only one facing the wrong way.[1] He's also the only one who isn't laughing. For normal people that's a nightmare, not a career aspiration. What complex array of hideous psychological deformities could drive a man (or sometimes even a woman) to stand up in front of a different bunch of strangers every night and invite them to laugh? Marty Feldman once said, "Comedy, like sodomy, is an unnatural act. After all, it's not normal to parade yourself in front of other people and invite them to laugh at you. All the comics I've met felt themselves to be somehow social freaks, at odds with their environment because of their background, or maybe the way they looked."

[1]Of course it could be "she." But in reality it's a man standing behind the mic about 90 percent of the time. We'll try to find out why in Chapter 7; meanwhile, we'll be referring to the comedian as "he."

When it comes to telling jokes, the difference between the amateur and the professional can *seem* very slight. Unlike an actor in a play, the comedian breaks through the "fourth wall" that separates the stage from the auditorium; he speaks directly to the audience. Although the comedian's onstage persona may be every bit as assumed as the

Outside of a dog, a book is a man's best friend. Inside of a dog, it's too dark to read.—*Groucho Marx*

character played by the actor, it will usually be presented as the real deal: this is me, exposing the humorous side of my life. And unlike a musician or singer, there's no apparent craft involved—no instrument to learn to play. Some comedy audiences refuse to believe the material is prepared at all, expecting comedians to produce a new set of jokes every night, as though they were evangelists speaking in tongues. These peculiarities of the art make stand-up comedy look easy—at least when it's done well. It's a reasonable-seeming aspiration for anyone who's ever been told they are funny. Most of us, or at least all those of us who've ever felt ourselves to be "social freaks," have watched someone tell jokes to a crowd and thought, "On a good day with the right material, I could do that."

In fact, the gulf between the gifted amateur and the successful professional joke-writer/joke-teller is massive, and filled to the brim with blood, sweat and more than a little involuntary pee. In this precarious and unforgiving profession, the character trait that unites all successful performers is a kind of masochistic compulsion to make people laugh. It's pure, naked need: a need for love, for popularity, to be noticed, to show off. The great attraction of stand-up as a balm for the fragile ego—as opposed to, say, writing a book or appearing in a radio play—is the instantaneous nature of the audience feedback. Do they love me? Yes, they must—they're laughing. Obviously it's a double-edged sword: the medium's greatest attraction is also its cruelest disappointment, because when they don't laugh, it must follow that they don't love me. Actually, maybe they hate me. No, I know what it is—they don't get my jokes. I'm just *too funny* for them to deal with. . . .

We might as well face it—stand-up comedians may be

I find the "theme" in most theme parks is "Wait in line, fatty."—*Demetri Martin*

funny, but they are not in the least bit cool. In fact, you probably have to discover just how inadequate you are before you can be funny. Cool is distant, mysterious; cool doesn't care. If it's cool you're after, buy some dark glasses and join a band instead.

But if you *are* uncool enough to want to tell jokes for a living, consider this. Being on stage at a comedy club is like a nightmarish amplification of that moment at a dinner party when you've just launched into a spicy little anecdote and you suddenly realize the whole room has gone quiet. Everyone else is not only listening to you but judging you too, and you have no choice but to plow wildly on with your story. When a joke is a little bit "clever," there's an agonizing pause while you wait for the audience to get it, and then pass judgment. From your vantage point on the stage it seems like a pitiless binary system—yes or no. Even if some laughs are bigger than others, there's no gray area in between getting a laugh and getting nothing. Live comedy audiences are ruthless and insatiable. If they smell fear, you're done for. And you're only ever as good as your last joke. Not even your last show—your last *joke*. Every comic has a back pocket full of "bankers"—the funny lines that always get you out of trouble. But even one of those doesn't buy you very much time; thirty seconds of sympathy before they want the next one.

This sounds brutal, and it is. It's no accident that the language of professional comedians is full of violence and death: "He died on his arse tonight" being the nadir, and "He really killed out there" being the pinnacle of achievement. Woody Allen once said that he preferred doing stand-up in nightclubs to TV shows, because "you've got all the time in the world to kill the audience. . . . Over the

I was in a bookstore last week. There was a third off all titles. I bought "*The Lion, The Witch . . .*"—*Jimmy Carr*

course of the show you can kill 99 percent of them." It's as though a comedy club is the chosen arena for a fight to the death, where either the audience or the comic gets out alive—but never both.

Supposing the preceding description hasn't put you off, you may just be foolhardy enough to make it through the first fifty miserable, unpaid open spots. Even to survive the first three will require heroic levels of persistence, the hide of a rhinoceros and a certain masochistic streak. Once you've made it that far, you might get lucky with your first paid gig—perhaps as much as $50. Then again, you might only get a free pint, and once you've drunk it you realize you've missed the last train home and have to pay for a taxi. And tomorrow, you have to get on the phone again and try to get another gig. In his first year as a stand-up, Jimmy clocked up over two hundred gigs, mostly unpaid or in exchange for gas money. And if you manage to keep at it for a year, you are definitely suffering from compulsive joking disorder. Only now can you consider making a career of it.

When the green, unknown "open spot" comedian steps out onto the comedy club stage (or "shabby, ill-lit back corner of pub," as it's also known), he is entering an extremely hostile social environment. The pressure is immense. He must suppress the powerful instincts that possess any human being confronted with a crowd of jeering strangers. He must reject the triggers for "fight or flight" and find a way to dominate the crowd using only his wit. On no account must he allow them to glimpse his naked terror. On the other hand, when he does tell a joke, no one's that

Just what is the handicapped parking situation at the Special Olympics? Is it still just the two spaces?—*Jerry Seinfeld*

surprised—he's on stage, microphone in hand, in a place where people come to laugh. Everything that comes out of his mouth is assumed to be part of a joke, which is why the reaction is so damning if it's not funny. It's also the reason why a very well known comedian can get a laugh just by opening his mouth, because the collective assumption—that what emerges *will* be funny—is so strong.

Joking in private works a little differently. When you tell a joke to a group of friends, you need to create your own metaphorical stage and microphone; you have to let them know they're about to laugh. Most people automatically start with a formal signal that what follows is a joke. You might simply say, "Here's a joke for you. . . . Have you heard the one about the . . ." The wording of the jokes themselves helps too. They are formulaic; in the same way that "Once upon a time . . ." announces a fairy tale, "A man/priest/horse walks/drives/runs into a bar/doctor's office/church . . ." primes the assembled company for a laugh. You couldn't, in the midst of conversation, casually say, "My father hugged me only once, on my twenty-first birthday. It was very awkward. I now know what it was that made me feel so uncomfortable: the nudity." At least you could, but you would be greeted with a slightly embarrassed silence and a niggling feeling that people were edging away from you, muttering, "What an arse." But Ray Romano can get a big laugh with this, because the rules we apply to the things he says on a comedy club stage override the everyday rules about signaling your jokes.

However, the average amateur has one massive advantage over any professional joke-teller: you know your audience, and they know you. That's why you can sometimes tell your friends a joke completely back to front, mess up the

I can't smell mothballs. Because it's so hard to get their little legs apart.—*Steve Martin*

punch line and *still* all end up on the floor: the whole purpose of private joke-telling is not to judge the quality of the performance but rather for everyone to laugh together, signaling how much they're enjoying one another's company.

Contrast this with the artificial atmosphere of a comedy club, where the teller of the jokes is expected to laugh little, if at all. And his audience's laughter is only partly shared with him. In one sense, the volume and pitch of the laughter is rewarding him, letting him know how successfully his jokes are going down. The audience's laughter is essential to the rhythm of the comic's set; although they aren't talking to him (except for the red-faced drunk in the front row), for the set to be successful it must still function with the to-and-fro rhythm of a conversation, albeit a rather one-sided one. But as an audience member you are also interacting, continuously and automatically, with the people around you; your laugh is a signal to them as much as to the comedian. It might come as something of a blow to some stand-ups to learn that much of the audience's response is not directed at confirming what a funny man the comedian is but rather at letting the rest of the audience know what a good time they're all having together. But all good comedians understand that creating an atmosphere of community in the room is almost as important as having well-crafted punch lines, if you're going to judge your success by the length and volume of audience laughter.

Performers have sometimes been less than honorable in their attempts to pump up the audience response. The Emperor Nero, a keen amateur dramatist, employed profes-

Somebody complimented me on my driving today. They left a note on the windshield—it said "Parking Fine."—*Tim Vine*

sional clappers to attend his plays. Even earlier, at dramatic contests in Athens, hired hecklers and cheerleaders were secretly employed to try and sway the judges. These days, TV studio audiences carry on the ancient tradition of clapping on command, although they demand little more than a can of warm beer and a long, long afternoon of gut-crunching dullness for their troubles. TV comedy *without* a studio audience is even more problematic. In the 1950s, the early days of market research, studio executives realized that comedies that had been well received in test screenings were causing viewers at home to switch off in droves. They realized that they needed a way to recreate the element of audience participation in order to give solitary viewers an experience that was closer to social laughter. And so it came to pass that a CBS executive named Charlie Douglass invented canned laughter. Persistent rumors that he sold his soul to the devil in exchange for the technology remain unsubstantiated, but the company he later set up to exploit the invention (Northridge Electronics) made him millions. The original machine was a sort of laughter pipe organ, using a bewildering array of keys and pedals to activate tape loops of giggles, guffaws, shrieks and chuckles in infinite permutations to simulate an audience reaction. Douglass was incredibly secretive about his invention, but a story does persist that the original laughs were recorded at a Marcel Marceau show, to minimize the chance of spoken interference from the performer. The thought that all those terrible sixties sitcom scripts were jollied up with the sound of *people laughing at a mime* is almost too good to be true.

Although canned laughter has long since gone digital, there is still a real art to producing a convincing laugh track. The team of sound engineers at Northridge Electronics has

My uncle had a rabbit's foot for thirty years. His other foot was quite normal.—*Tom Griffen*

won at least ten Emmy awards, including a lifetime achievement award for Douglass himself. Industry professionals assure us that a skillful canned laughter engineer can produce a "much more convincing" soundtrack than a live audience. We refer you back to the Satan/soul-sale rumors.

Of course, besides the insane level of dedication to an almost totally thankless vocation, and the ability to sustain an unnatural social bond with a roomful of strangers, the third major distinguishing feature of professional joke-tellers is the material. A quick scan of the jokes we've peppered this book with will serve to confirm that the anonymous, traditional ones—the "old chestnuts," if you will—are somehow more archetypal, more joke-like than the ones attributed to a particular comedian. That's partly because they need to be universal so that lots of different people can tell them, whereas a comic wants his jokes to be personal enough to be closely identified with him. In fact, if you were to talk to many of today's comedians, they would find an opportunity to tell you that they "don't really do jokes, as such." (If this remark is followed by "it's more observational stuff" then what they mean is, "I'm not very good at punch lines.") This reluctance to identify stand-up with "jokes" usually seems to have something to do with wanting to be taken seriously as an artist, and feeling that "just telling jokes" isn't quite art. It's also a way of identifying the current generation of comics as distinct from (and, by implication, better than) the previous one; a way of rebelling against our parents. Now, it's obviously each individual's prerogative to define "joke" however he wishes. But

I don't like country music, but I don't mean to denigrate those who do. And for those who like country music, denigrate means "put down."—*Bob Newhart*

we would argue that any intentionally funny story told to an audience, which sets up a scenario, builds to a crescendo and peaks with a big laugh . . . well, if it looks like a joke and quacks like a joke, it might just be a joke. What we hope is apparent by this point is that there are lots of different kinds of jokes, and the jokes that get passed around most freely—therefore the ones that last—tend to be quite portable. They are jokes reduced to their very essence, highly concentrated nuggets from which all the distracting brilliance of individual performance has evaporated.

In the old days, all jokes seemed to belong to everyone, and no one. Writing jokes down was much rarer than it is today (partly because the Internet was but a distant nightmare in those far-off, innocent days), and linking them permanently with a single author almost unheard of. If the history of jokes were a piece of string three miles long, then the period of writing them down with an author credit could be represented by a very short piece of string quite near the bit that we're holding. Some jokes have survived for centuries, told but never written down, as part of an oral tradition that grew out of primitive religion and folk tales; we know this is true because social anthropologists have written about it in books. These adaptive jokes are nomadic, respecting neither geographic nor ideological boundaries. They are like living things, protean, parasitic—wherever they land they adopt the local idiom and change their surface details to most efficiently ensnare the laughter that feeds them.

Although we have anecdotal evidence that "jest books" existed as early as the fourth century B.C., the books themselves have been lost. Probably the earliest one that survives is a Greek text called *Philogelos*, meaning "the laughter-lover," a collection of 265 jokes put together in

If toast always lands butter-side-down, and cats always land on their feet, what happens if you strap toast on the back of a cat and drop it?—*Steven Wright*

the fourth or fifth century A.D. The original manuscript is lost, but some later copies give the authors as the otherwise unknown Hierocles and Philagrios; others omit to mention an author. What's clear is that, whoever these men were, they were compilers and collectors rather than the originators of the jokes. Even jokes collected and published like this were considered common property, not least because in an age where books were rare and literacy levels low, there was a fluid relationship between written and oral culture: the jest book was a record of tales that were commonly told, rather than a single author's creative effort. Many of the jokes contained in the *Philogelos* are somewhat cryptic to a modern audience. For example, there are a couple of jokes about lettuce that only make sense if you share the ancient superstition that lettuce is an aphrodisiac. But in form they are pithy and strikingly similar to modern jokes. This one in particular rung a bell with us:

> *Someone needled a well-known wit: "I had your wife, without paying a penny." He replied: "It's my duty as a husband to couple with such a monstrosity. What made you do it?"*

Fast-forward about fifteen hundred years, turn to page 17 of Milton Berle's *Private Joke File* and you'll find this:

> *A man comes home and finds his best friend in bed with his wife. The man throws up his hands in disbelief and says, "Joe, I have to—but you?"*

The European joke book industry had something of a setback during the early Christian era, when any book that

Milton Berle knows the secret of making people laugh. And he sure knows how to keep a secret.—*Arnold Strong*

didn't mention Jesus was considered a waste of ink. Meanwhile in the Arab world the joke thrived, often elaborated into longer humorous or satirical folk tales. Many of these stories eventually coalesced around a protagonist called Mulla Nasrudin, a slippery, semimythical figure who appears in stories not just in the Middle East but also in Greece, Russia and China; he is supposed to have served as court jester to the fourteenth-century Mongol king Timur Leng (Marlowe's Tamburlaine) and is also supposed to be buried in Turkey under a stone dated A.D. 386. Mulla Nasrudin is a wise man as well as a consummate fool, and the followers of Sufism, a mystical breakaway branch of Islam, still make use of his jokes as parables of a sort. Here's one of them, as told by Idries Shah:

> *Nasrudin used to take his donkey across a frontier every day, with the panniers loaded with straw. Since he admitted to being a smuggler, when he trudged home every night, the frontier guards searched him again and again. They searched his person, sifted the straw, steeped it in water, even burned it from time to time. Meanwhile he was becoming visibly more and more prosperous.*
>
> *Then he retired and went to live in another country. Here one of the customs officers met him years later.*
>
> *"You can tell me now, Nasrudin," he said. "Whatever was it that you were smuggling, when we could never catch you out?"*
>
> *"Donkeys," said Nasrudin.*

During the Arab conquests, collections of this sort of folk tale made their way back to Italy and Spain. And in 1451, about a thousand years after *Philogelos*, Europe got its

I was taking my dog for a stroll in the cemetery early one day and a woman passed me by and said, "Morning!" I said, "No, just walking the dog."—*John Mann*

next milestone joke book. *The Liber Facetiarum* (Book of Trifling Jests) was the lifetime's joke collection of a dazzling Vatican scholar named Poggio Bracciolini. As well as acting as a secretary to eight popes over the course of half a century, Poggio somehow found time to moonlight as a heroic book detective. He traveled to remote monasteries all over Europe, rescuing neglected manuscripts from their libraries and painstakingly copying them. Many of the priceless classical works he found would otherwise have been left to rot—including Lucretius's *De Rerum Natura* (valuable because it reminds us of a simpler time when a book about the whole known universe, incorporating an atomic theory and a theory of evolution, could be called "On the Nature of Things," which is really just another way of saying "About Stuff") and rather a lot of Cicero (valuable because sometimes public school boys need to be set punishment exercises). He was also the author of a number of viciously satirical accounts of contemporary ecclesiastical and scholastic life, an accomplished calligrapher who may have invented the earliest Roman font, and the father of some twenty children. After all that, he's best known for a collection of silly jokes he published at the age of seventy.

Given that many of the jokes are supposed to have come from the Bugiale, a sort of informal club of Vatican scribes and scholars that met to exchange a joke or two after a hard day of scribing, you might be surprised to hear that the themes are pretty racy. Fat men, drunk men, farts, erections, randy wives—and all in the best High Church Latin. In fact, that was probably why the Vatican failed to condemn the dirty little book—it could be enjoyed by the educated classes without fear of corrupting the non-Latin-speaking masses.

It's easy to distract fat people. It's a piece of cake.
—Chris Addison

The *Liber Facetiarum* circulated throughout Europe, and wherever it went it was shamelessly plundered by later joke-compilers. Which was only fair, considering a good number of the jokes in it were lifted in their turn, from *Philogelos* and other jest books. In fact, a number of them are still doing the rounds today, if not in so many words. For example:

> *Matteo Franco, whose cat mewed when he pulled its ears, threw it out of the window, saying: "Now, I will catch my own mice."*

Which is the great-granddaddy to this modern joke:

> *A man runs over a cat. The cat's address is on its collar so the man goes to apologize to the owner. He knocks on the door and a little old lady answers. The man says, "I'm so sorry. I've just run over your cat. Can I replace it?" "I don't know," replies the old lady. "How are you at catching mice?"*

At around the same time as Poggio's book first appeared, the future for joke books began to look brighter still when Johannes Gutenberg invented the printing press. However, it turned out there was a bit of a backlog of Bibles and so forth to be getting on with, so the joke book output was, in these early days, more of a trickle than a flood. The first to be printed in English was a collection of Aesop's fables, spiced up with some of Poggio's *facetiae* and published by William Caxton in 1484. Caxton's liberal, uncredited borrowings from the Italian writer wouldn't have been frowned on at the time: jokes were still treated in a very different way

A philosophy professor and a sociologist are holidaying at a nudist camp. The philosopher turns to his colleague and asks, "I assume you've read Marx?" "Yes," replies the sociologist, "I think it's these wicker chairs."

from the witty sayings and aphorisms of famous men. They were common property, freely available to any entertainer who wanted to adapt them to local tastes or even just use them as they came. The joke-teller's only prerogative was to make the joke *seem* fresh to the audience in front of him.

Even as recently as the 1950s and early '60s, it was considered perfectly in order for professional comics to lift jokes and whole routines from their peers. It was possible to put a superficially individual spin on the act by adding personal details or simply claiming that "my friend Manny asked the rabbi the other day . . ." or "I live next door to a man called Paddy MacNamara and he's so stupid that . . ." Audiences were happy to wink back at the performer and enjoy the jokes as works of pure dramatic fiction. This is still how jokes function on a personal level. If you receive a topical joke by e-mail, you can forward it without worrying about crediting it to its original writer. You aren't pretending to have written it yourself, and your friends don't care that you didn't. You have a separate and almost equally important role as the conduit of the joke. In the same way that jokes we tell to one another in private life are contagious, inasmuch as whoever gets them can pass them on in turn to others who haven't heard them before, so jokes circulated freely on the music hall stages and early wireless comedy.

But with the rise of radio and TV comedy, a new model began to develop. The new mass media allowed audiences of a size previously undreamt of to access a single comedian's performance, the upshot being that a joke would become irrevocably associated with the first person to tell it

Instead of getting married again, I'm going to find a woman I don't like and give her a house.—*Lewis Grizzard*

on TV. Recording technology meant that comedians had a new sort of record of ownership of their material. Even though much of that material was churned out by more or less anonymous backroom writers, the comic was identified with his jokes in a different way. Another sea change came in the sixties, with the rise of idiosyncratic characters like Lenny Bruce, where the material was genuinely autobiographical. Instead of invoking some fictional Jew-next-door as a character in a recycled gag, the jokes became much more personal, richly textured patchworks of genuine events and comic embellishments. A joke like this is so closely identified with the individual performer that it can't really be appropriated by another.

Then, in the UK, comedy started to become a legitimate career for highly literate Oxbridge intellectuals, who imposed an authorial stamp on their sketches and parodies that would have seemed absurd to the music hall stars of the previous generation. Soon enough, the invention of dedicated comedy clubs (the pioneering Comedy Store opened in Hollywood in 1972, with its London namesake following in 1979), where seven or eight comedians would share a stage, ensured that all circuit comedians had to try harder to come up with something new, so as not to antagonize the audience by trotting out duplicate jokes.

And so in the space of a couple of decades the question of joke ownership became a slightly more vexed one. Whereas in private circles jokes are still common property (in the same way that you can still sing "My Way" in the shower without paying royalties), stealing a joke from a professional comedian is no longer considered an homage. Misunderstandings quite often occur when comedians inadvertently duplicate one another's jokes. This is easier to do than you

I'm a compulsive gambler and as a result of my problem my wife has left me. How can I win her back?

might think: although each comic's point of view is unique, the universe of joke premises is a finite one. Just as musicians work within the confines of an eight-note scale and rules of harmony, so joke-makers must underpin their jokes with a fairly conventional set of human experiences, however individual a spin they put on them. For example, compare the following:

I found my first gray pubic hair the other day. It was in a kebab, but there you go.—**Jeff Green**

I found my first gray hair today. On my chest.
—**Wendy Liebman**

It is improbable that these two individuals have ever seen each other's act, let alone discussed the aging process, comedy potential thereof. Although the jokes work in subtly different ways, they bear a close family resemblance. Many comedians have their own variation on the "gray hair" bit—it's one of those universally relevant comedy staples. Here's another one, from the late great Dave Allen:

Shock can turn your hair gray. I found my first gray pubic hair the other day.
What did he see that the others didn't?

The notion that a joke belongs to a particular comic may be relatively new, but the pressure on a joke-teller to come up with something fresh and novel for each audience is as old as the hills. Jokes suffer from a particularly dramatic ap-

Two snakes in the middle of the jungle; one says to the other, "Just out of interest, are we poisonous?" "I don't really know," replies his friend. "Why?" "I just bit my tongue."

plication of the law of diminishing returns. It's funny the first time you hear it, raises a nostalgic smile the second time, and the third time it's just annoying. It strikes many of today's comics as more than a little unfair that, whereas the Rolling Stones can hardly make themselves heard above the noise of the audience shouting for "Satisfaction" (not to mention the buzz of their hearing aids), a stand-up comedian who dares to repeat a joke his audience has heard before is more likely to get booed. There are some rare exceptions to prove this rule. For example, Jimmy wrote a joke a couple of years ago that goes like this:

> *A woman came up to me to complain after a gig the other day—quite a large lady—and she said, "You're fattist." I said, "No, I think you'll find* you're *fattest."*

On several occasions an audience member at one of Jimmy's live shows has shouted out, "Do Fattist!" Flattering as it is that people like the joke enough to heckle for it, it might be more fun for everyone else if they didn't request it by shouting out the punch line.

When John Cleese grew fed up with responding to interviewers' questions about where he "got his jokes from," he replied, "I buy them from a little man in Swindon." Unfortunately there is no such character. And we've already ruled out the existence of an alien intelligence to beam jokes to Earth, as Isaac Asimov imagined. The truth about where jokes come from is much more prosaic. Ten percent inspiration and 90 percent whittling and crafting—much of it in front of an audience—

"Sort of" is a harmless thing to say. It's just a filler, it doesn't mean anything. Except after certain phrases, like "I love you . . ." Or, "You're going to live . . ." Or, "It's a boy! . . ."
—Demetri Martin

until the joke is finished. The mind of a joke-writer is specially adapted to transform ordinary humorous observations into neatly packaged jokes; sadly this means that said mind is generally maladapted to function in normal social situations. A comic goes through life constantly on the lookout for the funny angle. A trip to the doctor's with your ailing girlfriend, a humiliating night-bus escapade or even a death in the family—all become fodder for jokes. Jerry Seinfeld describes the comedian as a person with a "third eye," constantly watching proceedings with a certain ironic detachment.

Detachment and an ironic point of view are not enough, though. Practically speaking, joke-writing and -performing is a craft, and it is possible to identify some of the specific building blocks with which a successful joke is constructed.

SETUP, PUNCH LINE, LAUGH?

Many traditional jokes—especially one- and two-liners, riddles and puns—are written backward, inasmuch as the punch line needs to be sorted out first. This reflects the central importance of a good punch line—it's the payoff, the destination without which the joke wouldn't know where it was going. Jokes tend to operate on their own weird internal logic, and that logic can only be understood by working from the punch line backward. Here are some examples:

> *"Doctor, doctor, I keep dreaming about these horrible sexual acts—sadism, bestiality, necrophilia. What shall I do?"*
>
> *"Forget it, you're flogging a dead horse."*

No matter how much you give a homeless person for a cup of tea, you never get that tea.—*Jimmy Carr*

A Buddhist goes to a hot-dog stand. He says, "Make me one with everything."

A cowboy walks into a bar and orders a whiskey.

As the barman's pouring it, the cowboy looks about him.

"Where is everybody?" he says.

"Gone to the hanging," says the barman.

"Hanging?" says the cowboy. "Who they hanging?"

"Brownpaper Pete," replies the barman.

"Brownpaper Pete? Why do they call him that?"

"Well," says the barman. "His hat's made of brown paper, his shirt's made of brown paper, his jacket's made of brown paper and his trousers are made of brown paper."

"Really?" says the cowboy. "What they hanging him for?"

"Rustling."

Even a punch line on its own, with little or no narrative setup, can make us laugh in the right circumstances. Witness the hugely popular sketch comedy of *Saturday Night Live* or *Mad TV*, in which recurring characters get laughs from catchphrases that function just like punch lines to the situational jokes conjured up by the sketches. This is how an "in joke" works among a group of friends too. Life itself provides the setup, and a word or two, sometimes just a knowing look between two people who are in on the joke provides the punch line.

A professional comic's routine may be based on true personal experience, although personal experience doesn't tend to come with a neat punch line. This goes some way

I enjoy using the comedy technique of self-deprecation—but I'm not very good at it.—*Arnold Brown*

to explaining why most comics are such outrageous liars. In fact, the commonest lie they tell is "This really happened to me, I swear." Lots of jokes *start* with a true story. For example, when Jimmy says, "I gave my girlfriend a book entitled *Cheap and Easy Vegetarian Cookery* . . . ," that much is true. It's a real book, with a proud place on the Carr kitchen shelf. Luckily his girlfriend is a woman of great wit and charm, so she took it remarkably well when he followed that statement with the punch line, ". . . because not only is she a vegetarian . . ." Pathological observational comics may even begin to live their lives in search of a punch line, provoking "hilarious" denouements by deliberately forgetting their wedding anniversaries or leaving their children in the supermarket or simply drinking a lot of vodka every day. Blurring the line between life and art is all very well, but carry on like that and there'll be tears before bedtime.

SURPRISE!

Surprise is the fundamental joke mechanism. Most punch lines rely on an element of surprise for their effect—that's why they're not funny the third time you hear them. The joke-teller's skill lies in judging exactly how much of a surprise the audience is prepared to take. He must make a series of assumptions about what they will understand, what their reference points are and how relaxed they appear to be. Jerry Seinfeld once compared telling a joke to attempting to leap a metaphorical canyon, taking the audience with you. The setup to the joke is the near-side cliff, and the punch line is the far side. If they're too far apart, the lis-

I'm sitting at the opera, and I'm thinking, "Look how much work it takes to bore me."—*Dave Attell*

teners don't make it to the other side. And if they are too close together, the audience just steps across the gap and doesn't experience an exhilarating leap of any kind. The joke-hearers get far more pleasure from the joke if they have to do a little work.

Telling a joke to an audience is an odd sort of mutual conspiracy. Every punch line is a little surprise, but not an unexpected one. When you start to tell a joke, you're effectively saying, "Let's all agree to suspend the normal rules for a moment." That really ought to spoil it for everyone, but somehow it doesn't. "I've got a surprise for you in thirty seconds. . . . Here it comes. . . . Wait for it. . . . BOO!" And we're still surprised. We laugh delightedly and settle back to wait for the next surprise.

OH, AND TIMING! SORRY.

The surprise thing doesn't work without effective timing. Good comic timing is the technique, surprise is the effect, and (hopefully) laughter is the response. It's almost impossible to explain in print, because our eyes always cheat. We can't stop them from skipping ahead and glimpsing the punch line before we've properly digested the setup. But next time you listen to a comedian doing his stuff, listen to the pauses. They're not that funny on their own—obviously, they're just tiny silences—but the point is, *neither are the jokes*.

There's a particularly widespread technique for working surprise into a joke that's known among professional writers as "pull-back/reveal." The joke focuses your attention on a particular angle or detail of the scene, then suddenly

Brevity is the . . . —*Kevin Gildea*

pans out to show you the whole, surprising picture. Very often the success of these jokes hinges on the joke-teller's subtle control of the rhythm of the joke: a beat here, a breath there. American comedian Emo Philips is a master of this technique, and there's no better way to illustrate it than by reproducing one of his routines. Spot the pull-back/reveal moments—one in every line.

> *My sister had a baby. We could have company over and she'll be there with her breast out, feeding him . . . cereal, or whatever.*
>
> *The other day she took me aside and said, "Emo, can you babysit little Derek while I go to the carnival . . . and look for the father."*
>
> *I said OK. So I'm pushing him through the park, and he's crying . . . because I forgot the stroller.*
>
> *I take him home and I'm trying to rinse out his diaper in the toilet—you ever rinse out a baby's diaper in the toilet? Euch. Anyway . . . I accidentally let go of his foot.*
>
> *And he's spinning around, crying, and I'm trying to get him out with the plunger . . . because you can't use Drano, that* hurts *a kid!*

F***ING SURPRISE!

A very cheap and easy way of making people laugh at a joke is to throw in some random swearwords. Almost all comedians do this from time to time. What's more, it's become something of a tradition among the more iconoclastic ones to write a routine which is ostensibly aimed at depriving

I'm tired of all this nonsense about beauty being only skin-deep. That's deep enough. What do you want—an adorable pancreas?—*Jean Kerr*

taboo words and phrases of their power to shock, but which also conveniently harnesses the power of shocking words to make us laugh. One of Lenny Bruce's many contributions to the canon includes the phrase "niggerniggerniggerniggerniggerniggernigger." Ho ho ho! George Carlin gave us the justly celebrated monologue "Seven Words You Can Never Say on Television," a semantic dissection of swearwords that at the time were tacitly banned from the public airwaves (namely shit, piss, fuck, cunt, cocksucker, motherfucker and tits, fact-fans). The court case that ensued, after a California radio station broadcast the routine at 2 P.M. (in October 1973), led the Federal Communications Commission to establish a 10 P.M. watershed, after which indecent (but not obscene) material could be broadcast. Sure enough, Carlin's seven "filthy words" formed the basis of the new regulations.

Of course, despite their protestations, comics don't *really* want those words to lose their power to shock—at least not completely. If we were all quite happy to skip about the place shouting "cocksucker" at one another, they'd just have to find a new trigger word that would grab the crowd's attention.

Jerry Seinfeld dismisses swearing altogether, calling it "a trick. You can get a laugh with a dirty word even when the joke isn't funny." And for the defense, George Carlin says, "Shock is just another form of surprise, and comedy is based on surprise. This is a noisy culture. Television is babbling at us from fifty-five channels, twenty-four hours a day. . . . Everyone is yelling at you, trying to get your attention. If you want to be heard, then you have to raise your voice a little bit. And you can do that literally or figuratively by finding a verbal image, a subject or some language

If you can't laugh at yourself, make fun of other people.
—Bobby Slayton

that grabs their attention and brings them in. If it's the only thing going for you, it won't last long. But as long as it's just a device to draw them in . . ."

Too fucking right.

FAMILIARITY

We have a little pamphlet, lent us by a comedian friend, called "JOKES JOKES JOKES: Why spend 2/6 at a Music Hall Here's 2,000 laughs for a 1/3. Selected by IKE 'NSMILE LETTSLAFF'" (sic). There's no publication date, but our best guess puts it somewhere in the late 1940s. These examples are fairly representative:

> *"Lor' lumme, Bill," said a gentleman of the course to his pal, as a fashionably dressed lady passed, "look at 'er wiv all 'em buttons on 'er skirt and me 'olding up me trarziz wiv string."*

> *He was rather shy and it was the first time that he had dared to bring her flowers. She, delighted, threw her arms about his neck and kissed him. He suddenly grabbed his hat and started out of the door. "Oh!" she said. "I'm sorry if I have offended you." "Oh, that's not it," he called back, "I'm going after more flowers."*

We mean no disrespect to Mr. Lettslaff when we say that the volume failed to yield the promised two thousand laughs. Jokes such as these rely on the audience's instant recognition of incidental detail. In a world now sadly bereft of proper ladies and courting swains in hats, these jokes

I deserve someone who likes me for who I am . . . pretending to be.—*Arj Barker*

can't get any purchase on our sense of humor. We fully accept that the jokes in the volume you currently hold in your hands will seem similarly alien to anyone who stumbles across a yellowing copy in 2065—if bookshops still exist, and anyone has been taught to read. The throwaway details of the jokes we've reproduced will seem quaint and ridiculous; although they will be recognized as jokes, they won't make people laugh out loud.[2]

[2]Oh, God. It's all been for nothing. . . .

Beyond the surface details, some of the subject matters will age more gracefully than others. There are certain basic themes, joke archetypes, if you like, that appear to stand the test of time. Henpecked husbands and village idiots will continue to be joked about forever and ever, amen. Other topics come and go; for example, there are six or seven jokes in the Lettslaff collection dealing with seasickness, which was a staple topic for music hall jokes. Sea travel is such a rare occurrence these days that, although a green-about-the-gills ferry passenger still has comic potential, the notion isn't funny by default, as it seems to have been sixty years ago. In its place, the trivial indignities and annoyances that plague each successive generation become the furniture of their jokes.

Jokes are disposable. As we've established, until quite recently whoever came up with them didn't consider it worth the bother to claim ownership. Individual jokes tend to have short shelf lives—yet jokes are surprisingly durable too, flexing to accommodate themselves to audiences in different continents, even different centuries. To resolve this apparent paradox, you have to consider a joke as a sum of various parts. The basic structural component of the joke is its theme or premise—a stupid man who thinks he's clever, for example—and that's the bit that

If at first you don't succeed, skydiving is not for you.

crosses continents and survives the march of millennia. The second layer of the joke is in the way in which the story is told, and that's incredibly culturally specific. Individual jokes have finite significance because they rely on telling details with which the hearer can identify. Those details are firmly anchored in a time and place and language; joke and audience must inhabit the same world. Finally, jokes can't be considered in isolation. Each instance of the joke's appearance has a joker, a jokee, a flavor, a context all of its own. George Carlin, again: "Stand-up comedy is the only art form where the audience is included in the act of creation and they're allowed to participate in changing the form of the work." The same principle applies to individual, private joke-telling; the act of telling a joke makes it a new one every time.

One of Britain's best-loved current comedians is Bolton stand-up Peter Kay. His live gigs, particularly in the Northwest, are legendary. Hundreds, sometimes thousands, cry with laughter. But this isn't the comedy of incongruity—his stories seldom end in very unexpected places. Nor is his the comedy of superiority, however much he gently mocks his family and friends. And there's no great explosion of suppressed sexual neurosis—no material your grandmother couldn't handle. This is the comedy of the banal: carefully observed vignettes which both deflate and celebrate the minutiae of British life. Philosopher Simon Critchley writes, "Humour views the world awry, bringing us back to the everyday by estranging us from it. The comedian is the anthropologist of our everyday lives."

Anthropological comedy is dependent on place as much as time. Peter Kay could perform the same act to a packed comedy club in North Dakota and be met with mild

What's the quickest way to a man's heart? Straight through the rib cage.—*Jo Brand*

bafflement. But in the North of England—in fact, all over the UK—his audiences howl with recognition because the comic has given them a licence to find themselves ridiculous. It's inclusive and warm, a conversation with the audience that at times feels like some kind of community therapy. It's more than just local, it's parochial. And it takes a brilliant, big-hearted writer and performer to spin so much everyday drabness into comedy gold.

Conventional two-liner jokes aren't that important to Peter Kay, whose act owes as much to physical clowning as it does to verbal ingenuity. The few classically defined "jokes" in Kay's set are put to use to build a conversational rapport with the audience. They are old and terribly familiar—so much so that everyone can join in, if they're not too busy groaning.

> Kay: *What's black and white and looks like a horse?*
> *[holds mic toward audience]*
> Entire audience: *A zebra!*
> Kay: *How does Bob Marley like his donuts?*
> Entire audience: *Wi' jam in!*
> Kay: *You see?* That's *a joke, that. That's first thing you'll tell when you get 'ome.*

Aside from being a great way to get new laughs from old jokes, this is comedy as a bonding exercise, and in some ways it's the closest that onstage comedy gets to everyday, private joke-telling.

I'd like to thank me mam and dad. If it wasn't for them I wouldn't have low self-esteem and have to follow this empty and shallow profession.—*Johnny Vegas*

Michelangelo was hard at work on his latest sculpture, watched by a fascinated young pupil. "How do you do that, maestro?" asked the student, as a perfect facsimile of a horse emerged from the rough block of stone. "I look at the block, and I chip away everything that isn't a horse," said the artist. The young pupil picked up his own chisel and set about his own block of marble. The following day, Michelangelo happened upon the boy, gazing disconsolately at a pile of marble dust. "What happened to your block?" "Well, I looked, but I guess there wasn't a horse in mine."

The difference between a funny story and a joke is often a function of verbal economy. That's not to say that long, wordy jokes can't be funny, but the skill lies in what goes unsaid. If too much is explained, there's no logical leap for the audience to make, and the paradigm shift that elicits laughter is lost. Compare:

I'm not a homosexual. Mind you, I might be mistaken for one if I went to the North of England. In places like Newcastle, there's such a culture of macho posturing that they go out in their shirtsleeves in all kinds of weather, so if you wear a coat they think you're gay.

Chip away all the bits of that story that aren't the joke, and you've got this joke:

I'm not gay. Unless you're from Newcastle and by "gay" you mean, "owns a coat."

If all the world's a stage, where does the audience sit?

Remember all those pages ago, when this joke was funny?

So just to recap: the setup is a cliff, the punch line is another cliff, the joke-teller is a stuntman/sculptor, and the whole joke is a marble horse. We're not even going to try to explain shaggy dog stories, for fear of a fatal metaphor pileup.

Oh, all right then. A shaggy dog story is a joke with a long, repetitive and overelaborate setup that ends in a massively anticlimactic punch line. The origin of the name (according to a helpful 1953 monograph by Eric Partridge called *The "Shaggy Dog" Story, Its Origin, Development and Nature*) is the following joke:

> *A grand householder in Park Lane, London, had the great misfortune to lose a very valuable and rather shaggy dog. He advertised repeatedly in* The Times, *but without luck, and finally he gave up hope. But an American in New York saw the advertisement, was touched by the man's devotion, and went to great lengths to seek out a dog that matched the specification in the advertisement and which he could bring over to London on his next business trip.* [The teller at this point should elaborate at great length on said great lengths.] *He presented himself in due course at the owner's impressive house, where he was received in the householder's absence by an even more impressive butler, who glanced at the dog, bowed, winced almost imperceptibly and exclaimed, in a horror-stricken voice, "But not so shaggy as that, sir!"*

This sort of joke is as likely to evoke a groan as a laugh, but if the audience guesses what's in store, there's a sort of

A comedian is sitting at the bar of a comedy club late one night when a beautiful woman comes up to him and says, "I saw you perform tonight, and you're the funniest guy I've ever seen. I want to take you home and give you the hottest night of sex you're ever had." The comedian looks at her and says, "Did you see the first show or the second show?"

giddy masochistic delight in waiting to be let down. It can only exist in a society which is saturated with jokes. In fact, it's a commentary on the way a punch line usually works, a joke about jokes. A meta-joke. In some ways it's closer to a practical joke than to a conventional verbal joke: a joke is played on the hearer, who has his expectations of a funny punch line utterly confounded. The old chestnut "Why did the chicken cross the road? To get to the other side!" works on exactly the same principle.

The art of the shaggy dog story rests entirely on the personality of the teller and his skill at embellishment and exaggeration, rather than on a carefully weighted and worded punch line. We can admire and laugh at a joke as a masterpiece of storytelling even if the punch line is unsatisfactory or entirely absent. At first glance this sort of yarn-spinning, not to mention the verbose flights of fancy of a comedian like Robin Willliams, Eddie Izzard or Ross Noble, might appear to be the antithesis of the necessary economy we describe above. Not so; listen carefully to any of those three masters of waffle and you'll see that their immense skill lies in leading us up the garden path and right to the cliff edge, setting carefully judged leaps of imagination for the audience to follow them across. The triggers for laughter are in the gaps between the words.

SOUNDS PECULIAR

Native English speakers seem to have a particular relationship with certain sounds and syllables that are almost always funny. In Neil Simon's play *The Sunshine Boys*, old Vaudeville entertainer Willy tries to explain this to his nephew:

I once saw a wino who was eating grapes and I said, "Dude, you have to wait!"—*Mitch Hedberg*

"Fifty-seven years in this business, you learn a few things. You know what words are funny and which words are not funny. Alka-Seltzer is funny. You say Alka-Seltzer, you get a laugh. Words with K in them are funny. Casey Stengel, that's a funny name. Robert Taylor is not funny. Cupcake is funny. Tomato is not funny. Cookie is funny. Cucumber is funny. Cleveland . . . Cleveland is funny. Maryland is not funny."

British radio comedy of the 1960s proved to be the high watermark for the art of making up funny names. *Round the Horne* writers Barry Took and Marty Feldman deserve particular mention: thanks to them the airwaves thronged with creatures such as Mr. Throbwalloper, Reg Pubes, Obadiah Loombucket, J. Peasemould Gruntfuttock and, of course, fading starlet Dame Celia Molestrangler and "aging juvenile Binkie Huckaback," her costar in many, many, many parodies of *Brief Encounter*. It's not at all certain why all these k and oo sounds are funny, but some speech experts maintain that the combinations of tiny facial muscles we use to make these particular sounds might subconsciously remind us of smiling or laughing. Whatever the reason, tweaking the words in a joke to include more of these sounds can make it even funnier.

As well as the individual sounds, the overall rhythm of a performer's speech plays an important part in that strange alchemy that takes a tolerably amusing incident and turns it into a routine. One of the reasons that Ireland has produced so many great comics is undoubtedly that Irish people have a rhythm to their language that goes beyond accent, a rhythm that seems somehow made for telling funny stories. This may reflect the fact that English was imposed on the Irish nation fairly recently, and

Two lions are walking down the aisle of a supermarket. One turns to the other and says, "Quiet in here today, isn't it?"

the singsong rhythms of the Gaelic tongue persist as a powerful undertow that tugs at the formal surface of the language. The rhythms of Jewish English also lend themselves well to comic performance—again, the cadences of Yiddish can clearly be discerned. But even performers not blessed with a naturally rhythmic way of speaking can exaggerate the rhythms of everyday language for comic effect. A performer like Kenneth Williams or Rowan Atkinson can distort the sounds and rhythms of quite ordinary BBC English to find jokes or innuendos you never thought were there. Think of Atkinson as Blackadder, rolling the name "Bob" around his mouth and out like a bubble. Language play is at the heart of joke-performance as well as joke-writing.

Opinions differ as to whether you can ever teach someone to be a comedian. Most professionals agree that really great comedians are born, not made: they have "funny bones." Woody Allen's take on the subject is characteristically pessimistic. He once said that in order to succeed as a stand-up comic you need the "funny bones," then you also need to study the greats and work like a dog, and *then* you need a lot of lucky breaks. Standing up and telling jokes isn't actually an art form, no matter what some stand-up comedians would like to believe. Sometimes, the very best comedians manage to elevate it to the realm of art. But the rest of us should be content enough to call it a noble craft.

The great thing about craft is that it can be worked at and improved. Apprentices can become masters in time. So

I don't want to achieve immortality through my work. I want to achieve immortality through not dying.—*Woody Allen*

in the spirit of self-improvement, we leave you with five basic rules for telling a joke.

1. Pick your moments. It's easiest, of course, to tell a joke when everyone's relaxed and enjoying himself. Telling a joke to relieve tension is a high-risk strategy, but potentially hilarious. Besides, there'll be other funerals.

2. Know where you're going before you start. Hopefully, in the direction of the punch line. It sounds obvious, but it's amazing how often people embark blithely on a joke they think they know without rehearsing the all-important ending, only to find themselves completely lost.

3. Don't be tempted to over-elaborate—using fewer words often works better. Eddie Izzard makes it look easy, but remember that one man's surreal flight of fancy is another man's rambling incoherent humiliation.

4. Project a demeanor of relaxed confidence—it gives your listener permission to laugh. You can try deadpan if you like, but normal social joke-telling usually requires the teller to laugh too.

5. Enjoy it. If you're all tense and competitive about sharing a joke with friends, if your entire self-esteem is resting on the outcome, then you're doing it for the wrong reasons. On the other hand, you are showing signs of the borderline personality disorder that characterizes all the best comedians; perhaps you should consider doing this for a living?

I did have trouble getting here tonight. I know a lot of comics say that, but I did genuinely have a lot of trouble getting here tonight. It was quite traumatic actually, when I think about it. Started out: unhappy childhood . . . —*Sean Lock*

DIVORCE ATTORNEYS 1, ROMANCE 0

People say to me, "You're not feminine." Well, they can just suck my dick.—*Rosanne Barr*

I met a girl at a barbecue. A very pretty blond girl, I think. I don't know for sure; her hair was on fire. And all she talked about was herself. "I'm on fire!" You know the type. "Jesus Christ, help me! Put me out!" Come on, can we talk about me a little bit?—*Garry Shandling*

The Five Secrets to a Great Relationship: 1. It's important to find a man who works around the house, occasionally cooks and cleans and who has a job. 2. It is important to find a man who makes you laugh. 3. It is important to find a man who is dependable, respectful and doesn't lie. 4. It is important to find a man who's good in bed and who loves to have sex with you. 5. It is important that these four men never meet.

A couple are lying in bed. The man says, "I'm going to make you the happiest woman in the world." The woman replies, "I'll miss you."

My girlfriend said, "Jimmy, we're at a crossroads in our relationship. Down one road is hard work and commitment but, ultimately, happiness. Down the other road . . . well, the other road is a dead end." And I said, "That's not a crossroads, that's a T-junction."—*Jimmy Carr*

My wife, God bless her, was in labor for thirty-two hours, and I was faithful to her the entire time.—*Jonathan Katz*

One of my friends told me she was in labor for thirty-six hours. I don't even want to do anything that feels *good* for thirty-six hours.—*Rita Rudner*

My wife gets so jealous. She came home from work and was mad at me because there was a pretty girl on the bus she thought I would have liked.—*Ray Romano*

I asked my date what she wanted to drink. She said, "Oh, I guess I'll have champagne." I said, "Guess again."
—*Slappy White*

My fiancé and I are having a little disagreement. What I want is a big church wedding with bridesmaids and flowers and a no-expense-spared reception; and what he wants is to break off our engagement.—*Sally Poplin*

A woman wins the lottery. She says to her husband, "I've got it made! Start packing." He says, "Am I packing for cold weather or warm?" She says, "How the hell should I know? Just be out by the time I get back."

I saw six men kicking and punching my mother-in-law. My wife said, "Aren't you going to help?" I said, "No. Six should be enough."—*Les Dawson*

The basic conflict between men and women sexually is that men are like firemen. To us, sex is an emergency, and no matter what we're doing we can be ready in two minutes. Women are more like the fire. They're very exciting, but the conditions have to be exactly right for it to occur.—*Jerry Seinfeld*

Last night my wife met me at the front door. She was wearing a sexy negligee. The only trouble was, she was coming home.
—*Rodney Dangerfield*

Never tell. Not if you love your wife. . . . In fact, if your lady walks in on you, deny it. Yeah. Just flat out: "I'm telling ya. This chick came downstairs with a sign around her neck, 'Lay on Top of Me, or I'll Die.' "—*Lenny Bruce*

There is one thing I would break up over, and that is if she caught me with another woman. I won't stand for that.—*Steve Martin*

A blonde walks into a doctor's office. "Doc, I hurt all over," complains the blonde. She touches herself on the leg and winces. "Ouch! I hurt there!" She touches her earlobe. "Ouch! I hurt there too!" She touches her hair. "Ouch! Even my hair hurts!" The doctor says, "You've got a broken finger. . . ."

A redhead, a blonde and a brunette escape from jail and hide in a barn. The police close in, so the three women each hide in a sack. The police search the barn, and to check each sack, a police officer kicks it as he walks past. The officer kicks the redhead's sack, and the redhead says, "Meow!" The officer kicks the brunette's sack, and the brunette says, "Woof, woof." The officer kicks the blonde's sack, and the blonde shouts, "Potatoes!"

A blonde goes to the hospital to give blood and is asked what type she is. She tells them she's an outgoing cat-lover.

What do blondes put behind their ears to attract men?
Their feet.

CHAPTER SEVEN

Take My Wife . . . No, Please: Take My Wife

In which we encounter clichés about women and jokes, and tiptoe around an angry lady with a rolling pin.

You know “that look” women get when they want sex? Me either.

STEVE MARTIN

In the course of selecting the four hundred or so jokes that we thought would most delight our readers, and which now decorate these pages, we accidentally conducted an interesting experiment. We had started out by scanning close to twenty thousand jokes between us, and gradually boiled them down to a shortlist of nine hundred. The final editing process involved each of us, separately, picking our favorites from this list. Sorting the wheat from the chaff. Now, we do realize it's not a totally scientific experiment, given a sample group of two people and no controls to speak of. But we had always believed we had fairly similar senses of humor, so we think it's interesting that we agreed only 56 percent of the time. We agreed to discard 40 percent of the jokes, and agreed to include another 16 percent. Another 27 percent made Jimmy laugh but not Lucy, and the final 17 percent made only Lucy laugh. From this we choose to conclude several things: Firstly, that Jimmy likes jokes more, or at least likes more jokes than Lucy. Secondly, that we are each quite often baffled by a joke that the other finds amusing. And lastly, that a small but

I'm in a relationship at the moment. Sorry, girls. It's going to have to be your place.—*Lee Mack*

significant part of the difference between our choices can be explained by the fact that one of us is a girl.

The assumption that men and women have very different senses of humor is nothing new. Things that women are supposed to laugh at: periods, menopause, funny things children say. Things that men are supposed to laugh at: the humiliation of their enemies, the humiliation of their friends, the humiliation of a perfect stranger. Global ad agency JWT did some focus group hocus-pocus on the subject in 2005. They concluded that women find humor in "the little issues . . . a household chore, or something silly that somebody says to them at work." Men, on the other hand, "want to be funny to show off and to get people to admire them. It's all about scoring points, whereas with women humor is much more a way of creating an attachment, bonding and getting intimacy with people."

Now, advertising agencies have never been shy about pushing to the front of the queue when the clichés get handed out. The whole story is a lot more complex, but it's undeniable that our gender does influence not just the jokes we laugh at but also the way we use jokes from day to day.

Since your authors are well placed to examine the gender politics of joking from both sides, we suppose it's confession time. Yes, Lucy is terrible at telling jokes. She hates it; whenever someone says, "Tell us a joke, then!" (which they often do these days, worse luck), she is filled with dread, comes out in a rash, forgets every joke she ever knew. She is most comfortable with the silliest jokes, mainly ones with animals as protagonists. Two monkeys in a bath, a rabbit

A study in *The Washington Post* says that women have better verbal skills than men. I just want to say to the authors of that survey: Duh!—*Conan O'Brien*

with its ears nailed to the floor, a dog in a blender—that sort of innocent fun. And she really likes the joke about Freud (see page 92), but lots of people don't get that one because it involves knowing how to count in German, which leaves her looking both nerdy and unfunny. She worries about telling ironic jokes—what if someone doesn't realize that those aren't really her opinions? And she doesn't get the appeal of telling a genuinely offensive joke. Understanding it intellectually is one thing—she likes to think of herself as broad-minded—but actively going out of your way to shock someone seems like terribly bad manners. So far, so depressingly ladylike. Conversely, she has never knowingly laughed at a joke about sanitary napkins or the menopause or "household chores," whatever they are. And although she is deeply unimpressed by the deadly serious competitive joke-capping that goes on in a room full of comedians, all her favorite stand-up comics are men. ("Traitor!" hisses the sisterhood.)

Jimmy, on the other hand, thrives in the competitive atmosphere of stand-up comedy. He acknowledges that jokes are a way of asserting power over an audience. They are his route to alpha-maleness, a verbal equivalent of territorial pissing or the peacock's display of plumage. He loves to make people laugh at things they shouldn't and he has an embarrassingly good memory for jokes. He recognizes very few taboo subjects or situations for humor—pretty much anything goes, as long as it's funny. Again, we're ticking all the conventional boxes so far. But Jimmy rates his mother as one of the funniest people he's ever known. She didn't exactly return the compliment; she was very proud of him but he's pretty sure his act left her underwhelmed. Nevertheless, Jimmy inherited his sense of humor from her.

There should be a birth control for men. It makes more sense to take the bullets out of the gun than to wear a bulletproof vest.—*Greg Travis*

It's true that she didn't tell jokes as such—she knew perhaps four or five to which she remained faithful for years, getting quite excited when someone who might not have heard one of them came to the house. But she was funny all the time, in gestures and anecdotes and teasing remarks. Her humor wasn't restricted to the supposed female preoccupations, the small-scale and the domestic. She was funny about many of the same subjects that Jimmy's jokes explore; she just used a different format.

Our sense of humor—what we choose to laugh at—seems to be determined by culture first and gender second, inasmuch as it differs far more between two different societies, or even two different families, than it does between the men and women within a particular social group. Men and women alike learn from their tribe what they should laugh at and, by extension, how they can make each other laugh. But the shape that our sense of humor assumes when it shows itself to the world, and the subtlety with which we wield it, do seem to reveal some basic gender differences.

When you look at the history of comedy—its roots, so to speak—one thing in particular sticks out, and it's not something women can ever really compete with. We saw in Chapter 3 how mythological trickster figures juggled their commitments vis-à-vis mischief and joking with the challenges presented by their enormous (and sometimes detachable) sexual equipment. The earliest staged comedies of ancient Greece were the Satyr plays, in which the actors playing the randy mythological creatures—half-man, half-

My "current girlfriend" is always saying to me, "You never tell me how much you love me." I don't want to upset her.
—Jimmy Carr

goat—wore hairy trousers incorporating a large and shameless leather phallus. The plays of Aristophanes dress up this slapstick with more sophisticated verbal wit, but the preoccupation with penises is undeniable. Just one example, from *The Knights:*

> Sausage Seller: *Here is a camp-stool to sit on, for your comfort. And to carry it, an incredibly well-hung young slave. And if you fancy it, just turn him over and use* him *as a camp-stool.*
>
> Demos: *Dear me, I am back in the good old days.*

Traveling troupes of comic street performers in the Middle Ages and early Renaissance continued the classical tradition of phallic innuendo, enlivening their mystery plays with all manner of buffoonery. The actors of the Italian commedia dell'arte, which flourished in the sixteenth and seventeenth centuries, wore grotesque masks with dildos for noses; the whole genre of slapstick is so called after a long, split stick, commonly used by the protagonist of this early form of sketch comedy to belabor another actor over the behind, producing an exaggeratedly loud (and therefore humorous) noise. Waving big sticks around is only a slightly less subtle way of strapping on a big fake erection. Medieval court jesters carried a stick called a bauble, with either a tinkling bell or an inflated bladder tied to the end. (Taste and decency obviously preclude us from employing the words "bell" and "end" in closer proximity than that.)

Behind (or beside or in front of) many a successful comic is a phallic symbol. Charlie Chaplin has his cane, Groucho Marx his cigar. Ken Dodd clutches his tickling stick and sings a song about "a penis" (he spells it "happiness,"

I would never be unfaithful to my wife for the simple reason that I love my house too much.—*Bob Monkhouse*

but it's all in the delivery), while Mr. Punch favors a truncheon. Even little Norman Wisdom endlessly strums his banjo—that is, when he's not leaning on an appropriately suggestive lamppost. For today's comics, as we hinted in Chapter 4, a fistful of microphone (or its hard, shiny, comforting stand) will have to do. We should point out that Jimmy generally uses a clip-on radio mic. Make of this what you will.

In May 2005, *The New York Times* published an article by Warren St. John entitled, "Seriously, the Joke Is Dead." St. John's premise was that the classic short-story-with-a-punchline joke has been completely superseded by "the din of ironic one-liners, snark and detached bon mots that pass for humor these days." Comedians, he argued, just don't tell jokes on stage anymore. Blame for the joke's demise is variously laid at the door of political correctness (because good jokes are mean-spirited, and that's no longer acceptable), the Internet (for diluting the power of what was essentially an oral culture), the atom bomb (which destroyed our innocent delight in absurdity and turned us all into cynics) and, finally, women.

Women killed the joke. Emasculated the traditional comic, took away his weapon. It's a pretty weighty charge, and the *New York Times* article wheeled out some big guns to back it up. One of the experts quoted in the article was Professor John Morreall, who observed that telling old-style jokes was a masculine pursuit while women's humor was historically based on personal experience—a familiar argument, and a sound one. But Morreall goes further, mapping

My girlfriend says there's never an excuse to raise your hand to a woman. What if you've got a question?—*Jimmy Carr*

the rise of observational humor to the progress of the women's movement.

> *"The golden age of joke-telling corresponded with a time when men were especially loathe to reveal anything about their inner lives,"* Mr. Morreall said. *But over time men let down their guard, and comics like Lenny Bruce, George Carlin and, later, Jerry Seinfeld embraced the personal, observational style.*
>
> *"Women's-style humor was ahead of the curve," he said. "In the last thirty years all humor has caught up with women's humor."*

It sounds as though women are finally getting some rare credit for influencing the development of the craft of stand-up comedy. But if it's true that modern stand-up is "women's humor," why haven't women achieved more equality on the comic stage? Let's take a quick (arbitrary, unscientific) survey of professional joke-tellers. In 2005 an edition of the weekly *Time Out London* listings magazine, chosen at random, named a total of 621 comedy performances. One hundred and two of these were by women—that's just over 16 percent. On the peak weekend nights (Friday and Saturday), the percentage of female performers dropped sharply to just under 6.5 percent, with not a single woman on the bill at either the flagship Comedy Store or any of the large Jongleurs chain of comedy clubs. All this in a week that should have been something of a high-water mark for female comics; it included the final of the Babycham Funny Women competition, an all-woman bill of twelve comics. You'll notice too that the great majority of the contemporary jokes we quote in this book are written

We have a saying in Russia, "Women are like buses." That's it.—*Yakov Smirnoff*

and told by male stand-up comedians—another reflection of the comedy scene's gender imbalance.

There's a problem with St. John's suggestion that women are responsible for killing the joke. His evidence for the death of jokes is that nobody tells them anymore and that observational comedy is something completely different. But he's confusing the natural life cycle of a particular style of joke with the extinction of the whole species. Comedians absolutely do still tell jokes, *just not the same ones*. Maybe we're indulging in a bit of semantic hair-splitification, but we think there are more fundamental similarities between an old-school "man walks into a bar" joke and a contemporary observation-based stand-up routine than there are differences. When U.S. comic Lisa Lampanelli says, "You don't tell joke-jokes on stage, ever, because then you're a big hack," what she means is that it's very old-fashioned and unfashionable to tell generic jokes that you obviously haven't written. The trend is for individualism, for one-off observations and stories that unfold in a more subtle, idiosyncratic way than the previous generation of jokes did. This may be a less aggressively masculine style, but it's not a whole new feminine art form; a joke is still a joke.

And a joke is still a fairly blunt instrument of communication. It's functional, to the point; it requires very little emotional investment. In fact it often helps to conceal the degree of our personal involvement with a subject or situation. Horace Walpole wrote, "The world is a comedy to those that think, a tragedy to those that feel." Of course he wasn't distinguishing between men and women: for people of either gender, telling jokes can be a good way of substituting thinking for feeling. Nevertheless, we can't help

I'm not a breast man. I'm a breast person.—*John Wilson*

feeling (*and* thinking) that "joke" is a fundamentally masculine noun.

The vexed question of gender politics on the comedy club stage reflects the convoluted role of joking in the everyday battle of the sexes. A 1996 study of over three thousand personal ads in American newspapers found that 13 percent of all advertisements mentioned GSOH: Good Sense of Humor. While 5.7 percent of female advertisers offered a GSOH of their own, more than twice that number (13 percent) were looking for a GSOH in their male partner. Conversely 6.5 percent of men offered their GSOH as an asset, while only 4.9 percent required it in their chosen female. It seems there's a pretty good reciprocal arrangement going on here: women want men who make them laugh, and men want to make women laugh. And furthermore, any woman on the hunt for a husband would do well not to make him laugh too much. Another survey published recently in the journal *Evolution and Human Behavior* seems, depressingly, to confirm the notion that men aren't interested in "humor-producing women" for long-term relationships. However, they showed a preference for funny girls when it came to one-night stands. The same study concluded that women seek out people who make them laugh in all types of social relationships, whereas men only look for people who respond to their own jokes, especially in sexual relationships.

This is borne out by a third study which found that women are more generous with their laughter at other people's jokes, while men may even withhold laughter in a

A lot of women complain about periods, but I don't because I think they're brilliant. Especially if you know somebody who lives next door who you can't stand who's got a white sofa.
—Jo Brand

spirit of "humorous" competition. In the words of *The Office* and *Extras* cowriter Stephen Merchant, "I'll laugh *at* a woman, never *with* one" (it's only fair to point out that he was in character at the time). The study showed that men laugh most in an all-male group and least when a woman tells them a joke—in fact, a man is almost twice as likely to laugh when he tells his wife a joke as when she tells him one. And women are gender-biased too, laughing more at remarks made by men than by other women.

One depressing implication of all this is that a female stand-up comedian might always have to work harder to get laughs than her male colleagues, without even the consolation of a groupie or two. That in itself is a very good reason why fewer women are interested in careers in stand-up. Whichever way you look at it, funny women face more risk for less reward.

Differences in the use of humor according to gender—with males as the principal instigators of laughter and females as the ready providers of it—show themselves early. By the age of six, boys show a far more competitive interest in provoking laughter than girls do. It seems women generally don't have the same hunger that men do for making people laugh, so they have no need to devote as much attention to inventing or retaining jokes. There's an unhappy parallel here with the differences in laughing behavior between different levels of a highly stratified society. Among the Tamil people of India, members of the inferior Harijan caste adopt a high-pitched, giggling tone of voice when addressing their social superiors. There's also a famous study of

I love women, though I couldn't eat a whole one. But I think I know where I'd start.—*Jonathan Ross*

joking behavior in a hierarchical business environment, where joking was found to be the privilege of management at the expense of junior staff, and laughter the automatic response of said juniors. We're willing to bet that the Queen gets big laughs with indifferent material too. Laughter seems often to signal submission to the joker's will.

But hang on—isn't it time we gave men a break here? Making people laugh may indeed be a way of dominating them, but it's also a way of giving pleasure. One theory suggests that men like to make a woman laugh because her response mimics an orgasm. The physical symptoms are similar: a rush of blood to the face, throwing back the head to reveal the neck, squeezing the eyes closed and opening the mouth to emit harsh panting sounds. Many women use laughter to signal a certain openness to romantic negotiation—perhaps a teasing precursor of things to come—and a sexy laugh can be a powerful weapon in the modern gal's flirting repertoire. It's quite possible to seduce a man simply by laughing delightedly at everything he says—as long as you stop laughing when he takes his pants off.

Once the object of one's wooing is actually in one's arms, compulsive joking can be more of a hindrance than a help. A teetering scaffold of complex social rules encircles the precarious topic of joking about sex. A 1966 study of joking relationships in a Glasgow printworks showed that obscene jokes were commonplace between men, and between old men and old women; that young men were permitted a modicum of "mildly obscene banter" with old women if the women initiated said banter; and that old men "would routinely engage in highly obscene banter with young women." Lucky girls. The situation between the

I went out on a first date, but I don't think I'll be seeing her again. She got mad when I didn't open the car door. I just swam to the surface.—*Emo Philips*

young men and women was quite different: although a certain amount of mildly suggestive chat was allowed, obscenity and any sort of public bodily contact was frowned upon—although no doubt plenty of private groping went on behind the presses. If the offices we've worked in are anything to go by, young men and women are a great deal more tolerant of each other's obscenities these days. But anxieties about sexual jokes are persistent: they tend to shift shape and location, rather than going away completely.

In August 2003 a man named Royston Vasey was fined £200 (plus £150 costs) for battering another man with his golf umbrella on Blackpool's North Pier. Vasey admitted that he had hit the man but claimed that he had done so to uphold traditional values. The man had shouted out, "How are you, Chubby? How are you, you fat bastard?" "I just wanted the man to stop swearing and being abusive in front of women and children," said Vasey, who works as a comedian under the stage name Roy "Chubby" Brown. His act is so famously "blue" that he is rarely seen on UK television, and although his live shows play to fairly large audiences and his annual X-rated video is eagerly anticipated by a certain demographic, to most of the population his name is a byword for old-fashioned end-of-the-pier smut.

There's a touchingly 1950s sort of hypocrisy about the suggestion that women and children and traditional values are in need of protection, while it's perfectly all right to create an environment inside certain seaside theaters and workingmen's clubs where men can gather to laugh at crude

A very common male fantasy is to have two women at the same time. One to cook, one to clean, I think.—*Jimmy Carr*

and sometimes violent jokes about women and children. It's a notion that belongs to the era of dirty postcards, marital discord and mother-in-law jokes, that time before equal rights and marriage guidance counseling when men were so emotionally inarticulate that they had to pretend to protect women from crudity while simultaneously inventing, through jokes, an acceptable way to express their aggression toward them. And it's doubly anachronistic now that women are all binge-drinking, potty-mouthed harridans with bigger balls than their men, right?

Jokes against the mother-in-law or the nagging or faithless wife aren't always violent or hateful. Lots of them are very funny, even affectionate; they poke fun at the henpecked male most of all, sidelined and stifled by domestic life. "My wife went swimming last summer and lost two stones. I don't know how, I tied them round her neck tight enough." That's one from Les Dawson, the archetypal downtrodden husband of the 1970s—a sort of British Rodney Dangerfield. His crumpled, careworn bulldog's face and tone of utter resignation somehow took the sting out of what's really a pretty cruel joke. We can look back fondly at jokes like this one—almost a museum piece now. But jokes still work as weapons in the battle of the sexes, and the ones that men tell against women far outweigh their opposite numbers. It's like lining up the entire U.S. military against, say, the Swiss army. And the size and variety of weapons in the male joke arsenal are clues to the anxieties they feel. As the social stigma of divorce eased and the influence of the feminist movement made itself felt, mother-in-law jokes were replaced by other kinds. (How many feminists does it take to change a lightbulb? ONE!) The relentless and terrifying rise of the independent workingwoman aroused new

I'm dating a homeless woman. It was easier talking her into staying over.—*Garry Shandling*

strains of anxiety in certain men. Jokes that question women's intelligence and sexually objectify them into the bargain—blonde jokes, or Essex Girl jokes in England—may help these men to deal with the threat that the female brain appears to pose. That's not to say that we can't all laugh at blonde jokes, if they're clever and funny, but it does indicate that there may still be an issue around *women* who are clever and funny. The jokes don't create the issue; they do hold up a mirror that shows our flaws only too clearly.

In the same week that the authors of the advertising survey we quoted earlier claimed that women are amused by "household chores," readers of men's magazine *FHM* voted the UK's funniest woman as "none of them." It appears that a sizeable section of the male population doesn't find women funny, and that these men feel quite aggressive about it. They don't *want* women to be funny. They won't let women make them laugh. This certainly supports the advertising company's suggestion that men's approach to joking is competitive—even downright aggressive.

A comedy club stage feels like a much more dangerous place for a woman than it does for a man. Comedy nights are magnets for young, drunk men. And in every group of young, drunk men there will be at least one who wants to take advantage of the instant audience feedback mechanism that comedians love so much, by articulating his personal critique of the show. Brevity and pungency are his watchwords. "You're shit," "Tell us a joke," "Get off" and so on. Female comics get heckled more than the men, and an overwhelming proportion of their critics feel moved to sug-

I was on a date with this really attractive model. Well, it wasn't really a date date. We just ate dinner and saw a movie. Then the plane landed.—*Dave Attell*

gest that the only way a woman can possibly entertain a pub full of men is by removing her clothes. Few male comedians are welcomed on stage with a chorus of "Get yer tits out!" Yet for a female comic this greeting is standard.

Gershon Legman, the Freudian joke theorist we met in Chapter 5, believed that any joke with a sexual theme was an act of "verbal rape." He went on to say, "Compulsive jokesters express almost openly the hostile components of their need, by forcing their jokes upon frankly unwilling audiences. . . . Often they proffer this openly as their only social grace." Ouch. But really, that's going a bit too far; we obviously can't agree with Legman's implication that all comedians are a little bit rapey—and socially inept, to boot. The very thought! On the other hand, if Legman was right to identify sexual violence (in its most metaphorical sense) as the underlying motive for telling "dirty" jokes, then that would explain why this kind of humor is such a male preserve: a boy's club that a few daring women enter at the risk of their reputations. It would also go some way to explaining the extreme hostility of the insecure male heckler to a woman who tells jokes. In some dull recess of his pickled-walnut brain, he understands that she's trying to rape him.

Now that we've safely deconstructed all of this, perhaps post-feminists can allow themselves to laugh at some contentious jokes without feeling themselves to have been "verbally raped"—just "verbally pinched on the bum and winked at." Much of the aggressive sexism that Legman identified resided in the attitude of the joke-teller and not the joke itself. But the landscape of stand-up comedy has become a whole lot more complex since Legman's sixties heyday. Comedians like Larry David, Ricky Gervais, Sarah Silverman and Sacha Baron Cohen (who appears as Ali G

I don't have a girlfriend. But I do know a woman who'd be mad at me for saying that.—*Mitch Hedberg*

and Borat) use an ironic stage persona to tease the audience's notions of acceptable humor. Sam Anderson, writing in the online magazine *Slate*, coined the term "meta-bigots" to describe their approach. This school of comedy addresses social issues indirectly, by satirizing the lazy clichés of public opinion. As Anderson points out, "They manipulate stereotypes about stereotypes. It's a dangerous game: If you're humorless, distracted, or even just inordinately history-conscious, meta-bigotry can look suspiciously like actual bigotry." It's often impossible for the audience to distinguish, with any certainty, the comedian's true intent behind the layers of misdirection and subtext. By cloaking their own opinions in this way, they can keep the audience guessing. They can also up the ante as far as shock is concerned, with the get-out clause that they are exposing hypocrisy. A sample joke from Sarah Silverman runs,

> *I was raped by a doctor. Which is so bittersweet for a Jewish girl. . . .*

Ironic sexism may be mistaken for actual sexism, but it's partly this ambivalence that gives jokes like this one of Jimmy's their particular comic charge:

> *Feminists are always saying, "A woman's work is never done." All I'm saying is, maybe if they got themselves organized a little bit better? . . .*
>
> *I see you're shaking your head, madam* [to woman in audience]. *What you need to understand is that this is postmodern misogyny. It's steeped in irony.*
>
> *So don't you worry your pretty little head about it . . . love.*

I'm single by choice. Not my choice.—*Orny Adams*

Are men better at telling jokes than women? Well, perhaps—the aggressive, point-scoring aspects of stand-up comedy certainly seem to come more naturally to them. But then men are also better at football, fighting and forgetting significant dates. These special masculine talents are undoubtedly partly chemical—a side effect of that red fog of testosterone that enshrouds the male brain. But there's a large degree of cultural conditioning at work too. A patriarchal society molds its men into hearty jokers, and claims this as a virtue. The impulse to tell jokes seems to spring in large part from a certain competitive, attention-seeking quality that contemporary Western culture still tries to breed out of its womenfolk, despite the valiant efforts of Germaine Greer and the Spice Girls. So lady jokers tend to be filed in the same category as lady boxers: brave, contrary, entertaining in their own peculiar way but somehow fundamentally out of place in a man's game. And they must be sick of it. It's more or less impossible for a female comedian to get through a media interview without being asked, "Why aren't there more women in comedy?" Perhaps if they were allowed to spend more time telling jokes and less answering the same unanswerable question over and over, there would be more women in comedy.

We're not sure that there will ever be an equal number of male and female stand-ups; the evidence from children's joking behavior—that telling a joke is something boys just want to do much, much more than girls do—seems overwhelming. But maybe it's not too much to hope that some of the additional cultural barriers to

I broke up with a girl once because she lied about her weight. Well, I say that—actually she died in a bungee jumping accident.—*Jimmy Carr*

women's stand-up are slowly being dismantled, thanks to the sheer bloody-mindedness of women like Jo Brand, Joan Rivers, Jenny Éclair, Sarah Silverman and a host of others. Certainly there are many more role models for women contemplating a comedy career now than there have ever been before.

Finally, there's one more vexed issue we need to address: that of the average woman's supposed inability to tell jokes. "My wife knows all my jokes back to front. And that's exactly the way she tells them," runs an old, old joke. Men are from Mars; women can't remember punch lines. On such reductionism is many a lucrative self-help empire built. Actually virtually *nobody* has a good memory for jokes. While we were researching this book, Jimmy appeared as a guest on the UK's most popular breakfast radio show, gave out his e-mail address and asked people to send him their favorite jokes. Of the two-thousand-odd replies, over seven hundred of them were repetitions of a single joke:

> *I went to the zoo, and when I got there all they had was a dog.*
>
> *It was a shi-tzu.*

There's no way that is the all-time, lifelong favorite joke of 33 percent of the Radio 1 audience. It just happened to have done the rounds as a "Friday funny" e-mail the week before, and lodged itself temporarily in everyone's forebrain. And so we theorize—why depart from the cava-

My wife thinks I'm too nosy. At least that's what she keeps scribbling in her diary.

lierly unscientific approach that has served us so well so far?—that the average human brain has room to remember about three jokes properly and five or six other half jokes that remain frustratingly incomplete at just the moment when you need to tell them. The people who develop their joke memory beyond this natural (dare we say, "normal") capacity do tend to be a bit odd. Some are charmingly so; others are beyond infuriating and, we suspect, mildly autistic. Many of them are stand-up comics, and most of them are men.

I remember my brother once saying, "I'd like to marry Elizabeth Taylor," and my father said, "Don't worry, son, your turn will come."—*Spike Milligan*

MUST HAVE G.S.O.H

My sister was with two men in one night. She could hardly walk after that. Can you imagine? Two dinners!—*Sarah Silverman*

So I kissed Lucy, and I was very surprised to feel her tongue pop out.

It was my first real snog and I loved it. You can imagine that I fell in love instantly. Sadly the next year Lucy developed distemper and had to be put down.—*Hugh Laurie*

I was on stage last night and I said, "You know the diaphragm is a pain in the ass." Someone yelled out, "You were putting it in the wrong way."—*Carol Montgomery*

What is my favorite romantic spot? You mean in the whole world or on somebody's body?—*Jackie Mason*

I'm a great lover, I'll bet.—*Emo Philips*

I split up with my last girlfriend because she was terribly hypocritical. She used to say, "I love surprises," but when she found out I was sleeping with her sister . . . —*Jimmy Carr*

A honeymoon couple go into a hotel and ask for a suite. "Bridal?" asks the desk clerk. "No thanks," replies the bride, "I'll just hang on to his shoulders."

Sex is one of the most wholesome, beautiful and natural things that money can buy.—*Steve Martin*

If rhino horn is such a powerful aphrodisiac, why are rhinos an endangered species?—*Rory McGrath*

—Wanna fuck?
—Looks like you talked me into it, you sweet-talking bastard.
—*Australian joke*

How do girls get minks? The same way minks get minks.

Harry announces his plan to marry a nineteen-year-old stripper on his seventy-fifth birthday. His doctor says to him, "I think you ought to reconsider. Prolonged sex with a girl that young could be fatal." Harry shrugs and says, "If she dies, she dies."

A middle-aged man is told by his doctor that he only has twenty-four hours to live. He rushes home to his wife and says, "I've only got twenty-four hours to live. Can we have sex one last time?"

"Of course, honey," she says, and they go to bed.

Four hours later, he wakes her up and says, "Honey, could we have sex again? I've only got twenty hours to live and it could be our last chance."

"Sure, honey," she replies, and they have sex again.

Eight hours later, he nudges her again and says, "I've realized I only have twelve hours to live. Do you think we could do it one last time?"

"OK," says his wife, and they do.

Another four hours pass, then he asks her again. "I only have eight hours left now. Could we possibly . . ."

"Fine," she sighs, "I suppose it's the least I can do in the circumstances," and they have sex again.

Four hours later, he wakes her again. "Honey, I've just realized . . ."

"Listen," she snaps, "you may not have to get up in the morning, but I do."

If you run out of K-Y Jelly, a fine emergency substitute is something called "foreplay."—*Jeff Green*

I failed my audition as Romeo through a misunderstanding over a simple stage direction. My copy of the script clearly said: *Enter Juliet from the rear.—Lester Stevens*

People are always shocked when a celebrity gets caught in a hotel room with hookers and cocaine. But what else are you supposed to feed to hookers in a hotel room? Yogurt?
—Dylan Moran

I've had more women than most people have noses.
—Steve Martin

I've been thinking about S&M lately. Because if the guy ties you up, at least you know he wants you there for a while. It's a commitment.—*Janet Rosen*

I don't let men smoke in my apartment. But if I have a woman over she can barbecue a goat.—*Todd Barry*

Crossword clue in *Financial Times*: Listen carefully, or a sexual perversion (15 letters). Answer: Prick up your ears.

A chicken and an egg are lying in bed. The chicken is smoking a cigarette with a satisfied smile on its face, and the egg is frowning and looking put out. The egg mutters to no one in particular, "I guess we answered *that* question."

It's a fallacy that males stop masturbating after seventeen. Most usually stop after one.—*Jeff Green*

Ninety percent of men masturbate and the other 10 percent have no arms. Sixty percent of women masturbate and the other 40 percent expect you to believe it takes them that long to take a bath.—*Richard Jeni*

I discovered my wife in bed with another man and I was crushed. So I said, "Get off me, you two."—*Emo Philips*

I went out with an Irish Catholic. Very frustrating. You can take the girl out of Cork . . . —*Markus Birdman*

My girlfriend used to think magazines like *GQ* and *Maxim* were pornographic—until she found my real stash.—*Jimmy Carr*

CHAPTER EIGHT

Beyond the Pale?

In which we examine society's arrangements for giving, and taking, offense in the vicinity of a joke.

The aim of a joke is not to degrade the human being, but to remind him that he is already degraded.

GEORGE ORWELL

In 2001, the British Academy for the Advancement of Science launched an online experiment to find "the world's funniest joke." Hopelessly misguided though this exercise was, we are indebted to them for trying. Here's why the experiment was flawed: firstly, nothing, except perhaps a script for *The Simpsons*, was ever funnier because a committee agreed on it. There's simply no point in polling thousands of Internet users to decide what the world's funniest joke is. If you want to know, find the joke in this book that made you laugh hardest last time you saw it. That's the only world's funniest joke that matters.

Secondly, and more damagingly, they decided to leave out the dirty jokes. In fact, they say in their introduction to the published account, "Obviously we couldn't allow any offensive jokes onto the site, so each and every joke had to be vetted." The upshot of this tragic and fundamental misunderstanding of what constitutes the funny was that the following joke was voted into first place by . . . who, exactly? Come on, who voted for this?

We didn't have pedophiles when I was a kid. We had to buy our own sweets.—*Brian Damage*

A couple of New Jersey hunters are out in the woods when one of them falls to the ground. He doesn't seem to be breathing and his eyes are rolled back in his head. The other guy whips out his cell phone and calls the emergency services. "My friend is dead! What can I do?"

The operator, in a calm, soothing voice, says, "Just take it easy; I'm here to help. First, let's make sure he's dead."

There's a silence, then a shot is heard. The hunter's voice comes back on the line. "OK, now what?"

Actually, it's not that bad. But if it's offensive material you're looking for, you could argue that this joke requires that we laugh at a mentally retarded man who shoots his best friend dead in a macabre misunderstanding. If you're really determined to take offense, you can find it anywhere. Perhaps what the BAAS people meant was "We can't allow any jokes which could possibly be construed as dirty, racist or blasphemous." Fair enough—it was their experiment, and it was a family show. But excluding dirty jokes from the World's Funniest Joke competition doesn't stop them from being much, much funnier than most of the clean ones. As Mae West used to say, "When I'm good, I'm very good; when I'm bad, I'm better."

The self-appointed keepers of our public morals have a tendency to try and proscribe laughter by identifying fit or unfit topics for joking. Sometimes these rules are an extension of more general social mores: it's not polite to talk about sex, so it's definitely not polite to tell jokes about it. And

Most pedophiles wear glasses and a beard. What is it about that look that kids find so attractive?—*Frankie Boyle*

sometimes the rules prohibit joking specifically for its irreverence: when you talk about God, you must always do so with solemnity; disabled people deserve our pity, not our laughter; racial tension is a serious matter and joking makes it worse.

Norman Douglas, who published the definitive collection of filthy limericks in the 1920s, wrote testily of "that trying form of degeneracy which is horrified at coarseness." Hear hear. Still, if you are one of those trying degenerates, you probably want to skip straight on to the next chapter, and give this one a miss. The Reverend and Mrs. Greeves, although neither trying nor degenerate, are likewise encouraged to leave this particular stone unturned.

One of the most important functions of a joke is to shock. It's an acceptable way of giving vent to the unacceptable. A critic once described the incomparable Joan Rivers as "wickedly funny, delightfully vulgar, refreshingly—brutally—frank." Whether or not you agree that Ms. Rivers quite embodies all of these virtues, it makes a decent manifesto for dirty jokes—at least, the good ones. There's a very special noise that the comedy club audience makes when they hear a joke that hits their taboo right in the middle. It's a short bark of involuntary laughter that immediately turns into an "oooh" of disapproval. What's interesting is the order those two reactions come in. The laugh is always first. The joke has made them lose control of their social self-edit function, just for a moment. "The richest kind of laughter," said stand-up comic Bill Hicks, "is the laughter in response to things people would ordinarily never laugh at."

When jokes are told in public, people edit their responses unconsciously and continuously. All of us are much more likely to laugh out loud when we're part of a group

Why did Hitler kill himself?
He got his gas bill.

rather than when we're alone—we are signaling that we get it, that we are part of a group with a shared sense of humor. Equally, we understand, even if only subliminally, that when and how we laugh can give something away. In judging whether we should take offense at a joke, we apply a complex set of measurements of which we're usually only partially aware. We look at who is telling the joke, assigning differing degrees of licence-to-shock depending on their status. For example, stand-up comic Francesca Martinez, who has cerebral palsy, automatically gets the audience's permission to tell certain jokes about physical disability—permission that they may refuse to grant to an able-bodied comedian. Then we look around at the other listeners to see whether they are laughing and whether we're allowed to laugh in their company. Are there any representatives of the minority group against which the joke works? Any wheelchair users in the audiences are likely to find themselves at the center of a little oasis of silence. Perhaps some of us are lucky enough to be able to refer to some kind of moral code, to look within our soul or to our god(s) and ask whether we feel comfortable laughing at this. Each of us possesses some kind of yardstick to tell us what, for us, is beyond the pale. But of course in the heat of the moment, often we just laugh. Shock, tension, relief—it's a survivor's laugh.

Away from the comedy club stage, our boundaries of taste tend to be rather different, and usually wider. We laugh freely in the company of friends at jokes that we would feel compelled to disapprove of in front of strangers. "I know I shouldn't tell this one, but . . ." Nevertheless, most of us bring to all areas of our social lives an innate sense of when a joke is or is not appropriate. This cultural common sense

Why do Mike Tyson's eyes water during sex?
Mace.

governs not just the occasions where jokes are appropriate but also the relationships in which they are acceptable; it's what prevents us from telling Andrew "Dice" Clay jokes to our sister-in-law who works for the American Humane Association, for example. In the old days, before somebody coined the phrase "political correctness," they used to call this "good manners." One of the great things about knowing these rules is that we're allowed to test them, if we're that way inclined. Jimmy, for example, considers it his sacred duty in any given awkward situation to come up with the most inappropriate joke he can deliver without getting a smack in the mouth. He learned this from his mother, who cured him of social embarrassment during his teenage years by shouting across a crowded high-street chemist's shop, "Jim! D'you want me to ask if they've got condoms?"

In contrast, Lucy grew up in a family distinguished by four generations of Methodist ministers. But not in quite such stark contrast as you might expect. Once the vicarage tea has been cleared away, the Greeves siblings are not averse to a round or two of Obscene Scrabble. In this variant on the classic board game (which we'd like to point out is completely unofficial and in no way endorsed by the manufacturer), unorthodox spelling is encouraged, but every word must be rude. For example, the charmingly Gallic "wanquer" or Latinate "bollox" can produce particularly high scores, while a simple Anglo-Saxon "fuk" will often get you out of a tight corner. In cases where the obscenity of a particular word is disputed, the onus is on the player to convince his opponents by using the word in an obscene context. (The secret here is that almost any word sounds rude when you put it into a sentence involving an actress and a bishop. "Feather," for example. Or "bean.") Once all

Has anyone here been caught thieving in the Middle East? Let's have a show of hands.—*Jimmy Carr*

legitimate plays are exhausted, players must pool their remaining letters and work together to try and achieve an obscene "full house," where every tile is employed in the service of smut. There are no real winners, just a warm glow of naughtiness all round. And no real losers, save the moral reputation of a generation of Greeveses.

Our own two households are far from alone in sharing a sense of humor and certain habits of joking that become family rituals over time. Many tribal societies formalize this family bond in specific "joking relationships." Anthropologists define a joking relationship as one in which tribal tradition dictates that one party is allowed, sometimes even required, to make fun of the other, who is required not to take offense.

The commonest joking relationships are between siblings-in-law. This has led some anthropologists to conclude that the joking relationship developed as an extension of the incest taboo into in-law relationships. Now, anthropologists seem on occasion a little too preoccupied with incest, but it's true that strong cultural traditions prevail against it in almost all societies, handily preventing overconcentration of the gene pool. Witness the Pitcairn Islanders or certain sections of the English aristocracy if you want to see the consequences of allowing this prohibition to weaken. In the case of joking relationships, we think what they're getting at is that if custom requires you to conduct your relationship with your brother's wife on a wholly humorous level you are less likely to have sex with her, thus preserving filial harmony and ensuring that the other villagers aren't kept awake by late-night domestics.

Joking relationships are also documented among whole tribes or villages, within groups of men who were all cir-

If homosexuality is a disease, let's all call in queer to work. "Hello, can't work today. Still queer."—*Robin Tyler*

cumcised at the same time and groups of women who all began menstruating at the same time. The common factor in all these instances of joking rules is that they govern relationships where there's a certain ambivalence—a potential rivalry or a potential sexual relationship—which both parties, and the society as a whole, would rather avoid. By joking publicly at each other's expense, the joking partners can both acknowledge and safely contain the potentially unruly elements to their relationship. In most cases the joking is restricted to verbal teasing, but sometimes it gets quite brutal. In the 1940s, J. Radcliffe-Brown undertook some slightly mind-boggling fieldwork that revealed, among other things, that joking partners of the Dogon tribe exchange incredibly explicit insults about one another's parents' genitals, while the Lodagaba clown around at their joking partners' funerals, and the intrepid Kaguru "think it witty to throw excrement at certain cousins." Not so much "kissing cousins" as "shit-kicking cousins." Even the Carr family doesn't go that far.

"Horrible things may also be laughable. When we laugh at them, we often do so partly because we do not know what else to do. . . . Through laughter we achieve a provisional stance, outside belief and disbelief, in the face of the horrible." These are the wise words of William Willeford, a Jungian psychoanalyst and academic. And these are the unwise words of an unknown wit:

> *Two Palestinians are sitting in a café on the West Bank, comparing pictures of their families. "Here is*

My wife of eleven years—and that's quite old for a Filipino . . .
—Jim Tavare

Faisul. He died in a bus bombing last year. And this is little Amira, the apple of my eye—beautiful girl. And this is Kamil; sadly he was a suicide bomber too, just seventeen when he died. And little Abdul, who is twelve. Look at that smiling face!"

"Ah me," laments his friend. "They blow up so fast these days!"

What constitutes a safe joking distance? We have all laughed guiltily at a shocking joke relating to a recent, tragic event. Many of us have probably also angrily deleted a joke sent by e-mail that was too close to home, too tasteless—or simply not funny. Do we have any responsibility per se to avoid joking about certain topics, or is everything just a matter of distance? There's an old saying that comedy is tragedy plus time. And Charlie Chaplin is credited with the observation that "life is a tragedy when seen in close-up, but a comedy in long-shot." Some tragedies seem so cataclysmic that in the immediate aftermath it seems wrong to laugh at *anything*, let alone at jokes about the tragedy itself. In New York, following the suicide attacks on the Twin Towers in 2001, the comedy clubs were strange, furtive places for months. People wanted to laugh, but they needed to be given permission. The atmosphere in the media was one of near-hysterical solemnity, and any discussion of "the events of 9/11" that deviated from this tone was swiftly silenced. Comedian Bill Maher's satirical TV chat show *Politically Incorrect* was an early casualty of this stifling political climate. During a discussion on September 17, Maher's guest challenged the accepted view that the 9/11 hijackers were cowards. Maher agreed, saying, "We have been the cowards lobbing cruise missiles from

My girlfriend said to me in bed the other night, "You're a pervert." I said to her, "That's a big word for a girl of nine."
—*Emo Philips*

two thousand miles away. That's cowardly. Staying in the airplane when it hits the building, say what you want about it, it's not cowardly."

Several major advertisers immediately pulled their commercials from the show and seventeen local ABC networks refused to air any further episodes. Maher made a qualified apology, but the show was quietly dropped a few months later.

On September 29, less than two weeks after Maher's misstep, comedian Gilbert Gottfried was booked to perform at a Friar's Club Roast in front of an audience which included many of his comic peers. He launched into his set, and halfway through delivered a line about not being able to get a direct flight to California because "they said I'd have to stop at the Empire State Building first." The audience went cold. There wasn't even an involuntary bark of laughter, just boos and hisses. Someone shouted, "Too soon!" and it looked as though Gottfried had lost his crowd. Like a true comedian, he did the only thing he could. He plunged headfirst into the unknown and apparently icy waters of the audience's disapproval, with a joke as his only flotation device.

But what a joke! The one that Gottfried chose to tell was the Aristocrats, possibly the dirtiest joke of all time. The Aristocrats is an old vaudeville joke so filthy that it is traditionally reserved for professionals only, and strong-stomached professionals at that. Passed from comedian to comedian, a test of bravado and one-upmanship, it provides a perfect can in which to squish the obscene worms of the comic's troubled imagination. Each rendition of the joke provides an accurate reading of his desire to shock and provoke, on a sliding scale of audience reaction from gasping to passing out. It goes like this:

People always want to try on my glasses. That's rude. I don't go to people with hairpieces, "Hey, let me try on your wig." "Let me sit in your wheelchair. Oh my god, you are so crippled."
—Jim Gaffigan

A vaudeville talent agent is sitting in his office. A man comes in and says, "Boy, have I got an act for you!" "What kind of act?" asks the agent suspiciously. "It's a family act, but it's really unusual. You're going to love it." The agent shakes his head. "Sorry, pal, I don't take family acts. They're a little too cute for today's audiences." "Just give me five minutes to tell you about it," pleads the man. "I think you'll agree it's something special. There's me, my wife, our two kids and our dog, and . . ."

The next part of the joke is the ad lib—the only given being that the act(s) performed by the family should be criminally indecent, with no taboo left standing: incest, bestiality, coprophagy, dismemberment, extreme violence, whatever else you can imagine and a few things you wish you couldn't.

When the man has finished, the stunned agent says, "That's quite an act. What do you call yourselves?" "The Aristocrats."

Now, it's not a very good joke per se. The name of the act—the punch line—is supposed to contrast with their horrible antics, so it's particularly unfunny in the UK, where the aristocracy have never been exactly renowned for civilized sexual behavior. Gottfried's night was already going pretty badly, and it could easily have gone so very much worse. But on this occasion, the Aristocrats killed. The audience laughed so hard that, by the end of the joke, some of them were literally on the floor. He substituted low scatology and smut for the greater horror of the terrorist attack, and the audience gratefully seized the opportunity to lighten up.

I've done a little survey, guys, and size does matter. But not as much as smell.—*Danny Liebert*

This episode is grippingly recounted in a movie about the joke called (naturally) *The Aristocrats*. Made by comic magician Penn Jillette (of Penn and Teller fame) and stand-up Paul Provenza, it premiered at the Sundance Film Festival in 2005. The film, which features over 100 comedians telling or talking about the infamous joke, was subsequently turned down by AMC, a massive U.S. cinema chain, and generated acres of press coverage on both sides of the Atlantic. Made by comedians, about comedians, largely for comedians, the film keeps its gaze fixed resolutely upon its own navel. If one agrees even slightly with Freud's contention that the jokes we tell reveal our unconscious fears and desires, the comedians here are a pretty sick bunch. Doug Stanhope recounts a lurid version of the joke to his own baby. George Carlin gets about as graphic with his toilet tale of laxatives and coprophagy as it's possible to get. Sarah Silverman neatly subverts the text by turning it into a true story with herself as the daughter in the act, a victim of rape and worse.

But the overwhelming impression is not of dark, twisted souls unexpectedly revealed as the comedy mask slips. Rather, these are overgrown kids, over-impressed by their own bravado in discussing incest, pedophilia and human waste matter—speaking of forbidden things simply because they are forbidden. And what's interesting is how neatly most of them sidestep any discussion of the topics for humor that are properly taboo. Although they all share a desire to shock that far exceeds that of any "normal" individual, they too have boundaries they will not cross in the context of a joke. The acceptable taboos of sex and scatology provide a handy proxy for the still unacceptable taboos of race and terror and emotional pain.

Say what you want about the deaf. . . . —*Jimmy Carr*

As a professional comic who deals with edgy topics, your licence to tackle taboos without giving offense has to be negotiated, with your own conscience as much as with your audience. Perhaps the most straightforward way to approach this is to treat the audience like a bunch of friends. It follows that, if you would happily tell your friends an off-color joke and enjoy a tension-releasing laugh together, then you shouldn't censor yourself on stage. The audience are grown-ups; they can deal with it. That's fine in theory, but getting away with it is another matter. The ability to treat taboo topics in such a way that you carry the audience with you without giving offense is a mark of the joke-teller's skill. If a joke is written and told well, in a way that appeals to your sense of humor, it's hard not to laugh at it, in the heat of the moment, even if it's incredibly tasteless.

A skillful comedian can ease the audience into a "dirty" joke, playing a series of shocks and anticlimaxes. Here's Steve Martin:

> *Now, this doesn't happen very often, but the other day I met a girl and she took me back to her apartment. And she had the* best pussy *I have ever seen. . . . [audience reaction]* Oh, *now* COME ON! *I'm talking about her* CAT. *Now, that makes me sick. You can't say anything anymore without people taking it dirty and I'm sorry, that disgusts me . . . [beat] . . . That cat was the best fuck I ever had."*

These days it can appear as though we're edging tentatively toward a situation where there are no taboo topics for

A homeless person said to me, "I haven't had anything to eat for two days." I said, "I wish I had your willpower."
—Roy "Chubby" Brown

jokes, only taboo treatments of certain topics. The solidest taboo still standing is almost certainly not that good old double act, sex and God, but rather race. Yet even in that most sticky of wickets, context is all. So Chris Rock can joke about hiding money in books so that black people don't steal it, because "books is like Kryptonite to niggers." Neither that sentiment nor that vocabulary would be available to a white comedian, but in Rock's hands it becomes incisive social comment—and, more importantly, funny. Joan Rivers, who approaches taboos as though they were piñatas, famously told jokes on stage about her husband's death almost as soon as she had buried him. "I think I'm the one who caused my husband's heart attack. While we were making love I took the bag off my head. . . ." From a grieving widow, such levity is startling (particularly since Rivers's husband had taken his own life, rather than dying of a heart attack), but we're not really allowed to find it offensive. On the other hand, no one else is allowed to tell these jokes—no one else could make the story funny. Personal pain confers inalienable joking rights, even over the most sensitive issues.

So we can't necessarily blame the jokes themselves for causing offense. In fact, offensive jokes give the lie to the old adage that you shouldn't shoot the messenger. What can be hugely distasteful and offensive is the intention of the joke-teller, even if the joke, taken in isolation, seems quite innocent. Context is everything. We could make a strong case for there being a big difference between telling a whole series of jokes that denigrate, say, gay people and telling a set full of jokes that fulfill the audience's expectations of your sardonic stage persona by taking an ironic swipe at every stereotype in sight. It's the difference between knowingly telling a lie in order to be funny, and really meaning it.

An old woman is upset at her husband's funeral. "You have him in a brown suit and I wanted him in a blue suit." The mortician says, "We'll take care of it, ma'am," and yells back, "Ed, switch the heads on two and four!"

But how much of a difference is there, really? After all, some members of the audience may not have their irony detector switched on. As we observed in the last chapter, "meta-bigotry" can be a dangerous game. The laughter the comedian hears is an imprecise feedback mechanism: some may be laughing not because they appreciate the layers of irony that overlay the joke but because they really believe, for example, that black people are stupid, and the joke confirms them in their belief. Should comedians lose sleep over the misinterpretation of their ironic intent?

For a joke to give offense, offense must first be taken. Someone must hear the joke and respond to it with outrage. Most of us have had that uncomfortable experience, in everyday conversation with friends, of making a comment because it popped into our heads and sounded hilarious, only to realize too late that it has mortally offended one of the company. It's one of those horrible, I'm-shrinking-inside-from-shame-why-doesn't-the-ground-swallow-me-up sort of moments. But a stand-up comedian has a much larger audience, he doesn't know them personally, and they've all paid to be entertained: he serves the majority, and can seldom allow himself that degree of sensitivity to a single outraged individual. The committed joke-teller feels an overriding responsibility to be funny and will successfully detach himself from any concerns about offending an audience member, in ruthless pursuit of the big laugh. Frank Skinner once responded to an audience that hissed at an off-color joke, "How d'you think I feel? My parents were killed in a car crash swerving to avoid a chicken that was crossing the road—and my brother and sister were both electrocuted changing lightbulbs." For the audience too the social rules are different, and are further complicated by

I once saw my grandparents having sex, and that's why I don't eat raisins.—*Zach Galifianakis*

the fact that a great many of the individuals who take offense at a joke in a comedy show do so on behalf of a minority group of which they themselves are not members. A joke about "cripples" is far more likely to result in walk-outs than wheel-outs. One of Jimmy's more contentious jokes is based on the premise that British theme park Alton Towers is "essentially a poor man's Disney. It's the sort of place you might send a child who's dying of something that's not that serious. [Mimes answering phone.] "Yeah, what's he got? Asthma, you say? Well, we'll pass the hat round, but I'm making no promises. . . . Brittle bones? Has he been to Chessington? OK, but he'll have to bring his own cap.'" One night, the mention of "brittle bones" elicited a huge cheer from one man in the audience. He was in a wheelchair. "Hello," said Jimmy, not without a certain trepidation. "Have you got brittle bones, then?" The man's reply? "Brittle as *fuck*."

Comedians are not the kind of people you want to put in charge of protecting minority groups. As a breed, they're instinctively with the mob. Far from being fearless mavericks, riding roughshod across popular sensibilities in pursuit of a laugh, most stand-up comics, and most "offensive" jokes, are not taboo-busting at all: they are inherently conservative. By mocking situations that we would otherwise find uncomfortable, by legitimizing our anxieties about people who are different and hard to relate to, these jokes perpetuate the status quo. They don't make things worse for the people they mock, but nor do they help us to understand them. That's not their job: they are jokes. It isn't the function or purpose of jokes to enlighten. Their only use is to amuse. And as we established in our earlier look at the mechanics of the joke, cruelty alone isn't funny. What

I met an amazing girl on the Internet. Smart, sexy, uninhibited . . . Of course it turned out to be a twelve-year-old paraplegic boy. I'll be honest—the sex was disappointing.
—*Jimmy Carr*

makes an "offensive" joke work is that the cruelty rings true with some aspect of the listener's experience, and that's not always a pleasant aspect. It's often a prejudice, a resentment, a guilty pleasure, something we're ashamed of.

Henri Bergson tells us that the appreciation of a joke requires a "momentary anaesthesia of the heart." In order to laugh, we must experience a temporary failure to empathize with the victim of the joke. By this definition, every laugh is an act of cruelty. It's true that our laughter often takes a more uncompromising stance than we would readily adopt in normal conversation. The important thing about this is not the fact that our response is cruel, but that it's truthful. In that moment, we are dispassionate even as we abandon ourselves to the emotional release of the laugh. We take ownership of an honest, if unattractive, emotion—and we are allowed to do so. Our heartlessness is defused and sanctioned by the ritual of joke-telling.

It doesn't necessarily follow that the joke-teller should be absolved of all responsibility to ensure his material is not injuriously offensive. A black waitress successfully sued Bernard Manning after he and his white audience subjected her to sustained racist abuse while she was working at one of his gigs; most of us would find this completely right and proper, given that she had no choice about being there. In this context it's easy to demonize Manning, especially since he himself seems willingly to embrace the role of martyr to political correctness. But what is much less comfortable for us to grapple with, well-meaning woolly liberals that we are, is the audience's complicity in the episode. No court ruling or legislation can stop people from finding Bernard Manning funny as long as he pushes their buttons. Doesn't that make them equally racist? The man

A husband and wife are relaxing on their wedding night. He leans over her and asks tenderly, "How was it for you?" "It was alright, but I didn't think much of your organ." "Well," he retorts, "I didn't expect to be playing in an auditorium."

himself claimed, in an interview with the *Radio Times* in 2003, that alternative comedy is dead because "people won't wear it. Political correctness is finished. Everyone thinks the way I do, otherwise I wouldn't get applause."

But Manning's argument oversimplifies the interaction between comedian, jokes and audience. It's simply not true to say "everyone thinks the way I do" on the basis that an audience laughs at your jokes. For a start, not "everyone" goes to see Bernard Manning live. He's at the tail end of his career, and his opinions are much less relevant than he would like to think. And secondly, a comedy club is not a place where people go to learn the truth. They go to hear a man or woman tell amusing lies about things that haven't really happened. Their laughter is not simply an expression of agreement with the comedian's politics, worldview or attitude to minority groups. They may laugh harder if the jokes seem to them to touch on some aspect of their own experience—if the lies ring true. But if we had more skill to interpret the individual laughs that make up the general audience response, we would hear a whole spectrum of differently motivated chuckles and guffaws. Laughter can express the joy of transgression: "I can't believe he just said that." It can express community: "I'm so glad we came to this comedy club for Stig's stag do." It can express rage: "Yes! I HATE MY WIFE TOO!" It can express anxiety: "I must laugh at these jokes so the guys don't realize I'm gay." And it can express high spirits: "I just had six tequilas. Woooo!"

For some time now, cultural commentators have been expressing concerns that bigotry is creeping back into

I once had a large gay following, but I ducked into an alleyway and lost him.—*Emo Philips*

mainstream comedy, camouflaged with a fresh coat of irony; that the lazy, casual cruelty, in response to which the UK alternative comedy movement first developed in the 1980s, is once more the stuff of mass entertainment. Perhaps the hard thing for these people to swallow is that the casually cruel jokes have never really gone away; they may not have been on the TV, but they thrived, not just in Northern workingmen's clubs and end-of-the-pier shows, but in private exchanges and, since the Internet became ubiquitous, in the in-boxes of . . . well, everybody. And another thing that certainly hasn't changed is the predictable grousing of every successive generation since Adam about how coarse and degenerate things have become since their heyday.

It's a very good thing that we've managed to come so far since the days of freak shows and Saturday excursions to Bedlam to laugh at the inmates. It shows how much more enlightened we are as a society, doesn't it? Actually it shows how cleverly we shift our moral boundaries in order to scratch the same itch. We watch prurient documentaries about hirsuteness, hermaphroditism, obesity and Siamese twins instead of gawking at the Missing Link, the Bearded Lady and so on. We turn the socially dysfunctional and the "learning-disabled" (previously known as village idiots) into figures of fun in the forms of Mr. Bean, Woody the Cheers barman and all sorts of others. And *The Surreal Life* is surely the closest we can get to recreating a Victorian psychiatric ward without actually putting straw on the floor and calling it "The 1800s Mad House." The urge to mock those who are disabled and different doesn't go away. We find their difference both threatening to the homogeneity of our community, and useful as an anti-model against which we can reaffirm our normality. We laugh at the mad-

What's the difference between an oral thermometer and a rectal thermometer?
The taste.

man because it makes him seem harmless and because it makes us feel united in our sanity.

Of course all these jokes feel incredibly uncomfortable and excluding for some of those who identify themselves with the targets—just one more insult added to the injury of being thought different. There is an ever-present danger that we may allow the fact that people are laughing to legitimize prejudice and obscure the real offense being committed. Professional comedians with any kind of integrity ought to be on their guard against this, resisting the temptation to make cheap and exploitative jokes that pander to audience prejudices. A good test: do you have to look over your shoulder before you tell a joke? If not, if you're happy to look your audience in the eye whatever their age, race, gender, sexual orientation or state of physical and mental health, then you are probably on the right track. But if you prefer your audience to be restricted to like-minded, able-bodied, similarly colored individuals who will agree in advance with your personal agenda, then warning lights should begin to come on.

Many minority groups feel that something more should be done to stop negative or derisive stereotypes being rehearsed and reinforced through jokes. But what? The government could publish a list a mile long of topics about which joking is inadmissible. Given that even the most vehemently right-on exponents of alternative comedy still needed someone to mock—lawyers, ginger people, the middle classes, policemen—where would the list end? We'd just keep on shifting our taboos to soothe our consciences, pushing all of that contentious joking underground. Certain live comedy venues already seem to resemble nothing so much as comedy "fight clubs," where the deeply unfashionable and

Jesus walks into a motel, throws a bag of nails on the counter and says, "Can you put me up for the night?"

unpleasant opinions of embattled but defiant men are aired under a paper-thin veneer of humor. These are the almost-jokes that give ordinary, decent jokes a bad name, the ones that are little more than aggressive statements of bigotry post-rationalized as humor. At least let's air our opinions in the open, exercise our judgment as consumers of comedy and allow a certain amount of rough-and-tumble in the name of a good joke.

The truth is that a joke is seldom a victimless crime. Someone or something is usually the butt of it. And if we condemn all jokes that make fun of anyone, we are left with . . . a handful of puns and "knock knock" jokes. Human beings are at home with binary thought patterns: black or white, one or zero, us or them. Howard Jacobson, in his fascinating book *Seriously Funny*, writes, "When a community celebrates its shared pleasure in the ordinary, *something* perceived as extraordinary is going to get it in the neck." Our communities define themselves, in part, by looking at what they are not. So whichever social group you belong to, willingly or otherwise, the one thing you can be absolutely sure of is that someone, somewhere, will still be telling a joke at your expense. So try and get yours in first, and make it funnier.

Should crematoriums give discounts for burn victims?

TWO BIGOTS WALK INTO A BAR . . .

A man takes early retirement and leaves the big city for a crofter's cottage in the Scottish Highlands. After a month of isolation he hears a knock on his door. He answers it and sees an enormous Scottish farmer standing outside. "I hear you're new around here," says the farmer. "Yes, I am," replies the man. "I thought I'd introduce myself and ask you to a party I'm having," says the farmer. "That's very nice, I'd love to come," says the man. "I'd better warn you there'll be lots o' drinking," says the farmer. "I don't mind, I like a drink," replies the man. "And nae doubt they'll be a few fights breaking out," says the farmer. "That's OK, I can take care of myself," replies the man. "And things get a bit frisky in the wee hours," says the farmer. "There'll be lots of sex." "That's fine by me," says the man. "I haven't had any female company for a long time." "Och, there'll be no lassies," says the farmer. "It's just the two of us."

After a long and fruitful life Angus died. His widow called the local paper requesting that a death notice be published. Ever frugal, she asked that the notice simply say, "Angus Dead." The newspaper representative told her that the death notice must contain a minimum of five words.

"Fine," she said, "make it: Angus Dead. Volvo for sale."

Ireland's worst air disaster occurred early this morning when a small two-seater Cessna plane crashed into a cemetery. Irish search and rescue workers have recovered 1,826 bodies so far and expect that number to climb as digging continues.

A guy walked into a bar and said to the bartender: "I've got this great Polish joke."

The bartender glared at him and warned him: "Before you go telling that joke, I think you ought to know that I'm Polish, the two bouncers on the door are Polish, and most of my customers are Polish."

"OK," said the guy, "I'll tell it slowly."

A man boards a flight and is lucky enough to be seated next to an absolutely gorgeous woman. The man notices she's reading a manual about sexual statistics and asks her about it. "It's a very interesting book," she says. "It says that American Indians have the longest penises and Polish men have the widest. By the way, my name's Jill. What's yours?" The man replies, "Tonto Kowalski."

A Jewish father was very troubled by his errant son's behavior, and went to see the rabbi about it. "I brought him up as a Jew, spent a small fortune on his education and almost as much on his bar mitzvah. Then he calls me to tell me he has decided to become a Christian! Rabbi, where did I go wrong?"

"Funny you should come to me," said the rabbi. "Like you, I too brought my son up as a good Jew, put him through college—it cost me a fortune—and then one day he too came and told me he had decided to become a Christian."

"What did you do?" the man demanded anxiously.

"I turned to God for the answer," replied the Rabbi.

"And what did he say?" the father pressed.

"He said, 'Funny you should come to me . . .' "

A middle-aged Jewish man took his wife out to dinner to celebrate her fortieth birthday. He asked her, "So what would you like, Julie? A Jaguar? A mink coat? A diamond necklace?"

She said, "Bernie, I want a divorce."

He said, "Gee, I wasn't planning on spending that much."

Two old Jewish men were strolling down the street one day, when they happened to walk past a Catholic church.

Above the door of the church they saw a big sign that said, "Convert to Catholicism and get $10."

One of the Jewish men stopped walking and stared at the sign. He turned to his friend and said, "Murray, what's going on?"

"Abe," replied Murray, "I'm thinking of doing it."

With that, Murray strode purposefully into the church.

Twenty minutes later, he came out with his head bowed.

"So," asked Abe, "did you get your $10?"

Murray looked up at him and snapped, "Is that all you people think about?"

CHAPTER NINE

An Englishman, an Irishman and a Rabbi . . .

In which we plunge neck-deep into the murky waters of ethnic humor, and say nice things about the Irish.

Why be prejudiced against anyone because of their race, or nationality, or creed, when there are so many *real* reasons to hate others?

EMO PHILIPS

English people often make the mistake of claiming that the English are better at joking than anybody else. It's not necessarily a factual error; it's just a mistake to admit it because it's really nothing to be proud of. Anthropologist Kate Fox, in her painfully fascinating study, *Watching the English*, argues that what's uniquely characteristic of the English is not their ability to joke, but their willingness—even compulsion—to do so. "For the English, the rules of humour are the cultural equivalent of natural laws—we obey them automatically, rather in the way that we obey the law of gravity." In other words, we have two default states: sleeping and joking.

Most other cultures, she tells us, have a much more rigid set of rules governing the time and place for humor. In England (and the rest of the British Isles) humor is never far away. In particular, the arts of irony and understatement provide a constant undercurrent to our social dealings. So much so that it sometimes seems as though a sort of desperate facetiousness has romped through the nation like a flu pandemic. For some reason, we take enormous pride in this

Where would we be without a sense of humor?
Germany. —*Willy Rushton*

affliction. The richness of our mongrel mother tongue provides ample scope for another depressing national obsession: the pun. Among tabloid sportswriters at least, the habit has gone critical. There is even an annual award for the best headline. In December 2003, struggling, semiprofessional Scottish football club Caledonian Thistle scored a historic 3–1 victory over league-topping Celtic in the Scottish Cup. The *Sun* led with "Super Caley Go Ballistic, Celtic Are Atrocious." Puns and innuendo sometimes allow the tabloids to get away with surprisingly sexually suggestive headlines. They had a field day when Elton John and David Furnish celebrated their civil partnership. First there was the stag night: "Elton's Massive Bender." Then the ceremony itself: "Elton Takes David Up the Aisle" and so on. But it's not just the newspapermen who can't resist this sort of wordplay. Napoleon famously dismissed England as a nation of shopkeepers. Shopkeepers we may be, *mon brave*, but at least we are shopkeepers who can pun! Particularly if we are provincial hairdressers—Curl Up 'n' Dye, Hair Razors, The Smart Set, Right Hair Right Now . . . need we go on? A friend of ours briefly threatened to give up his legal career and retrain as a barber, so taken was he with the idea of opening a radical salon called Lunatic Fringe.

Quite apart from our affection for dreadful puns, we British are possibly unique in our wholehearted appreciation of jokes that aren't even funny. It's not because we have a particularly low quality threshold for humor. We don't confuse bad jokes with good ones, we just appreciate them in a different way. Take the Christmas cracker. Invented by a British confectioner named Tom Smith in 1860, the novelties were initially marketed as "Bangs of Ex-

They say travel broadens the mind. Except with Americans where it seems to widen the arse.—*Jimmy Carr*

pectation." To begin with, they had fortune cookie–style mottoes or literary quotations in them, which were gradually replaced by the now-familiar terrible jokes. If it seems that the jokes haven't changed since you were a child, it's because by and large they haven't: Tom Smith Crackers is still one of the largest cracker manufacturers in the world, and they've been using the same set of jokes since 1955. "People complain if we take them out," claims a company spokesman sheepishly, propping his feet up on his desk next to the dusty typewriter and knocking over a small Bakelite sign which reads, "Chief Joke Writer."

As we observed in our introduction, having "a good sense of humor" is absolutely vital to our social self-esteem—far more so than in most other nations. In fact, having got this far with the book, you could be forgiven for wondering whether foreigners (our lazy shorthand, if you please, for "non-English-speakers") actually tell jokes at all. If you were brought up in England, you are highly unlikely to speak another language to a level of proficiency sufficient to understand its jokes. But they do exist, and those clever (and effortlessly multilingual) Dutch folk have studied them so that we don't have to. The Germans and the Dutch, said psychiatrist Dr. Renatus Hartogs, are more inclined to scatological jokes. This is due, in his opinion, to "excessively strict and early toilet training." The English he finds to be overly preoccupied with homosexuality and incest, the Americans with oral/genital themes and racial stereotypes. The French, thanks to their "relatively non-traumatic" cultural passage to sexual maturation, joke amiably about "the refinement and variation of sexual technique." It must be said that they also joke about the ineptitude of the English with regard not only to said sexual technique, but also our lack of expertise in

You cannot underestimate the intelligence of the American people.—*H. L. Mencken*

other fields such as fashion and the culinary arts. Of course, being English, we are also better than them at taking a joke, *n'est-ce pas*? Yes, ha ha. *Ta mère ne rase pas ses aisselles.*[1]

[1] *Your mother doesn't shave her armpits.*

The fact is that, without foreigners and foreign-ness, there would be far, far fewer jokes. Some of the very earliest jokes for which there is any evidence are those that the ancient Egyptians told at the expense of the Nubians, a long-suffering people who are still the butt of jokes in Egypt today. We love to pick a regional, social or ethnic group to stereotype in our jokes, as a kind of shorthand for an undesirable character trait. This might be stupidity and laziness (Irish, Polish, Nubian) or excessive canniness and tightfistedness (Scots, Jews), poor personal hygiene (French, Polish again) or cowardice (Italians, French again). Once upon a time, "dumb" jokes tended to be about the next-door town. The village of Gotham in Nottinghamshire was the butt of such jokes for over four hundred years. During the reign of King Henry VIII, in around 1540, a book was published entitled *The Merry Tales of the Mad Men of Gotham*. It contained twenty humorous tales, most of them collected from earlier jest books and enriched with a little local detail. Jokes like this:

> *The men of Gotham were once greatly scared by a report that enemies were about to invade their country. They were anxious to save as much as they could from falling into the hands of the invaders; and first of all they decided to save their church bell, which they prized more than anything else. After a great deal of trouble they managed to get it down out of the church steeple. "Where shall we hide it so the enemy can't find it?" asked one of another.*

America is the only country where a significant proportion of the population believes that professional wrestling is real but the moon landing was faked.—*David Letterman*

At last someone said, "Let's sink it in the deepest part of our pond."

"Agreed!" said his fellows, and they dragged the bell down to the shore of the pond and got it aboard a boat.

Then they rowed out to the middle of the pond and hoisted the bell overboard. After it had disappeared, the worthy citizens of Gotham began to think they had been hasty. "The bell is now truly safe from the enemy," said they; "but how are we to find it when the enemy has left us?"

One of them, who was wiser than the rest, sprang up and cried, "That's easy enough. All we have to do is to cut a mark where we dropped it in!"

He snatched a knife from his pocket and cut a deep notch in the side of the boat where the bell had been thrown overboard. "It was right here that we heaved the bell out," said he.

Then the men of Gotham rowed back to the shore, fully assured that they would be able to find their bell by the mark on the side of the boat.

Don't open with it, would be our advice.

Which just goes to show how much *we* know. The book was so popular that it continued to be printed until the end of the nineteenth century, unchanged but for the title, where *Mad Men* was quickly replaced by the ironic *Wise Men*. The tales were exported to America by Washington Irving, who conferred the epithet "Gotham City" (i.e., City of Fools) on his native New York. Over time, the connotations of the name changed. The Batman comic books gave "Gotham City" a new implication of decadent, slightly sinister cool, which has persisted despite Adam

I can't figure out why Colombia isn't a superpower by now. They produce coffee and cocaine, so it's not like they can't figure out how to motivate the workforce.—*Margot Black*

West's wrinkly tights and George Clooney's equally preposterous rubber abs. The association between "Gotham" and "village idiots" has been all but forgotten.[2]

[2] . . . until we brought it up just now, that is. It's a good thing our publishers at Gotham Books have such a great sense of humor.

The original Gotham was only one of many put-upon settlements. The phenomenon of "fool towns" is widespread; history furnishes us with examples from ancient Greece, Egypt and Syria, and at least forty-five examples in England alone. The tradition survives in modern Europe, with Aarhus in Denmark, Lepe in Andalucia and Kerry in Ireland still resigned to having jokes cracked at their expense. It's important to note that many of these jokes are generic "dumb jokes," requiring only that the name of the town or perhaps the profession of the man in the joke be changed in order to make it locally relevant. It seems likely that the original Gothamites were singled out initially because of the village's relative isolation and perceived backwardness in comparison to the bustling city of Nottingham nearby.

When a community is looking for a butt for its stereotypical jokes, it tends not to cast its net too far. What's required is another community that mirrors the joke-teller's own closely enough that its traits are recognizable, but that can still be readily distinguished by certain real or imagined quirks of accent, dress or behavior. We rarely tell this kind of joke about a community very distant from our own, or about whose customs we know little; for example, in the U.S., pejorative Mexican jokes are common. These jokes aren't circulated in the UK, as Mexicans aren't commonly employed here as casual laborers or domestic staff. We look for borderlanders, people in our peripheral vision whom we can identify with, but choose to identify negatively with. He is stupid, therefore we are clever. The effect of the joke

My sister married a German. He complained he couldn't get a good bagel back home. I said, "Well, whose fault is that?"
—Emo Philips

is to foist on this parallel community all the undesirable characteristics of the joke-teller's own people, to comic effect. By singling out a nearby example of who you are not, you overcome anxieties about your own shortcomings and reaffirm your community identity. Max Miller, who lived all his life in Brighton, was once offered the opportunity to do a show in Glasgow; he declined, saying, "I'm a comedian, not a missionary."

Since the nationalization (and latterly, globalization) of our media, since we all became citizens of a small, overcrowded world, we tend to identify more strongly with our nation-state than with our local communities. There are notable exceptions such as Italy and Switzerland, where a tradition of decentralized administration means that strong local loyalties prevail; in such places you will still find a "fool town" in many provinces. Local rivalries between competing towns, or even competing football teams, also provide excuses to dust off the same old dumb-yokel jokes. But in the main, joke stereotypes have gone international—no doubt to the great relief of the good burghers of Gotham. For example, the Irish fit the bill admirably as the butt of the joke for their neighbors across the Irish Sea. They speak the same language, but with a strong and recognizable accent. The majority of them are Roman Catholics—same basic religion, many striking contrasts with the good old C of E. And until the Celtic Tiger economy sprang to life in recent years, the Irish were reassuringly down-at-heel, allowing the English to use them as a yardstick for lack of progress and economic failure.

Does this mean that English people really think the Irish are thick and lazy? Probably not. In fact, outside the world of jokes, the Irish are held in special affection all

What's the difference between toast and Italians?
You can make soldiers out of toast.

over the world and are generally characterized as quick-witted, poetic and pretty damn sexy. (In the interests of full disclosure, we should point out that your authors boast 75 percent Irish ancestry between them.) Even decades of sectarian violence in Northern Ireland, bombs in London and ludicrous political posturing from both Republicans and Unionists have failed to dent our enthusiasm for the craic. Irish bars are one of the twentieth century's great export success stories, and Irish music, culture and especially Irish comedy are not far behind. You can decide for yourself into which of those categories Riverdance falls, but for all the well-deserved insults you might wish to fling at Michael Flatley, "stupid" or "lazy" wouldn't stick. And it doesn't make sense to characterize as backward a country with the fastest-growing economy in Europe, where you can get Wi-Fi Internet access with your cappuccino, and writers don't pay income tax. Viva Hibernia! And thanks to the stag and hen parties that nightly choke the streets of Cork and Dublin with their fatheaded festivities, it's the English who look backward these days. But Irish jokes have become such an intrinsic part of the cultural landscape that we don't stop to think about these discrepancies; we're actually telling a joke about stupidity, not about the Irish at all.

The ease with which a joke about the stupid Irish can be adapted at the expense of another ethnic group—simply by substituting Polack for Paddy in the U.S., for example—would seem to confirm that the comic depiction of stupidity comes first, then casts around for a suitable social group to fasten on to. But if it's not really about the Irishness of the joke protagonist, why not just tell jokes about a stupid man of unspecified ethnic origin?

Heaven is an English policeman, a French cook, a German engineer, an Italian lover, and everything organized by the Swiss. Hell is an English cook, a French engineer, a German policeman, a Swiss lover, and everything organized by the Italians.—*John Elliot*

Two men are out driving and run into each other. The first man climbs out of the wreckage of his car and helps the second man, who is badly shaken, to the side of the road. "You had a nasty shock," he says, and offers a hip flask to the other man, who takes a long, grateful gulp. "Go on, have another."

"But what about you?" asks the second man. "Don't you want a drink?"

"No," replies the owner of the hip flask. "Not until after the police have been."

Now rerun that joke as it should be told: this time the man with the hip flask is a rabbi and the grateful drinker is an Irish-Catholic priest. The rabbi helps the priest to the side of the road and offers him a drink. And the joke works much better. It taps into tacitly accepted cultural stereotypes of the Jews as canny and calculating, and the Irish Catholics as gullible and fond of a drink. It's a very economical way of creating a backstory for the characters in the joke. By simply dressing them as a rabbi and a priest, the joke-teller can rely on the listener to fill in the gaps with a whole series of assumptions about their character and likely behavior. And of course, if the Jewish or Catholic angle seems too much of a political hot potato, he can make the man with the hip flask a lawyer instead. Whether or not these stereotypes have some vague basis in cultural reality, they are widely held and therefore comforting. The joke reaffirms the sense of community between the teller and the listener, because they both believe they understand something that has not been said.

The joke is not an outright expression of anti-Jewish or anti-Irish sentiment; the Jews and the Irish are adept at

Apparently, one in five people in the world are Chinese. And there are five people in my family, so it must be one of them. It's either my mum or my dad. Or my older brother Colin. Or my younger brother Ho-Chan-Chu. But I think it's Colin.
—Tim Vine

telling such jokes against themselves. Like all good jokes it is ambiguous. The rabbi is clever, and gets one over on the priest—in the joke world, he wins. But his initial gesture, which seems so kind, is revealed as calculating and manipulative. The priest is the idiot, fooled into taking a drink which may incriminate him. Nevertheless, our sympathy may ultimately be with him as the joke's victim. This ambivalence makes jokes slippery, and prone to misunderstanding; while it's true that the joke is not *in itself* an expression of anti-Semitism or anti-anything, if either the teller or the listener or both are anti-Semitic, it has the potential to be so too. The guilt must lie with the teller and not the tale.

Ethnic jokes always have this potential to expose an ugly prejudice on the part of the joke-teller. While a generous helping of irony, a skillful technique or your own membership in the race in question can help you to wriggle free of that particular charge, nevertheless every joke that pokes fun at someone purely on the grounds of their ethnic origin has a dark side. It has the potential to cause offense if heard by a member of the race it describes; if told in a circle that excludes that race, it is highly likely to confirm the unsavory prejudices of some of the hearers and to make them feel their opinions are legitimate and valid. We can categorically state that racist jokes are not nice.

The problem, which we touched on in the last chapter, is it's sometimes very hard to distinguish between an intentionally racist joke and an ironically racist joke that's appreciated in a straightforwardly racist way. The threat in the

What's the difference between an Irish wedding and an Irish funeral?
One less drunk.

latter type of joke lies in its ambiguity, not its apparent aggression toward a particular group of people. You could call it Alf Garnett syndrome. In 1965 Johnny Speight, a lifelong socialist, created a situation comedy called *'Til Death Do Us Part,* which ran on the BBC for ten years. Its monstrous antihero was a bigoted working-class cockney called Alf Garnett, whose xenophobic views on "yer coons" were entirely antithetical to those held by the writer and broadcasters of the program. Therein lay the show's humor and its popularity—or so they thought. In fact it quickly became clear that a very great many of the show's viewers, which at the peak of its popularity numbered twenty-four million in Britain alone, found in Alf a reflection of their own views. The intended antihero was a very *real* hero for many. But throughout its history the BBC refused to admit there was a problem with the interpretation of the show; the writer had intended the character of Alf Garnett as an anti-racist critique and any response to the show that cast him in any other light was simply the wrong response. "I didn't create Alf Garnett. Society created him," Speight once said. "I just reported him. I'm a grass [snitch]."

The show's premise was successfully exported to the U.S. as *All in the Family,* produced by Norman Lear and starring Anglo-Irish actor Carroll O'Connor as Archie Bunker. Once again the irony of the show's message was lost on a large portion of the audience: the Bunker character, intended as a satire on the uneducated American male, ended up as a hero to many. O'Connor, a very skillful actor, found the humanity underneath the grotesque. Although O'Connor was a liberal with no political views in common with Bunker, he still identified profoundly with his character. He once said, "I have a great deal of sympathy for him.

The only thing I know about Africa is that it's far, far away. About a thirty-five-hour flight. The boat ride's so long, there are still slaves on their way here.—*Chris Rock*

As James Baldwin wrote, the white man here is trapped by his own history, a history that he himself cannot comprehend and therefore what can I do but love him?" But in making Archie lovable, the show's creators laid themselves open to the viewers' misapprehension that they approved of his views.

British Asian actor and comedian Sanjeev Bhaskar remembers being taunted at school in the 1970s with lines quoted straight from the UK show. The real problem, he pointed out in a 2005 interview, was that Alf Garnett had all the juiciest lines. There were no retaliatory jokes for a young Asian boy to quote in his defense. Warren Mitchell, the Jewish actor who played Alf, has spoken of his distress at being identified with the character—and identified as a hero, as "one of us" who speaks for the silent majority. "There have been times when I've felt ashamed. When I've been doing Alf to a live audience and he says something like 'Enoch Powell had the right idea' or 'Adolf Hitler had his moments,' and somebody in the audience cheers."

The Jews are widely accepted as the "jokingest" group of people on earth. (There's an episode of *Seinfeld* in which a character converts to Judaism solely "for the jokes.") Looking at the history books, it's hard to see how they found much to laugh about. The Old Testament isn't conspicuously packed with gags; one can just about imagine the Book of Job as a Buster Keaton comedy but you'd definitely have to bring in some new writers. The Talmud, a collection of Jewish lore and law, begun during the Babylonian exile of the Jews in the sixth century B.C. and refined and

I'm very proud of this pocket watch. My grandfather, on his deathbed, sold me this watch.—*Woody Allen*

added to for the next millennium, has scarcely more to offer in the way of humor. On the evidence of these traditional texts, you wouldn't guess that the Jews would become famous for their jokes. But they may provide us with some clues. Alan King (born Irwin Kniberg), one of the great twentieth-century Jewish comedians, thought the Talmud laid the foundations for a joker's sensibility. "Basic Talmudic wisdom holds that there are two answers to every question. We got a lot of humor out of that. In the days when no one was flying, someone got sick in Albany, New York, and I had to be there that night. They were flying Ford Tri-Motors in those days, you know with rubber bands and taking off from a kneeling position. . . . And my mother panicked. She said, 'You can't get on an airplane!' My grandfather was the rabbi, so I went to him [for advice] and he said, 'You don't have to *fly*—you get on a nice train, you see America go by, they have sandwiches in the car, you read a book that you never read before . . . it probably stops in Poughkeepsie, you got an aunt in Poughkeepsie—you can call her on the phone. . . .' And I said, 'Grandpa! I gotta be there *tonight*!' And he said, 'Well, then you fly.'"

Over the last twenty centuries the Jews have been expelled from Palestine (A.D. 70), persecuted throughout Western Europe during the Crusades, slaughtered en masse in Norwich (1144) and York (1189), expelled from England at the end of the thirteenth century, burned at the stake by the Spanish Inquisition in the late fifteenth century and driven east into Poland, the Ukraine and Russia, driven back west by the Cossacks in the seventeenth century, persecuted by the Russians, Swedes, Prussians and Austrians right through to the end of the nineteenth century and slaughtered in their millions in Germany under

China has a population of a billion people. One billion. That means even if you're a one-in-a-million kind of guy, there are still a thousand others exactly like you.—*A. Whitney Brown*

National Socialism in the twentieth. Not so much "chosen" people as "singled out." What's to laugh at? Given that the Jews are the archetypal example of what sociologists call a transitional wavering people—without permanent territory, only partially assimilated into the societies on the edges of which they live, marked out as different by their customs and traditions—one would expect them to be the butt of other people's jokes. And they certainly have been. Anti-Semitic jokes go back at least as far as the reign of Augustus Caesar who, on hearing that Herod planned to kill all the boys in Judaea under the age of two, including his own son, is said to have remarked, "Better to be Herod's pig than his son."

But the Jewish people have taken hold of these jokes at their expense and turned them outward, gaining tremendous resilience through laughing at themselves. A combination of that Talmudic aptitude for intricate, ambivalent opinionating, a culture that reveres verbal cleverness far above physical strength or athletic prowess, and a certain survival instinct have certainly helped. And there's nothing like having your property repeatedly confiscated to focus your attention on living by your wits. The rich humorous tradition that is one of Jewish culture's great gifts to the world is made of equal parts defensive self-criticism, delight at one's own wit and determination not to take the world and its woes too seriously. Jewish humor has been an essential ingredient in the glue that binds Jewish communities together.

An old Jew lies on his deathbed. "Sarah, my wife, are you here?" he whispers.

"Yes, my love, I'm here."

Not only is there no God, but try getting a plumber on weekends.—*Woody Allen*

"Nathan, my son, are you here?"
"Yes, Father, I'm here."
"Esther, my daughter, are you here?"
"Yes, Father."
"Then who's minding the store?"

Even in the darkest depths of persecution, Jewish jokes have proven hard to suppress. Dr. Viktor Frankl, a psychiatrist who survived the Nazi concentration camps, wrote about an occasion when a group of prisoners were shaved and then pushed into the showers—the actual showers, that is, not the gas chambers disguised to look like showers. "The illusions some of us still held were destroyed one by one, and then, quite unexpectedly, most of us were overcome by a grim sense of humor. We knew that we had nothing to lose except our so ridiculously naked lives. When the showers started to run, we all tried very hard to make fun, both about ourselves and about each other. After all, real water did flow from the sprays!"

The persistence and pervasiveness of jokes in Jewish communities is testament to humor's efficacy as a remedy for the sort of seasickness that decades—centuries—of political instability can cause. The ability to make jokes about stressful situations not only reduces stress, as we saw in Chapter 2. It's also a good indicator of someone's adaptability to changing situations—his ability to ride out the storm. A poignant joke was told in the Balkans in 1942 and resurrected in Israel in the 1970s, although its origins may be much older:

A Christian priest, a Muslim imam and a rabbi are discussing what they would do if a second Great Flood were about to sweep over the earth.

The only thing more suspicious than a black man running is a black man tippy-toeing.—*Dave Chappelle*

"We would pray for God to save us," says the priest.

"We would accept our fate as kismet and go to meet Allah," opines the imam.

Says the rabbi, "We would learn to live underwater."

Other survivors of the Holocaust saw no room for jokes in Nazi Germany, and felt their loss keenly. Wittgenstein said, "Humor is not a mood but a way of looking at the world. So if it is correct to say that humor was stamped out in Nazi Germany, that does not mean that people were not in good spirits, or anything of that sort, but something much deeper and more important."

According to this analysis some conflict situations are just so terrible that they kill jokes, and the possibility of jokes, as effectively as they kill innocent victims. So the existence of a large number of playfully insulting ethnic jokes could be an indicator of a fairly healthy and sustainable cultural relationship between two groups. It's the complete absence of such jokes we should look out for. In fact, in *Mein Kampf* Hitler warned the bourgeoisie of the danger of making jokes about the Jews, on the grounds that laughing at such jokes would undermine their implacable opposition to the Jewish threat. In other words, it's very difficult to hate something that you are accustomed to find funny.

Now, no one likes to be told that they have common ground with the Führer, especially if they're committed to a peaceful solution to the Israeli/Palestinian conflict. So when we say that this belief is shared by Ray Hanania, a comic whose life's work is a foundation called Comedy For Peace, let's make it absolutely clear that we mean just the bit about it being hard to hate what makes you laugh, not the bit about Jewish jokes being a bad idea, nor indeed the

Ever wonder why so many of the great violinists of the last century were Jewish, but so few of the great pianists? Well, you try escaping with a piano under your arm.

whole pro-hate stance. Hanania is a Palestinian-American married to a Jew; the couple have a son who is being brought up as a Jew. Family life provides Hanania with endless opportunities to cut the conflict in Palestine down to a human scale.

"My son is very patriotic. . . . He turned me into the FBI three times just this week. . . . I bought him some Legos so he'd leave me alone. So what happened? He was building something and I asked: 'Are you building a wall?' He got up, kicked me and yelled, 'No, Dad! It's a fence.' "

Hanania set up the Comedy For Peace foundation alongside Jewish-American filmmaker David Lewis with the intention of using stand-up comedy to help heal the divide between Israeli and Palestinian communities in the conflict zone. The more the two communities can joke together, Hanania reasons, the less sustainable will be their hatred for each other. "If we can laugh together, we can live together." A similar mission motivates the three Muslim comedians who have recently toured the U.S. and beyond under the banner "Allah Made Me Funny." (Sample joke: What do Muslim extremists and Muslim comics have in common? They bomb.) But a joke thrown into a tense political situation can just as easily create chaos as promote understanding, as twelve Danish cartoonists discovered when their caricatures of the Prophet Mohammed became the center of an international political storm. The cartoons were submitted in response to the story of a Danish writer who was having trouble finding an illustrator brave enough to work on his children's book about Islam. Danish newspaper *Jyllands-Posten* ran this story in 2005, provoking some local complaint; when the paper issued a qualified apology the following January, the cartoons were reprinted

An Irishman wanders into a library and says, "Fish and chips, please." The librarian says, "I'm sorry, but this is a library." The Irishman whispers, "*Sorry! Fish and chips, please.*"

in France, Germany, Italy and Spain. The subsequent protests throughout the Muslim world led to the deaths of at least thirty-five people, including sixteen Christians in Nigeria, and called an effective halt to Denmark's exports to Muslim countries.[3] Some of the cartoons were undoubtedly provocative, arguably irresponsible, possibly racist—but they were intended to provoke debate, not violence. Nonetheless, taken out of context, hijacked by extremists to prove that the Western world despises Islam, these feeble jokes sparked a chain of events that left innocent people dead.

[3] Although how much bacon and beer were they selling in Saudi Arabia, exactly?

Perhaps one day the healing power of comedy will succeed where so many diplomatic measures have failed. It's certainly tempting to believe that wars are only waged by people who take themselves too seriously—people who don't get the joke. Unfortunately this isn't the case. Take your average tyrant: he may not find the satire of the resistance funny, but that doesn't make him humorless. There's an important difference between having a robust sense of humor yourself and allowing the poor sod under your jackboot the same privilege.

Black-bloused socialite and Adolf-groupie Lady Diana (wife of Oswald) Mosley was once asked what she remembered best about Hitler. "The laughs," she is said to have replied. Apparently she had fond memories of his party piece, a hilarious impersonation of Mussolini. Hitler himself reminisced about his experiences in the Great War: "A sense of humor and a propensity for laughter are qualities that are indispensable to a unit. On the eve of our setting out for the battle of the Somme, we laughed and made jokes all night." And according to historian Robert Conquest, Stalin also had a prodigious sense of humor. In his

Karate is a form of martial arts in which people who have had years and years of training can, using only their hands and feet, make some of the worst movies in the history of the world.—*Dave Barry*

book *The Great Terror* (not a title you'll find in the humor section), Conquest recounts a story of a banquet given by the Russian leader for the heads of the secret police on the anniversary of their foundation. "When everyone had drunk a good deal, Pauker, supported by two officers playing the parts of warders, played for Stalin the part of Zinoviev being dragged to execution. He hung by their arms, moaning and mouthing, then fell on his knees and, holding one of the warders by the boots, cried out, 'Please, for God's sake, Comrade, call up Yosif Vissarianovich [i.e., Stalin]!' Stalin roared with laughter, and Pauker gave a repeat performance. By this time Stalin was almost helpless with laughter, and when Pauker brought in a new angle by raising his hands and crying, 'Hear, Israel, our God is the only God!' Stalin choked with mirth and had to signal Pauker to stop the performance."

Such anecdotes remind us that joking and laughter can only promote peace, understanding and the brotherhood of man if everybody gets to join in.

For many years, the eminent social historian (and, arguably, the daddy of all joke scholars) Professor Christie Davies has been on a crusade to debunk what he sees as a politically correct cliché: that ethnic jokes are dangerous and inflammatory. He has collected huge and detailed bodies of evidence to show that there is absolutely no correlation between the number of jokes told at the expense of one people by another and the actual state of relations between the two. For example, in the years during and immediately following World War II, Japanese people in the U.S.

I went to a restaurant the other day called "Taste of the Raj." The waiter hit me with a stick and got me to build a complicated railway system.—*Harry Hill*

were herded into internment camps and became the object of widespread fear and suspicion. Yet there are no popular jokes poking fun at the Japanese in that period. Conversely, jokes about the allegedly stupid, dirty Poles have circulated in the U.S. for a century and more, yet U.S. citizens of Polish origin are happily and comfortably integrated into the society, well liked and respected, and have never been the victims of significant prejudice or violence at the hands of other Americans. This is not to say that ethnic jokes are harmless, or that they don't cause offense. It's just that the relationship between jokes and ethnic conflict is not a simple one of cause and effect: there's absolutely no evidence that these jokes contribute to the actual ill-treatment of the ethnic group in question, nor can we show that the conflict generates the jokes.

In an environment characterized by ethnic conflict, trying to diffuse the tension with humor can be a high-risk strategy. The jokes must send up the superficial differences between the two opposing sides while simultaneously affirming their common humanity and making all of them laugh at once—an immense stretch for something as flimsy and disposable as a joke. One social fault line which jokes have proved particularly inadequate to bridge is that between black and white people. Whisper it, but before the 1960s, derogatory jokes about black people were common in the U.S., and not particularly controversial. The stereotype of the black man that emerges through such jokes is lazy, stupid, dishonest, and sexually immoral, with a voracious appetite for fried chicken, watermelon and respectable white womenfolk.

In the good old days of vaudeville, the jokes on offer were fairly raw. Audiences enjoyed the antics of "nigger

I never believed in Santa Claus because I knew no white dude would come into a black neighborhood after dark.
—Dick Gregory

minstrels" in blackface makeup alongside equally racist stereotypes of Jews and poor Irish. In those days "nigger" joke books were common; now there are none, but Jewish and Irish joke books are still freely available, most of them produced gladly by Jews and Irishmen. There's no doubt that the vaudeville blackface sketches were rotten, but it's equally clear that, although this unhealthy joking relationship between the black and white communities has come to an end, a mutually comfortable arrangement hasn't yet evolved to take its place. It seems that the continuing social inequalities which are, in part, the legacy of racial segregation in the U.S. are too severe to joke about—certainly if you're a white man. It's much less controversial to joke about people who clearly aren't any longer the victims of profound economic or political inequality: it could be argued that the Irish (who put a man in the White House) and the Jewish (who walk tall in Wall Street and Hollywood) can rather more comfortably afford to take a joke. Especially the Jews, who have so thoroughly appropriated the jokes once told against them that they've turned Jewish humor into a multibillion-dollar entertainment industry. That's perhaps the sweetest Jewish joke of all.

James Baldwin wrote, in 1962: "At bottom, to be colored means that one has been caught in some utterly unbelievable cosmic joke, a joke so hideous and in such bad taste that it defeats all categories and definitions." When you consider the inglorious history of America's "nigger minstrel" shows, you begin to see his point. Black slaves on the plantations used to sing and dance to entertain themselves; in particular, they invented a humorous dance called the cakewalk which was actually a parody of their

Q: What do you call a black man who flies a plane?
A: A pilot, you *racist*.

masters' "European" airs and graces. In the places of entertainment frequented by slave owners, these songs and dances were parodied for humorous effect by white performers in exaggerated "blackface" makeup (who presumably didn't realize the cakewalk was a parody already). Blackface remained a hugely popular comic device from its origins in the 1820s until well into the twentieth century. To heap irony on insult, for a long time these "nigger minstrel" reviews provided black performers with their only chance to beat the color bar. Black singers and actors were still forbidden to perform in whites-only theaters. But men made up to *look* black were all the rage. Hence the not uncommon spectacle of a black man, in blackface makeup, trying to look like a white man who's trying to look like a bigot's idea of a black man.

Lest we British are tempted to shake our heads sadly over the American race issue, which seems rather far away and foreign to us, we ought to remember that *The Black and White Minstrel Show* was a mainstay of the BBC's weekend schedule from 1958 until 1978, for much of which period it constituted British television's only comic representation of black people. What's more, the godfather of black British stand-up, Lenny Henry, spent several seasons touring with the Minstrels in his late teens—at the time, it seemed like the only way to get his career started. "I think by '79, I'd had enough," Henry has said. "The jokes were boring— 'And now the only one of 'em who doesn't need makeup,' 'When Lenny cries he gets little white lines crawling down his face,' etc. I partook in these jokes because I didn't really know any better; it

Personally I prefer to be called a "person of paleness, if you must refer to my 'race.' "—*Dan Henry*

hurts thinking about it now." With the memory of this casual racism so raw and so recent, it's little wonder that the unwritten joking rules currently demand that white people make some token reparation by handling the subject with extreme care.

We're asking far too much of jokes if we expect them to heal racial divides. But nor should we banish them from all areas of cultural sensitivity on the grounds that they might "make things worse." What jokes can sometimes do is give different communities a safe mechanism for acknowledging their differences, as well as their common humanity. Jokes may not ever really help "us" understand "them"; it may never be quite clear who's laughing "at" and who's laughing "with." But we might just be able to laugh "next to," and move on.

Black crime tends to be stupid, not crazy. When you hear on the news that somebody chopped off his girlfriend's head, drank her blood and used her toes to play pool, chances are it was a white guy. An old lady kicked downstairs for her welfare check? A black guy. Someone cut out the old lady's eyes and used them as knickknacks? Definitely a white guy.—*Chris Rock*

THESE JOKES WERE NOT TESTED ON ANIMALS

If you have a green ball in your left hand and a green ball in your right hand, what do you have?
Kermit's undivided attention.

What do you do if you come across a tiger in the jungle?
Wipe him off, apologize and run.

What's black, white and red all over?
Half a cat.

What goes "Mark!"?
A dog with a harelip.

Does the name Pavlov ring any bells?

In the pursuit of scientific answers animals have been tortured for the past one hundred years. They're still not talking. I'm starting to think they don't know anything.—*Jimmy Carr*

A vampire bat comes flapping into its cave covered in fresh blood. All the other bats smell the blood and begin hassling him about where he got it. "OK, follow me," he says and flies out of the cave with hundreds of bats behind him. Down through a valley they go, across a river and into a forest. Finally he slows down and all the other bats excitedly mill around him. "Now, do you see that tree over there?" he asks. "Yes, yes, yes!" scream the bats. "Good!" says the first bat, "because I didn't!"

YOUR JOB'S A JOKE

Banks have this new image of being your friend. If they're so friendly, how come they chain down the pens?—*Alan King*

"Employee of the month" is a good example of how somebody can be both a winner and a loser at the same time.
—*Demetri Martin*

I hate my supervisor. Behind her desk it says, "You don't have to be mad to work here, but it helps." Mind you, she's written it in her own shit.—*Alan Carr (no relation)*

I call my lawyer and say, "Can I ask you two questions?" He says, "What's the second question?"—*Henny Youngman*

When you go to work, if your name is on the building, you're rich. If your name is on your desk, you're middle class. And if your name is on your shirt, you're poor.—*Rich Hall*

I called a temp agency looking for work, and they asked if I had any phone skills. I said, "I called you, didn't I?"
—*Zach Galifianakis*

My dad used to say, "Always fight fire with fire." Which is probably why he got thrown out of the fire brigade.
—*Jack Handey*

A man was sitting quietly in a bar when someone shouted: "All lawyers are assholes!"

The man jumped to his feet and said: "I resent that."

"Are you a lawyer?"

"No, I'm an asshole."

I had a job selling hearing aids door to door. It wasn't easy, because your best prospect never answered.—*Bob Monkhouse*

CHAPTER TEN

Sometimes the Joke Gets Elected

In which we examine the uneasy relationship between jokes and the Establishment; can our rulers afford to have a sense of humor?

If you want to tell a person the truth, make him laugh or he'll kill you.

GEORGE BERNARD SHAW

For a comedian on stage, the success or failure of a joke sometimes feels like a matter of life and death. There are other times and places where it really is. According to anthropologist Max Gluckman, the hunting Esquimaux of the Arctic Circle use jokes in place of a court system; they govern their society through humorous insult contests called drumming matches.[1] When Gluckman studied them in the early sixties they had no leaders and certainly no legal system. Whenever disputes arose, they were settled in formal song duels where each side would insult the other as devastatingly and hilariously as possible, judgment being given in the form of audience applause and laughter. That's a bit like swapping the U.S. Supreme Court for a Friars Club Roast. Sadly, Gluckman also broke the news that the murder rate among the Esquimaux was extremely high—not perhaps the most ringing endorsement of trial by comedy.

A more successful example comes from the Bambuti pygmies of the Congo, a happy tribe of hunters with an average height of less than four foot six. They too live in a

[1]Sadly no contemporary examples of the "hunting Esquimanx" jokes were available, but any excuse to slip this one in: An Eskimo takes his car to the garage for repairs. The mechanic takes a look under the hood and then turns back to his customer. "It looks like you've blown a seal, mate." "No, no," replies the Eskimo hurriedly, "that's just frostbite on my lip."

I can picture in my mind a world without war, a world without hate. And I can picture us attacking that world, because they'd never expect it.—*Jack Handey*

largely anarchic society. The only individual with anything approaching an official function in a Bambuti hunting band is the camp clown. (That's "camp" as in attached to a temporary settlement, not mincing around the bush in sequins.) The function of the clown is to diffuse tension as a sort of scapegoat or patsy. When two or more members of the band fall out, his job is to bring affairs to a nonviolent conclusion, either by distracting attention, with mime and clowning, from the original cause for disagreement, by taking the blame on himself for some misdemeanor or by ridiculing one or both of the disputants. According to anthropologist Colin M. Turnbull, the system serves the pygmies well. Their existence is one of remarkable good humor. "When pygmies laugh it is hard not to be affected; they hold on to each other for support, slap their sides, snap their fingers. . . . If something strikes them as particularly funny, they will even roll on the ground." Forget the Esquimaux and the Friars Club. Let's replace all the Supreme Court judges with Bambuti pygmies. Come on, who's with us? We could call it a cultural exchange program and get a grant from the UN.

The first recorded court jester bears a striking resemblance to a Bambuti clown. He was a pygmy called the Danga who served at the court of Dadkeri-Assi, a pharaoh of Egypt's Fifth Dynasty. His hilarious caperings proved vastly diverting to the early Egyptian nobility, and all we know of his origins was that he came from the "Land of the Ghosts"—the mysterious, barbaric regions south of the Sahara. From these ancient beginnings until the early seventeenth century, fools and jesters of one kind or another entertained and mocked the powers-that-be with extraordinary freedom. The tradition of tolerating frank talk from

I'd kill for a Nobel Peace Prize.—*Denis Leary*

a fool may have originated with the primitive notion that fools and madmen were "touched"—that is, touched by a god and therefore divinely inspired and sometimes full of unwitting wisdom—holy fools, in other words.

The original fools were genuine simpletons or grotesques, kept almost as pets by rich households. In Rome there was a special fool market, a sort of boutique adjunct to the main slave market, where you could buy a genuine idiot. These days you can't give them away, but in the first century A.D. they were reassuringly expensive. One of Martial's epigrams describes the disgruntlement we all feel when we realize we've been ripped off by a dodgy fool dealer.

> Morio dictus erat: viginti milibus emi.
> redde mihi nummos, Gargiliane: sapit.
>
> *They said he was a fool: I bought him for 20,000 sesterces.*
> *Give me a refund, Gargilianus: he is wise.*

In other words, the main quality required in a Roman fool was that he couldn't help it. If he was just pretending to gurn and drool, it wasn't nearly as much fun. But for subsequent civilizations it became apparent that a clever and entirely whole-witted man could turn this fooling around into a profession, and could be relied upon by his master not only to caper and joke on demand, but also to live longer and need less keeping-an-eye-on around the daughters of the house than a natural half-wit.

Richard Boston, in his lovely book *An Anatomy of Laughter*, points out that the position of the court jester is echoed by that of the joker in a pack of playing cards. Not

What do I think of Western civilisation? I think it would be a very good idea.—*Mahatma Gandhi*

only is he not part of the royal family, he is not a member of any suit—not even properly part of the pack. At the same time, he can become, at a stroke, the most powerful card in the deck. He is "wild," and can assume whatever shape he wishes. The joker is at once everything and nothing. An absolute monarch embodies authority, his jester lawlessness. At the epicenter of power where the king stands, outside the law and subject to no one, he is almost, but not quite, alone. The regal profile throws a jingling, capering shadow. The jester is royal antimatter; he is the intimate opposite of monarchy and must therefore be kept close to the throne.

Long before the principle of freedom of speech became a prerequisite for our notion of civilized society, before it even occurred to anyone to demand it, the court jester had it. Shakespeare exploits this license to the full; his fools are the only ones to tell aloud the human frailty of the king—like the little boy who says the emperor has no clothes. His fools are the voice of reason, giving clues to the audiences but often poignantly misunderstood by the other characters.[2]

In *King Lear,* Shakespeare explores the full tragic potential of the shifting relationships between king and fool, truth and flattery, wisdom and madness. From the outset, Lear allows the Fool to be openly critical of him, while requiring absolute obedience and flattery from everyone else.

> Lear: *Dost thou call me fool, boy?*
>
> Fool: *All thy other titles thou hast given away; that, thou wast born with.*

[2]*Mind you, many of them spout streams of such irritating nonsense that you can quite understand why the remaining dramatis personae stopped listening to anything they said a long time ago. "Cry to it, nuncle, as the cockney did to the eels when she put 'em i'th'paste alive. She knapped 'em o'th'coxcombs with a stick and cried, 'Down, wantons, down!' 'Twas her brother that, in pure kindness to his horse, buttered his hay." Oh, do shut up.*

Too much food in America, man. We got so much food in America we're allergic to food. Hungry people ain't allergic to shit. Do you think anyone in Rwanda is lactose intolerant?
—Chris Rock

This fool is knowing and wise, though he cloaks his insight with apparent nonsense. Dismayed that Lear has given away his kingdom to his scheming daughters, the Fool can't help but tell him the truth.

> *For when thou gav'st them the rod and putt'st down thine own britches,*
>
> *Then they for sudden joy did weep,*
> *And I for sorrow sung,*
> *That such a king should play bo-peep*
> *And go the fools among.*
>
> *Prithee, nuncle, keep a schoolmaster that can teach thy fool to lie: I would fain learn to lie.*

Lear welcomes these home truths, telling him, "An you learn to lie, sirrah, we'll have you whipped."

As the old king descends into madness and his own language and behavior become more and more nonsensical, it's clear that this "foolish, fond old man" is the genuine article—the Fool was only *playing* the fool. He finds himself taking care of his delirious master, out on the heath in a thunderstorm, trying to stop him from taking off his clothes. "This cold night will turn us all to fools and madmen," he prophesies. By the end of the third act, the king is irretrievably mad and the Fool disappears from the play: Lear is quite beyond the reach of his "voice of reason."

Of the real-life court fools and jesters whose stories survive, few seem to have used their freedom of speech in the cause of truth, preferring instead to enrich themselves, enrage their foes and protect their friends. One notable exception was Rahere, jester at the court of King Henry I and

Finish your vegetables! There are thousands of children in Hollywood with eating disorders.—*John Callaghan*

benefactor of the priory and hospital of St. Bartholomew at Smithfield, London. The church is still in use today, and "Bart's" Hospital is a London institution. Another timely intervention came from Yu Sze, jester to the court of Emperor Shih Huang-Ti who ordered the building of the Great Wall of China at around the time of the beginning of the Christian era. Once the wall was finished, the emperor had his heart set on having it painted. The cost of the wall, in terms of human life lost during construction and punishing taxes levied to fund it, had already brought the empire almost to its knees, but no one dared criticize the emperor's home improvement plans. No one, that is, except Yu Sze, who made so many good jokes at the expense of the painting project that the emperor eventually dropped it. Yu Sze's achievement is still unmatched, despite the combined efforts of every comedian in the UK to halt construction of London's disastrous Millennium Dome by similar means.

The natural habitat of a court jester is behind the throne of an absolute monarch. But that's no guarantee that the ruler will tolerate jokes from any of his other subjects. Joking is all the more dangerous when the tyrant in question is an ideologue rather than a hereditary monarch. Dictatorships are notoriously intolerant of humor. In a society where intellectual and cultural freedom is curtailed, where clubs of like-minded people are threatening to the regime, telling a joke can be a highly subversive act. Yet it is precisely in this sort of environment that political jokes thrive.

How many people died in the Irish Famine? I mean, it was just the potatoes that were affected. . . . At the end of the day, you will pay the price if you are a fussy eater.—*Steve Coogan*

Did you hear, they've announced a new competition for the best political joke?

First prize: Fifteen years.

The anarchy of jokes, with their robust insistence on the individual in all his human fallibility, sits ill with totalitarianism. During the Cold War years, versions of the joke above were recorded in Russia, Romania, Poland, Czechoslovakia—it was probably whispered everywhere that people suffered the daily privations and restricted freedoms of Communist rule.

For those of us who take for granted the existence of a more-or-less independent judiciary, a more-or-less free press and a more-or-less democracy, free (more-or-less) from police brutality, it's difficult to imagine a way of life where nothing and no one can be trusted. (Mind you, some would say it's getting easier every day. . . .) For its subjects, Soviet rule brought about a topsy-turvy situation where you had to spout the most ludicrous, counter-factual nonsense in order to preserve your skin—the stuff of nightmares, but also the essential stuff of jokes. There's a Russian joke in which a man runs, wild-eyed, down a Moscow alley. He bumps into a friend who asks what on earth he's running from. "Haven't you heard? It's illegal to have three testicles." "But surely you only have two?" "Yes, but the KGB tend to cut them off first and count them afterward!" A very similar joke was told in Romania under Ceausescu, where a fleeing donkey warns his fellows that the government has requisitioned all camels for compulsory labor. And compare this joke, current in Nazi Germany. One day, a multitude of rabbits appears at the Belgian border to

You have to remember one thing about the will of the people—it wasn't so long ago that we were swept away by the Macarena.—*Jon Stewart*

claim political refugee status. "The Nazis have ordered that all pigs should be rounded up as dissidents." "But you're rabbits!" "Try telling that to the Gestapo!"

In one of those wonderful leveling strokes that humor seems uniquely capable of producing, Fascism and Communism are revealed as essentially identical in the threat posed to innocent bystanders by their bureaucratic rigidity. And what's more, antecedents of that joke are found in Arabic texts from the tenth century (also featuring camels and donkeys) and Persian texts from the twelfth. It would very much surprise us if a version of the joke were not doing the rounds today in Iran, or Libya, or Turkmenistan. It's as though tapping into the absurdity of the joke somehow helps to counterbalance the absurdity of everyday life under an oppressive regime.

Such jokes shouldn't be taken as evidence that the plucky Russians laughed in Stalin's face; living in real, abject fear for your own or your child's life is not the best environment for comedy. The greatest flowering of anti-establishment jokes in authoritarian societies tends to come when the regime is in decline. According to joke scholar Christie Davies, the Stalinist terror produced far fewer popular jokes than the long, grinding years of the Cold War, and the last years of General Franco's regime produced many more jokes than those years in which his grip was absolute. After all, he reminds us, the exchange of jokes requires at the very least some freedom of conversation, if not freedom of speech. In fact, once the media become vaguely autonomous, the rich supply of underground antiauthority jokes begins to dry up.

Throughout the former Eastern Bloc, jokes characterizing the government and the Communist Party as subnor-

It's not enough to have every intelligent person in the country voting for me. I need a majority.—*Adlai Stevenson*

mally stupid was commonplace. These jokes dismissed the entire political class as illegitimate—an anti-meritocracy where peasant origins, dumb obedience and influential friends in the party guaranteed advancement, rather than any virtues as an individual or skills as a politician. In our own society, where the electorate must shoulder most of the blame for the variously flawed individuals who hold political office, the jokes tend to be more specific. After all, if we said all politicians were stupid it wouldn't reflect too well on those of us who voted for them. We single out the quirks in character or appearance of a particular politician, rather than tarring them all with the same "dumb" brush. But hold on a minute . . . illegitimate election process, influential friends in the party, no obvious virtues: so that explains why we tell all the "dumb" jokes about George W. Bush.

When Poland, Czechoslovakia and Co. got their democratic governments and their free press, the old underground jokes—what Berliners in the 1930s used to call *Flüsterwitze* or whispered jokes—started to die out. They just weren't needed anymore now that newspapers and TV shows could talk openly about individual policies and politicians. But a new kind of joke must come into being to fill the void, to subvert the *new* received wisdoms. Hypocrisy and corruption don't disappear overnight when an authoritarian regime is overthrown, and jokes still offer an important way for ordinary people to protest that hypocrisy and affirm their personal politics. Besides, attempts to control humor are not confined to totalitarian societies. It's striking to note that, although our media are free to joke about our rulers, they collude in ensuring that a certain kind of topical joke very rarely appears in print. We're talking about this sort of thing:

I'm all for gun control. Sometimes I shake a little; I've got to use two hands.—*Tom Kearney*

What's the weather forecast for Chernobyl?
8000 degrees and cloudy.

Did you hear O. J. Simpson's got a new Web site?
It's www.slash-slash-backslash-escape.

Why did Michael Jackson go to Kmart?
He heard boys' pants were half off.

Did you hear about the Thai businessman whose beach bar was destroyed by the tsunami?

Things were tough for the first week, but customers are starting to drift back in.

Those French are such sore losers.

[When the London Underground was bombed the day after Paris lost the bid to host the 2012 Olympics to London.]

This type of joke is distributed by word of mouth and by e-mail, but always under the radar. When the existence of these jokes is acknowledged in a public forum, it's in order to deplore the sick minds that conjure such taste-free horrors into existence. Here's the short list of joke topics to which our media apply this sort of temporary self-censorship: murder or violent death of a celebrity; suicide bombings in major European cities; high-profile criminal trials involving murder or sexual abuse; natural disasters; technological disasters. Any of these jokes may sheepishly poke it's head above the parapet in some late-night talk show or newspaper opinion piece—or in a book like this—after sufficient time has passed. Other subjects are perenni-

I believe that Ronald Reagan can make this country what it once was—an Arctic region covered with ice.—*Steve Martin*

ally off the mainstream media's menu, although they provide rich sources for word-of-mouth jokes; these include AIDS and its identification with homosexuality; pedophiles, especially Catholic priests; abortion . . . the list goes on. (For a full rundown, see one of Jimmy's live shows.)

Although our scope of tolerance in joking matters appears to have increased, all in all, since the 1950s, our media organizations still try to keep the many-headed beast in check. More and more it seems that the media are policing themselves and us, drawing a line between a joke that is simply in poor taste and one that constitutes a sacking offense. Rodney Marsh lost his job as a football pundit on *Sky Sports* in early 2005 when he made a joke live on air that punned on Newcastle United's fans—the Toon Army—and tsunami, about a week after the devastating tidal wave hit Indonesia and Thailand. Billy Connolly got into quite a lot of trouble for telling a joke that expressed the unfortunate opinion that the kidnappers of Ken Bigley (the civilian contractor then being held hostage by Iraqi militants) should hurry up and kill him. Oops. But if we had been there, would we too have swallowed a laugh because the joke gave voice to something we knew we weren't supposed to think, but thought nonetheless? Maybe it's just as well we have jokes to say this stuff for us, so that we can cling to an inch or so of moral high ground.

One of the reasons why our media eschew such guiltily pleasurable jokes is because it's widely accepted that there is a direct and causal link between the sentiment the joke appears to express and the general acceptance of that sentiment among the public. Telling jokes legitimizes prejudices, runs the argument, so if we stop the jokes getting around

Based on what you know about him from the history books, what do you think Abraham Lincoln would be doing if he were alive today? 1. Writing his memoirs of the Civil War. 2. Advising the president. 3. Desperately clawing at the inside of his coffin.—*David Letterman*

we'll diminish the prejudices too. But it's very hard, with the available evidence, to make this charge stick. People didn't tell jokes about the death of Princess Diana because they were violent anti-monarchists who were glad she had died, or because they intended maliciously to upset the young princes. They told those jokes because they wanted to puncture the suffocating atmosphere of compulsory national mourning. The media were running saturation coverage which suggested that the whole population of Britain was united in grief as for a close family member. The citizens of the former Soviet bloc found comfort in jokes at the expense of their illegitimate governments; the Internet Diana jokers dealt with the illegitimate emotions prescribed to them in a similar fashion, by joking about her death.

For any politician, taking yourself too seriously is an occupational hazard. Politics is, after all, a serious business and our leaders are sensitive to the threat a well-aimed joke can pose to the dignity of their office. It was not so long ago that George Bush (Senior) exhorted the American people to be "more like the Waltons than the Simpsons"—in other words, to be less alive to the black humor of everyday life; to assume a studied, earnest cheerfulness. Bart Simpson's response, on the show: "But we *are* just like the Waltons. We're both praying for an end to the recession." In the UK, the government retained powers to censor satirical plays until 1968, and the BBC imposed firm restrictions on the impersonation of public figures for the purposes of satire until at least the mid-1960s. Spike Milligan lamented that, despite Peter Sellers's amazing talent for mimicry (of

Dan Quayle is more stupid than Ronald Reagan put together.
—Matt Groening

"any politician in the land, the Queen included") his impressions could only appear on *The Goon Show* under heavy layers of disguise. When *That Was the Week That Was* came on air, with its truly groundbreaking satire of the Macmillan government, Home Secretary Henry Brooke wanted to ban it. Macmillan himself is reputed to have supported the program, on the grounds that it was better to be laughed at than ignored. He famously attended Peter Cook's Establishment Club, and sat with smile intact through a monologue in which Cook, in character as Macmillan, ad-libbed, "There is nothing I like better than to wander over to Soho and sit there listening to a group of sappy, urgent, vibrant young satirists with a stupid great grin spread all over my face." Perhaps Macmillan understood better than Cook that this sort of satire has limited influence on the real business of politics. The personal jibes may sting the victim in passing, but the system marches on.

The popularity of the satirical political puppet show *Spitting Image* in the 1980s inadvertently delivered a PR boost to the Thatcher government that subsequent prime ministers could only dream of: up to fifteen million viewers knew each of the cabinet by name. The program concentrated on attacking their personal shortcomings rather more than their policies. In doing so it probably damaged some politicians' careers, notably that of SDP leader David Steel, who was caricatured on the *Spitting Image* TV show as a squeaky dwarf in the pocket of his (relatively) handsome coalition partner David Owen. Steel has acknowledged that the puppet undermined his credibility and may ultimately have damaged his political prospects beyond repair. But *Spitting Image* didn't really prick anyone's conscience. It certainly didn't lead the British populace to

I'm going to leave you with this frightening fact. If you took all the money that we in the West spend on food in one week, you could feed the Third World for one year. I don't know about you good people, but I can't help feeling we're being overcharged for our groceries.—*Jimmy Carr*

rise up and smash the system. In fact, the Conservative government it existed to lampoon outlived the show by more than a year. Turning political leaders into laughable puppets might actually have mitigated our opinions of their more heinous sins, reducing political corruption to harmless Muppet slapstick.

This is the paradox at the heart of the joke as subversive political act. Even in highly policed totalitarian societies, where a misplaced joke can be severely punished as an unacceptable flowering of intellectual freedom, jokes can also serve an inherently conservative function. By providing a safety valve for anarchic sentiments, they may actually help people to endure the prevailing political climate and so perpetuate the status quo. Making light of things, we gain temporary relief by refusing to take them seriously. But in the long term we may fail truly to challenge the state of the nation because we joke it into familiarity instead. Enid Welsford, in her book *The Fool,* asked, "Does comedy act on the spiritual system as a vitamin or a narcotic?" In other words, does our enjoyment of a joke help us to access insights into the human condition and allow us to criticize the status quo with more accuracy, or is joking a deliberate escapism, a way of abdicating responsibility for the state of society?

Of course, that depends on the joke.

Some individuals still work tirelessly to preserve the ancient model of the fool as a licensed critic of society. Comedians like Michael Moore in the U.S. and Mark Thomas in the UK believe passionately in humor as a political weapon; they are at the forefront of a genre that you might call campaigning comedy. They use comedy as their medium, but the intent behind their (mostly practical) jokes is deadly serious; they are wolves in sheep's clothing. Michael Moore

I'm against picketing, but I don't know how to show it.
—Mitch Hedberg

once sent a choir of throat cancer survivors to sing "Happy Birthday" to the CEO of tobacco giant Philip Morris, through their tracheotomies. Mark Thomas drove a missile launcher to Westminster Abbey to highlight the Church of England's stockholdings in various arms companies. And U.S. stand-up comedian Bill Hicks, shortly before his early death (at age thirty-three, in 1994) began experimenting with similar comedy reportage, filming on location outside the siege at the Branch Davidians' headquarters in Waco, Texas, and exposing the inconsistencies in the CIA's reporting of the fiasco. Hicks was vehemently opposed to the use of comedy as a "narcotic," to return to Welsford's analogy. "If comedy is an escape from anything, it is an escape from *illusions*," he wrote. "The comic . . . *reminds* us of our True Reality, and in that moment of recognition, we laugh, and the 'reality' of the daily grind is shown for what it is—*unreal* . . . a *joke*. The audience is relieved to know they're not alone in thinking, 'This bullshit we see and hear all day *makes no sense*. Surely I'm not the only one who thinks so.' Good comedy helps people know they're not alone."

One of the most politically active comedians working in Britain today is Robert Newman. In the early nineties, Newman became the first comedy act to play at the twelve-thousand-seat Wembley Arena, along with his then-partner David Baddiel. If comedy was the new rock and roll, as the British media decided at the time, then Newman and Baddiel were its Beatles. After the double act dissolved, Newman reinvented himself as a novelist and radical political activist, publishing three novels and campaigning with grassroots organizations against globalization, media control and human rights abuses. He returned to stand-up in 2001 with a newly urgent political viewpoint.

I recently attended a pro-drug rally. In my basement.
—David Cross

Newman's latest shows tend to be packed with the kind of terrifying statistics that make the average happy-go-lucky consumer's mind simply shut down. Did you know that it's highly likely we've already exhausted half of the oil on the planet? And that if everyone used fossil fuel at the same rate as the average American does, we would run out completely within the next ten years? And that once it's gone, there IS NO MORE? Lalalalala, I'm not listening! Pass the remote. . . .

But people do listen. All right, so quite often this sermon is going out to the choir—a Robert Newman gig isn't the first choice of entertainment for a Young Conservative stag night. The people who come are generally liberal, educated and reasonably politically savvy. But still, only a small percentage of the people who digest and enjoy Newman's comedy would ever find themselves at an antiwar march or a local pressure group meeting. Yet here they are, effectively listening to a lecture about how we're all going to die. The jokes sort of soften them up. A spoonful of sugar, and all that. Laughter seems to lower certain defenses, to soften up our preconceptions so that a committed campaigner like Newman can slip in some consciousness-raising on the sly. Newman himself sees no contradiction between his choice of stand-up comedy as a medium of communication and the high seriousness of his message. It frustrates him that others can't match his sincerity. "Alternative comedy ruined a generation. It's encouraged all young stand-ups to speak in whiny voices and be incapable of saying anything unless it is ironic. It's like a disease."

What even Newman can't do is make the joke carry a serious message *all on its own*. A joke is always ambiguous; it cannot preach and it cannot bring down regimes, at least

Anyone who is capable of getting themselves made president should on no account be allowed to do the job.
—Douglas Adams

not if it's funny. When Newman jokes about the ridiculous optimism of the people who imagine that a totally clean fuel source is within reach of our scientific community, he does so by conjuring up for us a car that runs on cocoa butter and whose only emission is a walnut-whip chocolate. It's funny, but inherently silly too. All jokes trivialize their subject matter; they skim the surface of the debate, although they may help to expose its inherent absurdities. Newman's jokes make up a rich and savory gravy that both enhances and conceals his real political beef. As "humor studies" professor Dr. Virginia Tooper puts it, "When the mouth is open for laughter, you may be able to shove in a little food for thought."

Newman's implication—that political comedy can only aspire to real power when the comedian isn't afraid to combine the jokes with sincerely held beliefs—is well founded. But that trick requires enormous talent. It demands that the comedian be hilarious and affecting at the same time. Bill Hicks was one of the most celebrated (in the UK, at least) recent exponents of loud, impassioned political stand-up. When Hicks got it right, when he resisted the cheap shock tactics and hit his evangelical peak, it was awesome. By allowing you to glimpse the depth of his heartfelt rage, he added real texture to his jokes. But the truth is that even Hicks missed his mark a lot of the time, resulting in an act that was neither funny nor moving. Most comedians can't handle the heavy stuff—and why should they be expected to? They're comedians, for goodness' sake: just one evolutionary step above a mime. The comedy of rage is a very slippery soapbox. Get too angry—even by a fraction—and you aren't funny anymore. You're just a man shouting about politics.

According to some commercials, driving an SUV means you support terrorists. The answer is a hybrid gas-electric car, which only supports terrorists while going uphill.
—Jon Stewart

—Does the tailor Rabinowitch live here?
—*No.*
—Who are you?
—*Rabinowitch.*
—And aren't you a tailor?
—*Yes, I am.*
—Then why did you say you didn't live here?
—*You call this living?*

Ivan dies and his soul is directed to hell. In front of the gate a devil asks him, "Do you want to go to the capitalist hell or the communist hell?"

Ivan is hesitating, puzzled, when he hears his friend Vasily hailing him from behind the gate.

"Hi, Ivan, come in to our hell; in a capitalist hell they'll throw you in a huge cauldron full of burning tar where you will burn eternally."

"And in the socialist hell?"

"The arrangement is the same, only here they either run short of tar, or they run short of fuel, and when both fuel and tar are available, the devils have a trade union meeting."

Khrushchev is being driven in a limousine in a rural area of Czechoslovakia. Suddenly the car strikes and kills a pig which has wondered onto the road. The chauffeur asks Khrushchev if he wants to drive on, and Khrushchev replies, "No, we'd better go up to the nearest farmhouse and pay some damages."

And so Khrushchev sends his chauffeur off to the farmhouse on the hill with the instructions to offer the farmer some compensation. A half hour passes, and the chauffeur does not return. Then another half hour. Khrushchev begins to wonder what has happened. Still another half hour passes, and finally Khrushchev sees the chauffeur returning. To his surprise, the chauffeur is staggering under the weight of all sorts of packages and gifts.

"What happened?" asks Khrushchev. "I sent you to pay them."

"I don't know," replies the chauffeur. "All I said to them was: I have Khrushchev in the car and I killed the pig."

"OFFICER, I SWEAR THIS IS A SETUP."

Some people are against drunk driving. I call those people the cops. But sometimes, you've just got no choice. Those kids just gotta get to school.—*Dave Attell*

TV commercials now show you how detergents take out bloodstains, a pretty violent image there. I think if you've got a T-shirt with a bloodstain all over it, maybe laundry isn't your biggest problem.—*Jerry Seinfeld*

Remember: it takes forty-two muscles to frown and only four to pull the trigger of a decent sniper rifle.—*Mitch Henderson*

A couple are walking down the street when the girl stops in front of a jewelry store and says, "Honey, look at that necklace! It's so beautiful." "No problem," replies her man, throwing a brick through the window and grabbing the necklace. A little later the girl points to a bracelet in the window of another shop. "Ooh, honey," she says. "I'd love that too." "No problem," says her boyfriend, and again, he throws a brick through the window. A little later they pass another shop, where she sees a diamond ring. "Oh, honey. Isn't that lovely!" she says. "Hang on!" he says. "What do you think I am? Made of bricks?"

Two men are robbing an apartment in a block of flats when they hear police sirens. "Quick, let's jump out of the window!" says the first man. "Are you crazy?" replies the other. "This is the thirteenth floor." "Don't be ridiculous. This is no time to be superstitious."

Sherlock Holmes and Dr. Watson go camping. Sometime in the middle of the night Holmes wakes Watson up. "Watson, look up at the stars, and tell me what you deduce." Watson says, "I see millions of stars, and if even a few of those have planets, it's quite likely there are some planets like Earth, and if there are a few planets like Earth, there might also be life." Holmes replies, "No, Watson, the correct deduction is that somebody has stolen our tent!"

CHAPTER ELEVEN

Knock Knock. Who's There? The Police.

In which we examine how a joke can lead to a jail sentence, especially once God gets involved.

God is a comedian, performing for an audience that is too afraid to laugh.

NIETZSCHE

Ah, the opera. The highest flowering of the musical arts. The jewel in the crown of human civilization. The audience holds its breath, the baritone holds the stage: a large, imposing black man clad only in a white loincloth, fastened with an oversized safety pin. It looks for all the world like . . . a nappy. He strikes an operatic pose and loudly, proudly, he begins to sing, "I just wanna shiiiiiit my paaaants!" OK, perhaps you have to be there, but the collision of high opera and low farce is genuinely hilarious. Childish, crude and of questionable artistic worth, but *funny*. Later in the show, for reasons of plot too convoluted to explain here, the diaper fetishist reappears as Jesus. Satan taunts him with accusations of effeminacy and he admits, "OK, I am a little bit gay." The chorus line appears in Ku Klux Klan costume. A talk show host is sent to hell and God and Satan fight over his soul. About three hundred colourful expletives are sung in the course of the show, which is a satire on trash TV—specifically, the lurid confessional presided over by U.S. daytime talk show host Jerry Springer—via Milton's *Paradise Lost* and the music of

A lot of people say to me, "Why did you kill Christ?" I dunno . . . it was one of those parties that got out of hand.
—*Lenny Bruce*

Mozart, Wagner and Sondheim. It's a conceptual car wreck, but somehow it works. Audiences love it, and *Jerry Springer—The Opera* becomes the first piece of musical theater ever to pick up a "grand slam" of West End theater awards, winning Best Musical at the Olivier, Evening Standard, Critics' Circle and What's On Stage awards for its sell-out run at the National Theatre in 2003.

Two years earlier, all this popular success and critical acclaim would have sounded like a joke to the show's creator and composer, Richard Thomas, and its writer and director, Stewart Lee. In fact, it all started as a bit of a joke, when Richard Thomas gave a sparsely attended but enthusiastically received talk at London's Battersea Arts Centre called "How to Write an Opera about Jerry Springer." Stewart Lee joined him soon afterward to help turn the concept into a show. Lee is one of Britain's most challenging stand-up comedians, highly rated by comedy connoisseurs and a firm adherent to the belief that it's a comedian's job to challenge his audience's assumptions and push the boundaries of received notions of taste and decency. But he was about to find out that nasty things can happen to people who stick their heads too far above that particular parapet.

The musical became *the* runaway success of the following year's Edinburgh Festival. The phenomenon just kept on growing, a total sell-out at the National Theatre for six months of 2003 and then on to a successful West End run. Then in late 2004, BBC2 announced its plan to broadcast this modern comic opera the following January, with the intention of giving a broader audience access to an original and entertaining piece of popular theater. The commissioners knew it would be controversial, but they were totally unprepared for what actually hit them.

Going to war over religion is basically killing each other to see who's got the better imaginary friend.—*Richard Jeni*

The BBC received some forty-five thousand complaints, mainly by telephone and e-mail, prior to transmission. At this point, we should make one thing clear: we do understand that people are entitled to be offended by jokes that they feel belittle something that matters to them. The right to take offense is, in our eyes, very nearly as important as the right to cause it. The BBC's feedback mechanisms should be put to good use—along with the national broadcaster's programming, some of which may offend us, our license fees also fund our right to reply. But the complaints about this particular show went far beyond the legitimate concerns of individual viewers. All the evidence pointed to an orchestrated "spam" campaign by several special-interest groups, each of them pursuing a particular religious/political agenda. One of these organizations, Christian Voice, also published the home addresses and telephone numbers of several BBC executives on its Web site. Threats of violence subsequently made against its staff were serious enough for the BBC to contact the police and hire a private security firm to protect its employees. There was some unseemly squabbling over the number of profanities contained in the broadcast, Christian Voice claiming eight thousand while the BBC counted around three hundred. The broadcast went ahead. By the following Monday, just 317 further viewers had contacted the BBC, more than half of them to express their support for the show.

Christian Voice immediately approached the director of public prosecutions and asked the state to prosecute the BBC (and the Cambridge Theatre, where the show was still playing nightly) for blasphemy. When the DPP declined, saying that a prosecution would not be in the public interest, Christian Voice founder Stephen Green announced his

I told the traffic warden to go forth and multiply, though not exactly in those words.—*Woody Allen*

intention to bring a private prosecution. On his Web site, he says, "Clearly, if *Jerry Springer—The Opera* is not found in court to be blasphemous, then nothing in Britain is sacred. We have to take a stand. A line must be drawn. However, the costs of the action could exceed £75,000. Would you pray for the Lord to provide at least that sum, and prayerfully consider a donation yourself?"

Green raises one rather good point amid the tangle of fundamentalist rantings. "Why am I bringing a case when God is quite capable of looking after Himself? In truth, God could have struck the BBC electrical system with a thunderbolt as we prayed. He chose not to." Surely God can take care of himself? After all, he seems to have managed perfectly well throughout the Middle Ages, when the Feast of Fools was celebrated in His churches across Europe, with donkeys in the choir stalls and sausages in the censers. A few well-placed lightning strikes might have put an end to the fun, but He held back. He's been fairly good-humored about the Reformation and all sorts of other schisms too, letting Christians of various minutely differentiated persuasions shout "Heretic!" and burn one another alive without flinging weather at them. Surely by now there's a robust enough tradition of Christian debate to allow a patently silly piece of theater like *Jerry Springer—The Opera* to take place?

Stewart Lee now has a joke in his stand-up act about the attempted legal action against the show. "Someone tried to prosecute us for blasphemy, but the court threw it out, on the grounds that it's not 1508." In a modern, democratic society, the purpose of the laws that govern freedom of thought and expression is surely to prevent intimidation, not to enable it. In the case of Christian Voice versus *Jerry*

I don't believe in God, but I do believe that you shouldn't step on the cracks in the sidewalk.—*Jonathan Katz*

Springer—The Opera, it's pretty clear from which direction the intimidation comes. The Christian Voice campaign inflicted real nuisance and damage on the creative team responsible for the show, causing huge personal stress and effectively removing their livelihoods. Besides the intimidation of BBC staff, there were poisonous letters and e-mails to Stewart Lee and several of the performers. When the cast put on a gala performance in aid of a Scottish cancer charity, the charity was bullied into refusing the donation. A planned UK regional tour was scrapped after Christian Voice wrote to the theaters threatening demonstrations and negative publicity. U.S. investors were so badly spooked that the show's Broadway run was canceled. Although enough of the UK theaters rallied round to reinstate a smaller tour a year later, the damage had been done. Stewart Lee told us, "I've got to go around the country now, in advance of the show touring to various terrified provincial theaters, and do all these workshops—damage-limitation exercises. And I don't want to, because I think it's a shame to have to decode everything—ultimately what you want is for people to be able to come out and think about it for themselves." Thanks to the controversy stirred up by the BBC broadcast, it will be almost impossible for future audiences to appreciate *Jerry Springer—The Opera* as a straightforward piece of musical theater, and certainly impossible to see it as a big, gleeful joke. "It's ruined forever. It will always be seen through a grimy lens, as if it were pornography. No one will come to it clean—to that extent, the protestors have succeeded," Lee told us.

In one polemic against the show's regional tour, the Christian Voice Web site likens the show's producers to the Third Reich: "This tour can only bring the judgment of

I was raised half-Jewish and half-Catholic. When I'd go to confession, I'd say, "Bless me, Father, for I have sinned—and you know my attorney, Mr. Cohen."—*Bill Maher*

Almighty God on the United Kingdom. The whole nation prayed to God in the name of Jesus Christ just sixty years ago, and God delivered us from the Nazis in answer to that prayer." All this in response to a joke. A joke which many people might feel was in poor taste, but most agree was well executed and carried through to its logical conclusion with enthusiastic, even reckless commitment. *Jerry Springer—The Opera* was an artistic experiment, a satire on the degrading nature of popular television. It offended a number of Christians, but others quite enjoyed it. "*Jerry Springer—The Opera* is a piece of art," said Reverend Chris Newlands, chaplain to the Bishop of Chelmsford. "I don't see anything blasphemous in it."

While the controversy over *Jerry Springer—The Opera* was playing itself out, many comedians in the UK were becoming deeply concerned about proposals to splice a new prohibition into the existing law against inflammatory racist language and behavior. The wording of the new law would criminalize "incitement to racial *and religious* hatred" as part of the government's new measures to combat terrorism. Comedian Rowan Atkinson[1] spoke eloquently in defense of our right to joke about other people's ideologies, a right he and many others felt would be threatened by the new law.

[1] *Best known these days as worldwide superstar Mr. Bean.*

> *To criticize people for their race is manifestly irrational but to criticize their religion, that is a right. That is a freedom. The freedom to criticize ideas—any ideas—even if they are sincerely held beliefs—is one of the fundamental freedoms of society and a law which*

When I was a kid, I used to pray every night for a new bicycle. Then I realized that the Lord doesn't work that way, so I stole one and asked him to forgive me.—*Emo Philips*

attempts to say you can criticize or ridicule ideas as long as they are not religious ideas is a very peculiar law indeed. It promotes the idea that there should be a right not to be offended, when in my view, the right to offend is far more important than any right not to be offended, simply because one represents openness, the other represents oppression.

Supporters of the amendment assured us that it would be very hard to write a joke that actually "incites religious hatred." They said that the law was necessary in order to help prosecute the publishers of hate-filled British National Party pamphlets and neo-Nazi Web sites. But Atkinson's concerns were not groundless; religion is a ripe and tempting target for ridicule, and yet it's precisely the ridicule rather than the straightforward hate that gets under the collars of litigious evangelicals. The bill shuttled back and forth between the two houses, and had its teeth systematically extracted by the Lords. By the time the bill was finally passed in February 2006 its reduced scope was heralded as a victory for free speech. Only "threatening words" intended to cause offense are to be criminalized under the new law, leaving us free to proselytize, discuss, criticize, insult, abuse and ridicule religion, beliefs or religious practice without fear of prosecution. Hopefully that covers most of the jokes in this chapter.

Unlike inflammatory hate rhetoric, jokes don't set out to encourage violence. Nobody sent threatening mail to prominent Christians as a result of watching *Jerry Springer—the Opera*. What jokes are *very* good at doing, however, is pricking pomposity. And surely the Christian church can take a bit of that? After all, what was Jesus doing when he

When I was a kid I had an imaginary friend and I used to think he went everywhere with me, and that I could talk to him and he could hear me and that he could grant me wishes and stuff. Then I grew up and I stopped going to church.—*Jimmy Carr*

rode into Jerusalem on a donkey if he wasn't trying to burst the smug bubble of the religious establishment's self-image? But let's be careful what we say here—it's not so long since that sort of comment could put one in prison. The last person to be sent to prison for blasphemy in the UK, in 1922, received a nine-month sentence with hard labor. The prisoner, inaptly named John Gott, was a social reformer—sorry, make that "godless heathen"—who spoke out in favor of birth control and against the church. The state's case against him rested on a statement he made that Christ entered Jerusalem "like a circus clown astride the backs of two donkeys."

Less than half a century later, Harvard theologist Harvey Cox published a groundbreaking book in which he analyzed Jesus in terms of the archetype of the fool. Like the various mythological fools and tricksters we encountered in Chapter 3, Christ has his origins on the very margins of society: in Jesus's case, in a stable with the animals. He tells parables with a recognizable joke-like structure, complete with setup and punch line. He inverts expectations not only through his miracles (water into wine, feeding five thousand with a few loaves and fishes) but also in the manner of his triumph: riding into Jerusalem to be crowned king upon an ass. And like the original Lords of Misrule, he is killed in a mockery of coronation—in a crown of thorns, under a sign proclaiming him the King of the Jews, mocked and ridiculed by the crowd.

Speaking of legal action and martyred Jews . . .

Leonard Schneider was born in 1925 into a blue-collar

Taking Reservations For Eternity. Smoking or Non-Smoking. (sign outside church)

Jewish family in Long Island. Brought up by his mother, a burlesque dancer, he was a self-taught jazz philosopher and moralist who pursued a career of uncompromising, heroically antiestablishment attention-seeking, and came to a sticky end. His stage name was Lenny Bruce; posthumous mythmaking has made him modern comedy's first free-speech martyr. Bruce joined the U.S. Navy at eighteen and saw distinguished service aboard the USS *Brooklyn* in the Mediterranean. He obtained a discharge in 1945 by posing as a transvestite—it would have been a dishonorable discharge, but he managed to prove that he was not a homosexual, "based upon paid up accounts in numerous Neapolitan bordellos." After the war, Bruce began appearing as an MC for burlesque shows and a comic in vaudeville. In 1951, he was being praised as a nice clean comic, but by 1957 he was gaining a reputation for edgier sexual and religious material.

Bruce was a genuine iconoclast. In the late fifties and early sixties, he said things on stage that got him arrested, not once but over and over again. The more the authorities persecuted him, the more shocking his routines became. Preoccupied with sex and religion and the prevailing hypocrisies of the government, the "religion industry" and the media, Bruce had a quasi-religious fervor about him; his comedy was dark, despairing and intensely felt. In his misspent youth, he once masqueraded as a Catholic priest to solicit donations from old Floridian ladies. It's typical of the man that the charitable cause was almost legitimate—he claimed to have sent a third of the money to a leper colony in the Caribbean. Typical, also, that he justified his actions by condemning the rich pickings enjoyed by the legitimate church. "I knew in my heart by pure logic that any man who

I have personally experienced a number of miracles. Just the other day I saw the face of Jesus, *in a film.*—*John Oliver*

calls himself a religious leader and owns more than one suit is a hustler as long as there is someone in the world who has no suit at all." And he made a most convincing priest, collecting $8,000 in three days despite the fact that it would be very hard to find a man who looked more like a New York Jew in a stolen cassock. Perhaps the slightly manic gleam of missionary zeal in his eye transcended any limitations of specific religion: whether in the (fake) service of Jesus or the great God Comedy, he was a passionate evangelist.

Lenny forced stand-up comedy to take a great evolutionary leap, because he insisted that the sort of jokes that people told each other in private should also be heard in public. It enraged him that sex could be celebrated as an earthly delight in homes and bars, but must be denounced as "dirty" from pulpits and stages. "His only crime," wrote Ingmar Bergman, "was that he dared to tell people the truth." But this is to whitewash the man, who was not only far from being a saint in his personal life but was also a grade-A public provocateur. In his autobiography, Bruce writes, "As a child I loved confusion: a freezing blizzard that would stop all traffic and mail; toilets that would get stopped up and overflow and run down the halls; electrical failures—anything that would stop the flow and make it back up and find a new direction. Confusion was entertainment for me." Lenny Bruce's jokes are acts of sabotage: a snipped electrical wire, a bundle of rags down the toilet that force public opinion to back up and find a new direction.

Critic Kenneth Tynan had a slightly more poetic take on Bruce, of whom he wrote, "Constant, abrasive irritation produces the pearl: it is a disease of the oyster. By the same token, Lenny Bruce is a disease of America."

After his marriage broke down in 1959, Bruce's drug

Jehovah's witnesses don't take part in Halloween because it's against their religion. They don't like it when strangers come to their doors and bother them.—*Bruce Clark*

use began to increase and his jokes began to attract rather a lot of unwelcome official attention. His first vice squad arrest was for obscenity, after a San Francicso gig in 1961 at which the arresting officer objected to his use of the word "cocksucker." On that occasion he was acquitted, but the trial marked the beginning of a downward spiral of persecution and paranoia. Between November 1962 and February 1963 Bruce was the subject of three further obscenity charges and a narcotics bust.

Listening to a live recording of one of these controversial concerts, in Chicago in 1962, is an odd experience today. By this stage, he was recording most of his appearances in case he needed the tapes as evidence in court. Sure enough, the police actually arrest Bruce, on stage, toward the end of his set. He is obviously stoned, barely audible in parts and a long way from his comedy prime. Many of his bits of material tail off into slightly paranoid rants about police persecution. And the audience response is all wrong. Even on this old, scratchy reel-to-reel tape recording, you can almost hear them gawking and you understand that few are there to have their minds opened or to show solidarity with the man on stage—or even to laugh at his jokes. They are there to see someone get arrested, and the comic is in cahoots with them; he's there to get arrested too.

There's genuinely edgy material here, and even from a twenty-first-century viewpoint—coarsened by repeated exposure to blasphemous operatic parody to the point of being near-as-dammit unshockable—you glimpse what all the fuss was about.

One particularly blistering routine imagines Christ and Moses turning up at St. Patrick's Cathedral in New York. Cardinal Spellman recognizes his unexpected guests because

Thank God, I am an atheist.—*Luis Buñuel*

Moses is "a dead ringer for Charlton Heston" and is particularly agitated when a group of lepers begins to gather, attracted by the holy visitors. He puts a call through to the Pope: "Hey, woppo, what's happening? Listen, I've got a lot of grief here. The Kid's dropped in. . . . Yes, it's him. . . . I don't want to hear that horseshit, I'm up to my eyeballs in crutches and wheelchairs here. What are we paying you protection for?"

In the Chicago prosecution a Catholic judge and an all-Catholic jury found him guilty of obscenity and sentenced him to a year in jail and a $1,000 fine. Interestingly, Bruce was never prosecuted for blasphemy, perhaps because legal precedent would have made it very hard. The Supreme Court ruled, in refusing to censor a movie in 1952, that the state "has no legitimate interest in protecting any or all religions from views which are distasteful to them. It is not the business of government in our nation to suppress real or imagined attacks upon religion." Fortunately for the state of Illinois, it was still possible to prosecute someone for using certain words or phrases, including (in this case) "piss," "tits," and "fuck their mothers for Hershey bars" (the last from a satirical monologue about why the Japanese don't like the Americans much since the war).

By 1966, after a fifth prosecution for obscenity in New York resulted in a one-year jail sentence, Lenny was officially bankrupt and effectively barred from performing, pending his appeal. According to the man himself, he never used drugs illegally. He was certainly prescribed intravenous amphetamines for an ill-defined lethargic condition (said to date from a spell of hepatitis during the war)

It is no accident that the symbol of a bishop is a crook and the symbol of an archbishop is a double-cross.—*Gregory Dix*

and subsequently treated for his dependence on them. But his drug use was well known not just among the showbiz community but also to police in California and Illinois. He was found dead in the bathroom of his Hollywood home in 1966, his life ended by a morphine overdose. Dead at forty, Bruce had accidentally found what journalist Seamus McGraw calls "the ultimate loophole in America's moral code." Live fast, die young, and they'll eventually make you a hero, whatever they said when you were alive. Lenny's contemporary and one-time rival Mort Sahl, still performing in his late seventies, has this to say: "I found Lenny Bruce to be a funny comedian, a great impersonator and a very sentimental guy. I did not find him profound, and I disagree with those who now put him on a cross. Even Lenny knew that only you can kill yourself."

It's a beguiling legend: the man who had to die because his jokes were just too real, man; the martyr to the system who advanced the cause of free speech. And Bruce was probably the last comedian in the West to come up against quite that level of *de facto* state censorship. It's interesting to speculate whether he would have been prosecuted so vigorously if he had merely lectured on the topics of church corruption and sexual liberation, rather than performing stand-up comedy. Was it his opinion of the Catholic Church that rankled, or the fact that he *told jokes* about it? In the case of *Jerry Springer—The Opera*, it seems that the miscalculation the BBC made was in assuming that the obvious humorous intent of the piece would soften the impact of its startling assault on received notions of taste and decency. In fact, the complaint from the more liberal Christians who protested was that they might

What's a Hindu?
Lays eggs.

have taken the shocks on the chin if the opera had been altogether more serious in its artistic ambitions—had tried to educate rather than amuse.

The celebrated clown and satirist Dario Fo, born in 1926 in a small town near Milan, is also fond of a joke or two at the Church's expense, for which predeliction he was persecuted by the Italian government for much of his career. A political activist and one-time Communist Party member, he devised sketches and plays with his wife, Franca Rame, that were banned from Italian state television, and he was banned from working in the U.S. for a number of years. Far worse, his wife was kidnapped, tortured and raped by a fascist organization angry at the pair's passionate and popular art, which mocked the Church and celebrated the workingman.

Fo and Rame's agenda is much more explicitly political than Bruce's was, their rage more disciplined and perhaps less ruinously personal. They are more comfortable with their roles as educators as well as entertainers. But much of the ground they cover is strikingly similar. Although Fo is generally studied as a dramatist, he belongs to a tradition of minstrels and jesters that have more in common with stand-up comedians than with the mainstream theatrical establishment. Like a stand-up, he is concerned with breaking through the "fourth wall" that separates audience and performer, talking directly to the crowd and incorporating their reactions into an ever-evolving text. One of his best jokes is the title of his 1973 play, *Pum pum, chi è? La Polizia!*, from which we borrowed the title for this

If there was no capital punishment, there'd be no Easter.
—*Bill Hicks*

chapter. It's a joke that has had its punch line stolen by the state. Once the police are at the door, the joking is over.

In Fo's *Mistero Buffo,* a modern reading of the medieval mystery plays, one scene set in the early fourteenth century reads like a long-lost twin to Bruce's "Christ and Moses" bit. This monologue was denounced as sacrilegious by the Vatican and directly precipitated Fo's seven-year ban from the national airwaves when it was first performed in 1969. In it, the unpopular and tyrannical Pope Boniface VIII is leading a Good Friday parade when some of his entourage spot Jesus himself in the crowd, struggling under the weight of the cross. Boniface recognizes that it will be a great PR coup for him if he is seen to be helping Christ to shoulder his burden. He quickly rids himself of all his finery, saying, "Don't let him see all the glittery stuff. He's got terrible fixed ideas, that one." When Jesus accuses him of persecuting the monks, the pope summons an acolyte. "You! Go get me a monk, quickly. Where are you supposed to find one? The prison, you fool. It's full of them." The scene ends with Christ kicking Boniface in the backside, and the pope raining down curses on him in return: "If your father gets to hear about this . . . I don't mind telling you it will give me great pleasure to see you nailed up . . ."

Had Lenny Bruce survived the sixties, he and Dario Fo would be celebrating their eightieth birthdays within a year of each other. But Fo's trajectory could hardly be more different. His sixty-year career has taken him from enfant terrible to cuddly national treasure. In 1997 he received the Nobel Prize for literature. In his acceptance speech he spoke about his passionate belief in art, and particularly comedy, as a form of popular protest. Fo also paid tribute to Molière and commedia dell'arte dramatist Ruzzante Be-

Did you hear about the yogi who had his wisdom teeth extracted without anesthetic?
He wanted to transcend dental medication.

olco: "They were despised for bringing onto the stage the everyday life, joys and desperation of the common people; the hypocrisy and the arrogance of the high and mighty; and the incessant injustice. And their major, unforgivable fault was this: in telling these things, they made people laugh. Laughter does not please the mighty."

From an objective viewpoint, it's clear that society has far more to fear from the publishers of pamphlets, the webmasters, even the street-corner bullhorn prophets, than from men who stand on stages, in theaters or in smoky nightclubs and tell jokes. But there's something about the levity of the joker, the slippery, devil-may-care attitude, that gets under the skin of reactionary moralists. To the outraged Catholic cop, undercover in the audience at a Lenny Bruce gig, the insult is threefold. First, he is accusing the Church's officers of corruption, right up to and including the pope himself. Second, he is making light of this terrible accusation by presenting it in a routine or skit. Third, and perhaps worst of all, a roomful of people are listening; he has gathered disciples to his cause and they are all laughing in agreement, mocking the established order. Although the breathtaking hypocrisy of the Bruce obscenity trials is that his prosecutors never openly expressed their outrage about the opinions he held or the sentiments he expressed, but rather took refuge in feigned outrage over his use of language. No wonder he developed a persecution complex.

Bruce received a posthumous pardon from New York governor George Pataki in 2003. Was this a belated victory for intellectual freedom, free speech and dirty jokes? Well,

Never before have I encountered such corrupt and foul-minded perversity. Have you considered a career in the church?
—Rowan Atkinson

you still can't say "cocksucker" on *The Tonight Show*, or on the BBC before the watershed, but it's certainly a lot harder to get arrested for saying it on stage. Comics have to try really hard if they want to swing an obscenity charge these days, let alone a prosecution for blasphemy. The politicians have realized that, in an era defined by MTV and twenty-four-hour Internet access, our children's minds are unlikely to be further poisoned by the rantings of a few angry young men with microphones.

Comedians these days may not need to fear the long arm of the law. The British legal system is broadly tolerant of humor. But the experiences of the *Jerry Springer—The Opera* team at the hands of a few minority pressure groups show that telling jokes can still be dangerous for your health. Their show was hijacked and demonized to serve a political agenda they deeply oppose, then sacrificed in an almighty media shit-storm over which they had no control. Then again, Stewart Lee didn't end up dead on the toilet, like Lenny Bruce. Nor was he exiled by the national media, like Dario Fo—after all, the BBC did use license-payers' money to broadcast *Jerry Springer—The Opera*, despite the tens of thousands of preemptive complaints. And no one died a violent death at the hands of rioters, like the unfortunate bystanders at the protests against the Danish Mohammed cartoons. Unlike the Danish cartoonists, the creators of *Jerry Springer—The Opera* wisely chose to be provocative within their own culture. There were demonstrations in Nottingham and Sheffield, but no riots in Afghanistan or Nigeria; Britain's overseas trade was unaffected.

The *Jerry Springer—The Opera* story even has a happy ending, of sorts. The show is touring again, it's available on

God *knows* that life sucks. It's right there in the Bible. The Book of Job is all about Job asking God to take away pain and misery. And God says, "I can't take away pain and misery because then no one would talk to me."—*Bill Maher*

DVD and Stewart Lee is keen to stress that his *annus horribilis* had its upsides: "In a way it's quite invigorating; always at the back of your mind you're worried about causing offense, worried about what they'll do to you, but in the end, it doesn't really matter. I'm still here and I'm still working. The thing is, I'm a thirty-seven-year-old, white, middle-class man with no family—I have nothing to talk about. Then this thing comes along . . . I got a new hour of stand-up out of it, at least. You could say it's been a godsend, creatively speaking."

Not every joke is dangerous, and very few comics are really free-speech heroes. Comedy is not the most effective instrument for iconoclasm. It's too ambivalent, too easy to brush aside. A joke, in the end, is only a joke. And yet . . . In Burma, in March 1996, two comedians known as the "Moustache Brothers" were sentenced to seven years in prison after performing a comedy show that made jokes about the ruling regime. Five years later, Amnesty International successfully campaigned for their release.[2] Amnesty still monitors the progress of too many writers and comedians around the world who are prisoners of conscience as a result of their jokes. A joke defies control, because it's a scrap of chaos pinned proudly to the lapel of the individual in defiance of society. The artificial collectives of state, of received opinion, of religious dogma, tend toward deep suspicion of jokes and the chaos they represent, their refusal to be suppressed or supervised. All the more reason to celebrate our freedom to joke, and our right, in the process of joking, to offend occasionally: that's something worth fighting for.

[2]The comedy community in the UK has since adopted the case of another Burmese prisoner of conscience, seventy-five-year-old journalist U Win Tin, who has now been incarcerated for sixteen years. You can join the campaign for his release at www.amnesty.org.uk.

There is a remote tribe that worships the number zero. Is nothing sacred?—*Les Dawson*

DIE, HERETIC SCUM!

St. Peter decides to take the day off to go fishing, so Jesus offers to keep an eye on the Pearly Gates. He is not sure what to do, so Peter tells him to find out a bit about people as they arrive in heaven, and this will help him decide if he can let them in. After a while, Jesus sees a little old man with white hair approaching who looks very, very familiar. He asks the old man to tell him about himself. The old man says, "I had a very sad life. I was a carpenter and had a son who I lost at a relatively young age, and although he was not my natural child, I loved him dearly."

Jesus welled up with emotion. He threw his arms around the old man and cried, "Daddy!"

The old man replied, "Pinocchio?"

I was walking across a bridge and I saw a man standing on the edge, about to jump. So I ran over and said, "Stop! Don't do it. There's so much to live for!" He said, "Like what?" I said, "Well, are you religious?" "Yes." I said, "Me too! Are you Christian or Buddhist?" "Christian." I said, "Me too! Are you Catholic or Protestant?" "Protestant." I said, "Me too! Are you Episcopalian or Baptist?" "Baptist." I said, "Me too! Are you Baptist Church of God or Baptist Church of the Lord?" He said, "Baptist Church of God." I said, "Me too! Are you original Baptist Church of God, or are you Reformed Baptist Church of God?" "Reformed Baptist Church of God." I said, "Me too! Are you Reformed Baptist Church of God, Reformation of 1879, or Reformed Baptist Church of God, Reformation of 1915?" He said, "Reformed Baptist Church of God, Reformation of 1915." I said, "DIE, HERETIC SCUM!" and I pushed him off.—*Emo Philips*

Some nuns are renovating a church and getting very hot and sweaty. The Mother Superior suggests they take off their clothes and work naked. The nuns agree but bolt the church door as a precaution. They've all stripped down when there's a knock at the door. "Who is it?" says the Mother Superior. A voice replies, 'It's the blind man!' The Mother Superior opens the door and the man says, "Hey, nice tits, Sister. Where do you want these blinds?"

The pope is visiting a town and all the residents are lining the street hoping for a blessing. The mayor is sure the pope will stop and talk to him, but is surprised when the pope ignores him completely and whispers a few words to a filthy old tramp standing on the other side of the road. "Of course!" thinks the mayor. "The pope cares more for the poor and homeless, not the rich like me!" With this he dashes over to the tramp, buys his clothes, gets into them, then runs to the end of the street and lines up again. Sure enough the pope sees the mayor and walks over to talk to him. "Hey, stinky," whispers the pope. "I thought I told you to get lost."

Saul is working in his store when he hears a booming voice from above: "Saul, sell your business." He ignores it. It goes on for days. "Saul, sell your business for $3 million." After weeks of this, he relents, sells his store. The voice says, "Saul, go to Las Vegas." He asks why. "Saul, take the $3 million to Las Vegas." He obeys, goes to a casino. Voice says, "Saul, go to the blackjack table and put it all down on one hand." He hesitates but knows he must. He's dealt an eighteen. The dealer has a six showing. "Saul, take a card." *What? The dealer has*—"Take a card!" He tells the dealer to hit him. Saul gets an ace. Nineteen. He breathes easily. "Saul, take another card." *What?* "TAKE ANOTHER CARD!" He asks for another card. It's another ace. He has twenty. "Saul, take another card," the voice commands. *I have twenty!* Saul shouts. "TAKE ANOTHER CARD!!" booms the voice. "*Hit me,*" Saul says. He gets another ace. Twenty-one. The booming voice goes: "Un-fucking-believable!"

A guy joins a monastery and takes a vow of silence: he's allowed to say two words every seven years. After the first seven years, the elders bring him in and ask for his two words. "Cold floors," he says. They nod and send him away. Seven more years pass. They bring him back in and ask for his two words. He clears his throat and says, "Bad food." They nod and send him away. Seven more years pass. They bring him in for his two words. "I quit," he says. "That's not surprising," the elders say. "You've done nothing but complain since you got here."

A religious man lived a good life and always felt God had treated him well. One day, a terrible flood struck the town where he lived. While all the neighbors evacuated the street, he stayed put and told them that he would put his trust in God.

As the water reached the first floor, a man came past on a makeshift raft and shouted at him to jump on. "No, no," said the religious man. "God will provide."

A little later, as he sat on his roof watching the still-advancing tides, a lifeboat came past. The captain begged him to come on board, but once again he refused, saying that God would provide.

Finally, as he clung to his chimney, a rescue helicopter dangled a ladder within reach of his hands. "I'm not budging!" he shouted. "God will provide!"

The helicopter flew off, and slowly but surely the floodwaters closed over his head.

At the gates of heaven, the man remonstrated with God. "I've been a faithful servant to you all my life. Why didn't you save me?"

"You idiot! I sent two boats and a helicopter."

CHAPTER TWELVE

The Last Laugh

In which we are determined to get to the punch line, if it's the last thing we ever do . . .

Seriousness, young man, is an accident of time. . . . In eternity there is no time, you see. Eternity is a mere moment, just long enough for a joke.

HERMAN HESSE, *STEPPENWOLF*

Two and a half thousand years ago, Aristotle observed that a baby begins to laugh from the fortieth day of life. His estimate seems a trifle premature; these days most babies don't produce their first laugh until they are at least ten weeks old. Was life for a baby in ancient Greece really that much funnier? Aristotle made many, many invaluable contributions to biology, zoology and mathematics, but he also believed that human beings thought with their hearts (the brain being a sort of cooling organ) and that snakes had no genitals.[1] So let's overlook the trifling question of timing and focus on the crux of his observation about baby's first laugh. For Aristotle, laughter is one of our defining features: no animal laughs, he says, save man. By laughing, a baby joins the human race.

[1] *We know a joke about that: Why don't snakes have balls? Because they can't dance.*

The Navajo Indians agree with Aristotle. A Navajo baby's first laugh is so portentous it requires a ritual—a solemn ceremony to give thanks for the laughter, and a party for the whole community. Howard Jacobson attended a first-laugh rite in the course of researching his 1997 Channel 4 series and book, *Seriously Funny*. He tells us that

How young can you die of old age?—*Steven Wright*

the person who causes the baby to laugh is expected to cough up for the party. On this particular occasion, the laugh came later than expected. "The Navajo had their own joke going about Calvin's timing. They'd known he was ready. They'd felt the imminence of the laugh. . . . But given how tight money was right now, they'd been passing him furiously from one to the other. As in pass the parcel."

When baby Calvin laughs, he gives his parents the first real signal that he's a contributing member of the community. By displaying that he has a sense of humor he shows that he has a sense of self, a sense of others and an ability to interact with them. If we look back to the origins of the word "humor," we find that it has a powerful function in early medical science. The Greek physicians, stealing a notion from their Arab predecessors, believed that the stuff of physical life consisted of four "humors": blood, phlegm, black bile (melancholia) and yellow bile. The balance of these substances pulsing round the body gave us vitality, health, life force. By medieval times, medical theory had moved on very little, but for one important detail. There were *two* court professionals responsible for restoring or rebalancing the king's humors: his doctor and his jester, which just goes to show that "humor therapy" is no New Age fad.

A sense of humor doesn't necessarily guarantee a long and happy life. In fact, one or two learned gloombuckets have suggested that being cheerful and taking things lightly may be detrimental to our health. Childhood optimism and sense of humor were found in one study to be inversely related to longevity—a conscientious attitude was a much better predictor of survival into old age, while those who died young presumably died laughing. But let's not

My dad used to say, "Whatever doesn't kill you makes you stronger." Until the accident.—*Jimmy Carr*

confuse an optimistic outlook with an ability to joke about life. Joking is for realists, not blind optimists. It's a coping mechanism that works because it acknowledges what a mess things are and celebrates the fact. Friedrich Nietzsche—a surprisingly funny man, as it happens, and sometimes even on purpose—wrote, "Man alone suffers so excruciatingly that he was compelled to invent laughter."

Laughter is indeed a serious business. It's a practice that finds the measure of our humanity. Laughter sets us going, marks the real beginning of our journey. If we're lucky, we count on it as a constant companion—for richer, for poorer, in sickness and in health. If we're very, very lucky, laughter bookends our lives. Laughter in the face of death is a great gesture of defiance, and it can be enormously comforting to think that our last human act might be to crack a joke. The last words of great men and women are often suspiciously quotable; in reality most of us sign off with an anguished cry of "Nurse! The bedpan!" Or, like Tallulah Bankhead, "Codeine . . . Bourbon!" Or even, like Union commander General John Sedgwick, during the American Civil War, "They couldn't hit an elephant from this dist—" But if we're lucky, our acolytes conspire to spread a nobler myth. For example, the ballerina Isadora Duncan met her end when her trailing scarf became entangled in the wheel of the Bugatti in which she was a passenger. The actual cause of death was a broken neck. In the circumstances, it seems somewhat unlikely that she piped up, "*Adieu, mes amis, je vais a la gloire!*" as she took her leave. And Lord Palmerston almost certainly didn't say, "Die, my dear doctor? That's the last thing I shall do!" but it's a good joke.

A slightly more reliable account exists of the poet A. E.

I want to die peacefully in my sleep like my father, not screaming in terror like his passengers.—*Bob Monkhouse*

Housman's last words, thanks to his doctor, R. S. Woods. Woods was accustomed to entertain his patient with a dirty joke as he took his leave. The night before Housman died, Woods told him the one about the judge who asks a witness to clarify a certain aspect of his evidence, to which the punch line goes, "Am I to understand by the expression 'platinum blonde' a precious metal or a common ore?" To which deathless wit the patient replied politely, "That is indeed very good. I shall have to repeat that on the golden floor."

A joke is the weapon of the underdog, the preemptive strike of a man who knows he's in a corner. To attribute a joke to a man on his deathbed is to console ourselves that he went out fighting, not railing ineffectually against fate but with a knowing wink, ironic and unbeaten. Perhaps the best throwaway deathbed line is the one attributed to Oscar Wilde: "Either this wallpaper goes, or I do." Two and a half thousand years earlier, a dying Socrates failed to remark on the décor—wallpaper being less of a hot issue in ancient Athens—but he set the standard for mordant wit. He committed suicide by swallowing hemlock, the proper action of an Athenian gentleman found guilty of a trumped-up charge of corrupting the nation's youth. Plato tells us that, as the poison gradually crept toward Socrates' heart, the great philosopher summoned one of his disciples and whispered, "Crito, I owe a cock to Aesculapius; will you remember to pay the debt?" It was customary to sacrifice a cockerel to Aesculapius, the god of medicine, to give thanks for the successful treatment of a disease. Some read his remark as a profound philosophical observation about life being a disease from which we recover, but it looks more like a black joke about hemlock to us: "This medi-

My auntie used to say, "What you can't see can't hurt you." She died of radiation poisoning a few months back.—*Harry Hill*

cine's working well." Even more courageous are the reported last words of St. Lawrence, martyred on a griddle. He remarked to the Roman soldiers tasked with roasting him alive, "You can turn me over now—this side is done."

Taking things seriously is no barrier against pain. And while laughter won't make you live forever, who wouldn't rather go to the grave joking? Spike Milligan took that literally, leaving instructions that his headstone should bear the inscription "I Told You I Was Ill." Joking at the moment of death is a profound assertion of life.

So if we laugh ourselves into existence, and aspire to be laughing still at the bitter end, the logical conclusion must surely be that life itself is a joke. Beethoven is said to have remarked, after he had been given the last rites, "*Plaudite, amici, comœdia finita est.*" (Clap, my friends, the comedy is finished.) Likewise Rabelais is credited with "*Tirez le rideau, la farce est jouée.*" (Bring down the curtain, the farce is over.)

In the course of this book we've told Jewish jokes and Christian jokes, met pagan trickster gods and even a comic hero of Sufism. But when it comes to laughing in the face of death, it's the Buddhists who can boast the most robust sense of humor. At least they could boast if they weren't Buddhists and above all that sort of thing. To be a Buddhist is to learn to take everything lightly, including your own death . . . and beyond. The heroes and sages of the Buddhist tradition are not noble warriors or fearsome prophets, but tiny wizened monks who don't care what people think of them. Like all holy fools, they say incredibly stupid things that turn out to embody enormous existential truths.

My son has taken up meditation. At least it's better than sitting there doing nothing.—*Max Kauffman*

A lot of Zen Buddhist teaching comes in the form of koans: little philosophical problems which, superficially at least, bear a close resemblance to riddles. Probably the best known are "What is the sound of one hand clapping?" and "If a tree falls in a forest and there's no one there to hear, does it make a sound?" The koans, while undoubtedly profound, are also playful. They sound like jokes because, to a Buddhist, there's a great big joke at the very heart of our existence. Being is nothingness. Reality is illusory. There's not only nothing to be taken seriously, there's not even really a "you" to take it, seriously or otherwise. Consider these words from mysterious Buddhist scholar Wei Wu Wei: "What we appear to be is a fleeting shadow, a distorted and fragmentary reflection of what we all are. . . . Why is it a joke? It is a joke because all the time we are nothing but the substance and have never for a moment been the fleeting and tormented shadow."

Traditional representations of the historical Buddha show a serenely handsome youth with a clear, impassive face. But all over China, you will also find a strikingly different depiction: a bald, fat, laughing monk who has come to represent a future reincarnation of the Buddha. According to legend, this Maitreya Buddha is due to arrive on earth in two thousand years or so, after mankind's immorality has reduced the whole world to a desolate battlefield, to teach us patience and tolerance. The size of the gap between our high opinions of ourselves and the dust to which we all come at last is a clue to the jolly face of the Chinese Laughing Buddha. Perhaps he understands that, faced with a true awareness of the human condition, the only responses open to us are laughter or tears, and he chooses the more enlightened path. The ability to *choose* to find the

I spend money with reckless abandon. I spent $5,000 on a seminar about reincarnation. I got to thinking, what the hell, you only live once.—*Ronnie Shakes*

world funny is a powerful survival tool; if only we could all remember more often that this choice is available to us, we would almost certainly improve our quality of life.

A good number of the theorists we've met in the course of this book believe that joking is an expression of latent fear or hostility. That's not where all jokes come from, but it's undoubtedly interesting that the physical composition of our brains dictates that the laughter response lives right next door to the fear and pain centers. Perhaps one of the functions of joking is a kind of civilized aggression—a third way in the classic "fight or flight" dilemma. Faced with a social threat, modern man can run and hide, stand and fight, or . . . make a humorous remark. A joke can be a useful equivocation between aggressive behavior and evasive action: neither an obvious attack, nor exactly a retreat.

When human beings are under stress, there can be an awfully fine line between cracking a joke and cracking up. It's a psychological high-wire act that fascinated Shakespeare, and one that he nailed most accurately in *Hamlet.*

> First Clown: *A pestilence on him for a mad rogue! 'A pour'd a flagon of Rhenish on my head once. This same skull, sir, was Yorick's skull, the King's jester.*
>
> Hamlet: *This?*
>
> First clown: *E'en that.*
>
> Hamlet: *Let me see.* [Takes the skull.] *Alas, poor Yorick! I knew him, Horatio; a fellow of infinite jest, of most excellent fancy. He hath borne me on his back a thousand times. And now how abhorred in my*

We have to believe in free will—we have no choice.
—Isaac Singer

imagination it is! My gorge rises at it. Here hung those lips that I have kiss'd I know not how oft. Where be your gibes now, your gambols, your songs, your flashes of merriment, that were wont to set the table on a roar? Not one now, to mock your own grinning? Quite chopfallen? Now get you to my lady's chamber, and tell her, let her paint an inch thick, to this favor she must come. Make her laugh at that.

If poor Hamlet had been a Buddhist, he might have been able to confront the bleached skull of his father's late jester with more equanimity. But even the deeply depressed Dane can conjure jokes in the face of death. These gloomy, febrile puns—addressed to the grinning skull of the clown, "chopfallen" not through sadness but because its jaw has literally fallen away—represent the escaping steam of a psyche under tremendous pressure. It's precisely this safety valve aspect of joking that political comedians appeal to when they tackle controversial topics on stage, and it's what Ray Hanania hopes to harness in the Middle East with his Comedy For Peace initiative. They offer us humor as the most civilized, enlightened response, not just to personal psychic turmoil but to political unrest too.

Devotion to a particular cause, be it religious, patriotic or political, is always in danger of becoming too solemn, too weighty to admit any challenge. The phrase "deadly serious" has deep and bloody roots. Jokes are the sworn enemies of absolutism, puncturing the pomposity of extremists and defusing the threat they pose to the rest of us moderates. Without the vent that jokes provide, fundamentalism can build up a dangerous head of steam.

Jimmy is a self-confessed recovering fundamentalist.

I saw that show, *50 Things to Do Before You Die*. I would have thought the obvious one was "Shout for Help."
—*Mark Watson*

He was brought up a Catholic—and not in the Jesuitical, let's-have-a-debate tradition, but steeped in proper, superstitious, fire-and-brimstone rural Irish Catholicism. Transubstantiation? You betcha. Sex before marriage? Hellfire. When He says Thou Shalt Not, it's not a suggestion. Jimmy credits (should that be "blames"?) comedy for the loss of his faith in his mid-twenties. Jokes are the chink in the fundamentalist's armor. Attack a committed believer and he can defend his beliefs indefinitely. Tell him a joke, *make him laugh* at something he knows his God thinks he shouldn't laugh at, and you've got a foot in the door. Now Jimmy has total faith in jokes instead. The stage is his new confessional.

Lucy grew up on the far side of the sectarian divide. If priesthood were hereditary, she would be five-eighths vicar. Father, grandfather, two great-grandfathers, two great-great-grandfathers—mostly Methodists, with a piquant seasoning of Anglican. The God who's been affiliated with the Greeves family for so many generations is a very English God: fair-minded, comforting and wry. Lucy has never had to choose between faith and jokes because she's absolutely certain that God (whoever or whatever that might be) has a robust sense of humor and, moreover, that an appreciation of the comic is a prerequisite for having faith in the first place. As Robert Frost once prayed, "Forgive, O Lord, my little jokes on Thee, And I'll forgive Thy great big one on me." Jimmy knows she's wrong, and is comforted by the thought that the God he no longer believes in is, at least, the real one. You see, fundamentalism can't be cured—only tempered, perhaps redirected.

But hang on a minute. We appear to be attempting a proof of the existence of God based solely on our

I'll always remember the last words of my grandfather, "A truck!"—*Emo Philips*

long-running argument about His ability to take a joke. Could it be we've started to take this joking business just a bit too seriously?

Actually, seriousness is not incompatible with joking. It's a common mistake to confuse "serious" with "solemn," and to assume that seriousness of purpose can only be conveyed by solemnity of tone. It's an understandable error; we do have a marked tendency, we Anglo-Saxons, to answer the big questions with furrowed brow and downturned mouth. An acquaintance of Dr. Johnson, on hearing of his reputation as a philosopher, remarked, "I have tried too in my time to be a philosopher; but, I don't know how, cheerfulness was always breaking in." But cheerfulness and thoughtfulness aren't mutually exclusive. It's simply wrong to assume that everyone who jokes about serious matters like death and pain is somehow failing to deal with them; that laughter is a childish, evasive response and that the only mature reactions are solemn, sober and sanctimonious. Telling a joke is not always a sign of "not taking things seriously." As George Bernard Shaw put it, "Life does not cease to be funny when people die, any more than it ceases to be serious when people laugh."

The ability to joke about the messy bits of life is a lot like owning a pair of lovely rose-tinted spectacles. Nothing, but nothing, feels quite as bad or scary or painful when you can look at it through the subversive prism of a joke. On the other hand, joking about absolutely everything that occurs is not normal. Constant flippancy is just as wearing as constant solemnity. There is indeed a time to weep and a time

My dad's dying wish was to have his family around him. I can't help thinking he would have been better off with more oxygen.—*Jimmy Carr*

to laugh, and all of us should cultivate a healthy understanding of when that is. Joking is, after all, a social skill. It takes place in the context of a community and helps to bind that community together. That joking achieves this partly by setting different communities against each other is just one of its paradoxes. Joking bonds us in laughing cliques; it almost always implies "laughing at" as well as "laughing with." Although sense of humor, laughter and joking are more or less universal human traits, if we narrow our focus to the next level of complexity, they are actually incredibly specific. We can very easily be convinced that the people of neighboring countries have no sense of humor at all, which makes the jokes we tell about them even more pleasurable. We are even baffled by what makes our parents laugh, and strangely gratified when they react to our jokes with shock rather than mirth.

The only real constant among all these laughing cliques is this very tendency to be shocked at the new. As each of us grows older, we are more and more likely to see the nation's sense of humor going down a long, inexorable slide toward moral degeneracy. In fact it regulates itself pretty well: there are jokes in Aristophanes and Rabelais quite as disgusting as any doing the rounds today. Explicit state censorship of jokes waxes and wanes, but it could certainly be argued that the unspoken cultural rules and restrictions that police our joking activities are just as stringent today as at any time in the past. Actually, we're quite looking forward to tut-tutting over our children's jokes and lamenting the passing of our comedy heroes, just as our parents had to accept that we would never, ever "get" *The Goon Show.*

No matter how risky the subject matter, no matter how

My uncle died of asbestos poisoning—took a long time to cremate him.—*Tommy Cooper*

much it shocks our elders and betters, there's something *safe* about a joke. It deals with the riskiness so neatly, taking all the sting out of it. Of course, it can be a false sense of security—some jokes are stealth bombers, creeping under our radar and exploding our settled preconceptions—but the illusion of safety is comforting nonetheless. We prize jokes partly for this ability to render scary things harmless, reflecting the distant origins of laughter as an expression of relief at a threat diffused. We give our powers of reason and logic a break, just for a minute, and the sense of release is palpable. A joke allows the everyday to collide with the utterly outlandish, letting us play with dangerous notions in a safe place. Some of the simplest, most archetypal jokes for children encapsulate this perfectly. For example:

Q. What's yellow and dangerous?
A. Shark-infested custard.

A joke is self-contradictory: socially excluding some while it bonds others together, disposable but enduring, dangerous but safe. But it's more than a simple oxymoron. The joke doesn't so much contradict itself as partake in the nature of contradiction. A joke is a tiny world where everything is provisional; everything can be in two states at once. A joke takes the primordial comic chaos of the trickster, the fool and the clown and contains it. It's a plastic snowstorm globe, which we shake every which way and enjoy the tornadoes raging inside.

Joking does have its sinister side. Our jokes can reveal more than we might suppose about aggression, shame and fear. But a joke isn't only dark, as some Freudians suggest. Nor is it composed of sunlight and kittens—to characterize

I'm going to live forever, or die trying.—*Joseph Heller*

jokes as childish, harmless fun is just as reductive as the opposite position. Joking is bitter and sweet in equal measure. Joking is a game. OK, so quite often there are tears before bedtime, but that doesn't mean we won't be playing just as enthusiastically tomorrow. The high, entrancing sparkle of a child's first laugh wouldn't dazzle half as brightly without the wink of Satan's dark, unspeakable bumhole that underlies the joker's art. A joke is neither good nor evil—it's just excess energy, a bubble thrown up by the creative chaos of human consciousness. Jokes are sly, jokes are anarchic, jokes are . . . profoundly insignificant.

To say that "life's a joke" is not so much to belittle life as to correctly identify the elusive nature of the joke. Jokes have the measure of us. They change in the telling, defy capture, slip through our fingers like water. And they outlast us all. They are trifles, fragments, nothings that turn out to be all that's left: the aptest metaphor for our pathetic species' struggle to survive. Curtain up—the comedy is just beginning.

You live and learn. Then you die and forget it all.
—Noël Coward

ACKNOWLEDGMENTS

WE'D LIKE TO THANK:

Our indomitable agents, Hannah Chambers ("Bad Cop") and Simon Trewin ("Good Cop") for making sure it happened.

The team at Gotham Books for their passion, integrity and hard work. (Can you tell we're hoping to pitch a sequel?) But seriously, Brendan Cahill, Patrick Mulligan, Andy Heidel and Co. have been patient, accommodating and enthusiastic about the project from the word go and we'd like to thank them most sincerely. (For the money.)

All our friends and acquaintances who told us jokes and helped us think about them, but especially Ruli Manurung and Graeme Ritchie at the University of Edinburgh, James Campbell and Melissa O'Brien of Comedy 4 Kids, Stewart Lee and Robert Newman.

Dan Schreiber for helping to draw up the long, long list of jokes that we began with.

JIMMY WOULD ALSO LIKE TO THANK:

Karoline Copping, for putting up with all my jokes that begin, "My girlfriend says . . ."

My brothers, Colin and Patrick Carr.

My mother, for telling her small repertoire of jokes really rather well.

Every stand-up comic and comedy writer I've ever had the privilege of working with.

Last but not least, Her Majesty the Queen, whose warm friendship and wise advice have been an invaluable source of comfort to me down the years.

LUCY WOULD ALSO LIKE TO THANK:

The Greeves tribe, both immediate and extended, which is glued together not least by its sense of humor; in particular my sister Susanna for generous and incisive early comments on the manuscript. My mother and father for being, unshakeably, there. And Emily and David, co-creators of Obscene Scrabble.

My extraordinary friends, who have been extra-extraordinary this past year.

Most of all, love and gratitude to Luke Hacker for patience and grace beyond all reasonable bounds, for keen-eyed editing and insightful criticism. Without its first and best reader this book might never have remembered its punch line.

NOTES

CHAPTER 2

pg. 16 Chimpanzee "laughter" experiment: Robert Provine, *Laughter: a Scientific Investigation* (New York: Viking Penguin, 2000).

pg. 16 Laughing rats: J. Panksepp and J. Burgdorf, "Laughing rats? Playful tickling arouses high-frequency ultrasonic chirping in young rodents," *Toward a Science of Consciousness* III (1999), MIT Press.

pg. 17 Washoe the joking chimp: Roger Fouts, *Next of Kin* (New York, William Morrow, 1997).

pg. 18 Nonverbal communication in infants: Desmond Morris, *The Naked Ape* (New York: Vintage, 1994).

pg. 19 "Laughter circuit" in the brain: V. S. Ramachandran and Sandra Blakeslee, *Phantoms in the Brain* (New York: Fourth Estate, 1998).

pg. 21 Social laughter releases oxytocin: Experiment cited in an article in *The Independent*, October 12, 2005.

pg. 21 Laughter boosts the immune system: L. S. Berk, S. A. Tan, D. B. Berk, and W. C. Eby, "Immune system changes during associated laughing," *Clinical Research* 39 (1991): 124A.

pg. 21 Laughing raises the heart rate: W. F. Fry and C. Rader, "The respiratory components of mirthful laughter," *The Journal of Biological Psychology* 19 (1977): 39–50.

pg. 22 *Patch Adams* the movie: dir. Tom Shadyac (1998) DVD.

pg. 23 Patch Adams on comic relief: Patch Adams with Maureen Mylander, *Gesundheit!* (Vermont: Healing Arts Press, 1998).

pg. 23 Anthony Trollope laughs himself sick: J. N. Hall, *Trollope: a Biography* (Oxford: Clarendon Press, 1991).

pg. 24 Laughter is mental conflict resolution: Terrence Deacon, *The Symbolic Species* (London: Allen Lane, 1997).

pg. 26 World record puns: *Tim Vine Live* (2004) DVD.

pg. 26 Multivac, the joke computer: Isaac Asimov, *Earth Is Room Enough* (New York: Doubleday & Co., 1957).

pg. 31 No one laughs in the lab: Robert Provine, *Laughter: A Scientific Investigation* (New York: Viking Penguin, 2000).

CHAPTER 3

pg. 54 Ronald McDonald statue accident, "McDonald's Found Negligent in Statue Accident," *Philadelphia Law Intelligencer,* October 27, 1995.

OTHER READING

Richard Boston, *An Anatomy of Laughter* (London: Collins, 1974).

Mikita Brottman, *Funny Peculiar* (Lawrence, KS: The Analytic Press, Inc., 2004).

Howard Jacobson, *Seriously Funny* (New York: Viking Penguin, 1997).

Enid Welsford, *The Fool: His Social and Literary History* (London: Faber, 1935).

CHAPTER 4

pg. 63 Nonsense makes sense to children: Kornei Chukovsky, *From Two to Five* (Berkeley: University of California Press, 1963).

pg. 69 What's black and white and Freud all over?: Martha Wolfenstein, *Children's Humor* (Bloomington: Indiana University Press, 1978).

pg. 73 Childlike qualities important to mental health: Oliver James, "Directions Home," *Observer Magazine*, October 16, 2005.

pg. 73 Comedy persona inspired by an intelligent eight-year-old?: Steven Wright, *I Have a Pony* (1996) CD.

pg. 73 Mel Brooks on comedy and heartache: Alan King, *Inside the Comedy Mind* (2004) DVD.

OTHER READING

Janet and Allan Ahlberg, *The Ha Ha Bonk Book* (London: Puffin Books, 1982).

CHAPTER 5

pg. 79 Learn about jokes and never laugh again: Max Eastman, *Enjoyment of Laughter* (London: Hamish Hamilton, 1937).

pg. 81 Joking numbs the heart: Henri Bergson, "Laughter and the Meaning of the Comic," trans. Brereton and Rothwell (Los Angeles: Green Integer, 1999).

pg. 82 A joke has only one winner: Charles R. Gruner, *The Game of Humor: A Comprehensive Theory of Why We Laugh* (Somerset, NJ: Transaction Publishers, 1997).

pg. 89 Freud's theory of humor: Sigmund Freud, *The Joke and Its Relation to the Unconscious*, trans. Joy Cook (London: Penguin, 2002).

pg. 95 Later support for Freud: Gershon Legman, *No Laughing Matter: The Rationale of the Dirty Joke* (London: Panther, 1972).

OTHER READING

Mikita Brottman, *Funny Peculiar* (Lawrence, KS: The Analytic Press, Inc., 2004).

Leonard Feinberg, *The Secret of Humor* (Amsterdam: Editions Rodopi, 1978).

Egon Larsen, *Wit as a Weapon* (London: Frederick Muller Ltd, 1980).

John Morreall, *Taking Laughter Seriously* (Albany: State University of New York, 1983).

Jerry Palmer, *Taking Humor Seriously* (Oxford: Routledge, 1994).

John Allen Paulos, *I Think, Therefore I Laugh: The Flip Side of Philosophy* (London: Allen Lane, 2000).

Stephen Potter, *The Sense of Humor* (London: Max Reinhardt, 1954).

Alison Ross, *The Language of Humour* (Oxford: Routledge, 1998).

CHAPTER 6

pg. 103 Marty Feldman quote: *The Times* (London), June 9, 1969.

pg. 105 Woody Allen quote: *Woody Allen on Comedy* (2001) Laugh.com CD.

pg. 113 Nasrudin and the donkeys: Idries Shah, *The Pleasantries of the Incredible Mulla Nasrudin* (London: Octagon Press, 1983).

pg. 120 Jerry Seinfeld quote: *Jerry Seinfeld on Comedy* (2001) Laugh.com CD.

pg. 122 Emo Philips routine: Emo Philips, $E=mo^2$ (1990) CD.

pg. 125 George Carlin's dirty words: George Carlin, "Seven Words You Can Never Say on Television," *Class Clown* (reissued 2000) CD.

pg. 125 George Carlin interviewed: Alan King, *Inside the Comedy Mind* (2004) DVD.

pg. 126 Out of date jokes: Ike 'NSmile Lettslaff, *Jokes Jokes Jokes* (UPL, date unknown).

pg. 128 Peter Kay jokes: Peter Kay, *Live at the Bolton Albert Halls* (2003) DVD.

pg. 128 Humour views the world awry: Simon Critchley, *On Humour* (London: Routledge, 2002).

pg. 132 K sounds are funny: Neil Simon, *The Sunshine Boys* (New York: Samuel French Inc., 1976).

pg. 133 J. Peasemold Gruntfuttock and chums: Barry Took and Marty Feldman, *Round the Horne* (London: Futura, 1975).

pg. 134 Woody Allen, *Woody Allen on Comedy* (2001) Laugh.com CD.

OTHER READING

Oliver Double, *Stand Up! On Being a Comedian* (London: Methuen, 1997).

Steven Jacobi, *Laughing Matters* (London: Century, 2005).

Gene Perrett, *Comedy Writing Step by Step* (New York: Samuel French Inc., 1990).

CHAPTER 7

pg. 142 Advertising report on women's humor: *Trend Report: Finding the H Spot* (2005) JWT, and an interview with the report's authors in *The Independent*, September 30, 2005.

pg. 146 Article on the death of the joke: Warren St. John, "Seriously, the Joke Is Dead," *The New York Times*, May 22, 2005.

pg. 149 Personal ads study: Robert Provine, *Laughter: A Scientific Investigation* (New York: Viking Penguin, 2000).

pg. 149 Men don't marry funny women: Eric R. Bressler et al. "Production and appreciation of humor as sexually selected traits," *Evolution and Human Behavior* 27, issue 2 (2006): 121–130.

pg. 150 Women are more generous with their laughter: Robert Provine, "Laughter Punctuates Speech: Linguistic, social and gender contexts of laughter," *Ethology* 95 (1993): 291–298.

pg. 151 Management gets the last laugh at work: Rose Coser, "Laughter among colleagues: A study of the social functions of humour among the staff of a mental hospital," *Psychiatry* 23 (1960): 81–95.

pg. 155 Sexual jokes are "verbal rape": Gershon Legman, *Rationale of the Dirty Joke* (London: Panther, 1972).

pg. 156 Meta-bigotry: Coined by Sam Anderson in Sarah Silverman article at *www.slate.com.*

CHAPTER 8

pg. 165 World's funniest joke experiment: British Association for the Advancement of Science, *LaughLAB: The Scientific Quest for the World's Funniest Joke* (London: Arrow Books, 2002).

pg. 167 Norman Douglas quote: From the introduction to *The Norman Douglas Limerick Book: Collected for the Use of Students & Ensplendour'd with Introduction, Geographical Index, and with Notes Explanatory and Critical* (London: Anthony Blond, 1969).

pg. 167 Joan Rivers review: Mark Lewisohn, *Radio Times Guide to TV Comedy* (London: BBC Books, 2003).

pg. 167 "The richest kind of laughter": Bill Hicks, *Love All the People: Letters, Lyrics, Routines* (London: Constable, 2005).

pg. 170 Joking relationships studied by J. Radcliffe-Brown: Richard Boston, *An Anatomy of Laughter* (London: Collins, 1974).

pg. 171 "Horrible things may also be laughable": William Willeford, *The Fool and His Scepter: A Study in Clowns and Jesters and Their Audience* (Evanston, IL: Northwestern University Press, 1969).

pg. 175 *The Aristocrats* the movie: dir. Paul Provenza and Penn Jillette (2005) DVD.

pg. 176 "The best pussy": Steve Martin, *A Wild and Crazy Guy* (reissued 1989) CD.

pg. 177 "Kryptonite to niggers": Chris Rock, *Bring the Pain* (1996) DVD.

pg. 178 Frank Skinner heckle comeback: William Cook, *Ha Bloody Ha: Comedians Talking* (New York: Fourth Estate, 1998).

pg. 180 "Momentary anaesthesia of the heart": Henri Bergson, *Laughter and the Meaning of the Comic*, trans. Brereton and Rothwell (Los Angeles: Green Integer, 1999).

pg. 184 "When a community celebrates . . .": Howard Jacobson, *Seriously Funny* (New York: Viking Penguin, 1997).

CHAPTER 9

pg. 189 The rules of humour: Kate Fox, *Watching the English* (London: Hodder & Stoughton, 2004).

pg. 191 National joking characteristics: Renatus Hartogs with Hans Fantel, *Four-Letter Word Games: The Psychology of Obscenity* (New York: M. Evans / Delacorte Press, 1967).

pg. 194 List of historical "fool towns": Christie Davies, *Jokes and Their Relation to Society* (New York: Mouton de Gruyter, 1998).

pg. 195 Max Miller quote: Steven Jacobi, *Laughing Matters* (London: Century, 2005).

pg. 200 Warren Mitchell interview: Lyn Gardner in *The Guardian*, February 16, 2000.

pg. 201 Alan King anecdote about flying to Albany: Alan King, *Inside the Comedy Mind* (2004) DVD.

pg. 203 "Real water did flow from the sprays": Viktor Frankl, *Man's Search for Meaning: An Introduction to Logotherapy* (New York: Washington Square Press, 1969).

pg. 204 "Humor is not a mood": Ludwig Wittgenstein, *Culture and Value* (Oxford: Basil Blackwell, 1980).

pg. 204 Ray Hanania and the Comedy For Peace foundation: *www.comedy4peace.org*.

pg. 205 Muslim stand-up comedy: *Allah Made Me Funny—The Official Muslim Comedy Tour* (2005) DVD.

pg. 206 Stalin's sense of humor: Robert Conquest, *The Great Terror* (London: Macmillan, 1968).

pg. 207 Jokes not an indicator of ethnic conflict: Christie Davies, *Jokes and Their Relation to Society* (New York: Mouton de Gruyter, 1998).

pg. 210 British *Black and White Minstrel Show*: Lenny Henry, in his biography at *www.lennyhenry.com*.

OTHER READING

Ted Cohen, *Jokes: Philosophical Thoughts on Joking Matters* (University of Chicago Press, 1999).

Alan King, *Alan King's Great Jewish Joke Book* (New York: Crown Publishers, 2002).

Richard Pryor (with Todd Gold), *Pryor Convictions and Other Life Sentences* (London: Revolver Books, 2005).

CHAPTER 10

pg. 217 Eskimo drumming matches: Max Gluckman, *Politics, Law and Ritual in Tribal Society* (London: Basil Blackwell, 1967).

pg. 217 Bambuti pygmies: Colin M. Turnbull, *The Forest People* (London: Chatto & Windus, 1961) and *Wayward Servants: The Two Worlds of the African Pygmies* (London: Eyre & Spottiswoode, 1966).

pg. 218 The Danga, ancient Egyptian jester: Enid Welsford, *The Fool: His Social and Literary History* (London: Faber, 1935).

pg. 219 Joker's wild: Richard Boston, *An Anatomy of Laughter* (London: Collins, 1974).

pg. 223 "First prize: Fifteen years": Alan Dundes and C. Banc, *You Call This Living? A Collection of East European Political Jokes* (Athens, GA: The University of Georgia Press, 1990).

pg. 224 Jokes under Stalin and Franco: Christie Davies, *Jokes and Their Relation to Society* (New York: Mouton de Gruyter, 1998).

pg. 228 Restrictions on satire in the 1960s: Ben Thompson, *Sunshine on Putty* (London: Fourth Estate, 2004).

pg. 230 "Vitamin or narcotic": Enid Welsford, *The Fool: His Social and Literary History* (London: Faber, 1935).

pg. 230 Comedy activism: *Mark Thomas Comedy Product* (1996–2002), Channel 4, *www.mtcp.co.uk*.

pg. 231 "The comic reminds us of our true reality . . .": Bill Hicks, *Love All the People: Letters, Lyrics, Routines* (London: Constable, 2005).

pg. 231 Geopolitical analysis, with jokes: Robert Newman, *Apocalypso Now* (2005) CD at *www.robnewman.com*.

OTHER READING

Ron Jenkins, *Subversive Laughter: The Liberating Power of Comedy* (New York: The Free Press, 1994).

Bill Hicks, *Relentless* (reissued 2006) DVD.

CHAPTER 11

pg. 239 *Jerry Springer—The Opera:* Stewart Lee, Richard Thomas, and Cast (2005) DVD.

pg. 241 Campaign to prosecute *Jerry Springer—The Opera* for blasphemy: *www.christianvoice.org.uk*.

pg. 244 Rowan Atkinson's speech against the Religious Hatred bill: Published in full on *www.timesonline.co.uk*, October 20, 2005.

pg. 246 Jesus and the Fool archetype: Harvey Cox, *The Feast of Fools* (Cambridge, MA: Harvard University Press, 1969).

pg. 248 Lenny Bruce's autobiography: *How to Talk Dirty and Influence People* (London: Panther, 1975).

pg. 249 "Hey, woppo, what's happening?": Lenny Bruce, *The Historic 1962 Concert When Lenny Got Busted* (1998) Viper's Nest CD. (For another version of the routine see Lenny Bruce, *The Essential Lenny Bruce* (London: Panther, 1975).)

pg. 253 "Don't let him see all the glittery stuff": Dario Fo, *Mistero Buffo*, trans. Ed Emery (London: Methuen Drama, 1992).

OTHER READING

Ronald Collins and David Skover, *The Trials of Lenny Bruce: The Fall and Rise of an American Icon* (Naperville, IL: Sourcebooks MediaFusion, 2002).

Dario Fo, *The Tricks of the Trade*, trans. Joe Farrell (London: Methuen Drama, 1991).

Stewart Lee, *Stand-up Comedian* (2005) DVD.

CHAPTER 12

pg. 263 Aristotle on laughter: *Historia Animalium (The Natural History of Animals)* and *De Partibus Animalium (On the Parts of Animals)* (c. 350 B.C.), in *The Complete Works of Aristotle: The Revised Oxford Translation*, ed. Jonathan Barnes (Princeton University Press, 1984). Text also available via the Internet Classics Archive at *http://classics.mit.edu/*.

pg. 263 Navajo naming ceremony: Howard Jacobson, *Seriously Funny* (New York: Viking Penguin, 1997).

pg. 264 Childhood optimists die younger: Howard S. Friedman et al. "Does childhood personality predict longevity?" *Journal of Personality and Social Psychology* 65, no. 1 (1993): 176–185.

pg. 265 Famous last words: Brian O'Kill, *Exit Lines* (London: Longman Group, 1986).

pg. 266 A. E. Housman's last words: Bernard Ruffin, *Last Words: A Dictionary of Deathbed Quotations* (Jefferson, NC: McFarland & Company, 1995).

pg. 268 "What we appear to be is a fleeting shadow": Wei Wu Wei. *The Tenth Man: The Great Joke (Which Made Lazarus Laugh)* (Boulder, CO: Sentient Publications, 2003).

pg. 272 "I have tried too in my time to be a philosopher": James Boswell, *The Life of Samuel Johnson* (London: Penguin Classics, 1986).

pg. 272 "Life doesn't cease to be funny when people die": George Bernard Shaw, *The Doctor's Dilemma* (London: Penguin Books, 1987).

FURTHER READING/VIEWING

Tests show that books and CDs bought from your local independent retailer are 20 percent funnier.

TEN GREAT BOOKS ABOUT JOKES

Janet and Allan Ahlberg	*The Ha Ha Bonk Book*	The all-time classic English children's joke book
Richard Boston	*An Anatomy of Laughter*	Humane and erudite look at laughter in literature
Lenny Bruce	*How to Talk Dirty and Influence People*	Freewheeling autobiography of comedy's enfant terrible
Ted Cohen	*Jokes*	Philosophical investigation of the social value of joking—with great jokes
Peter Cook	*Tragically I Was an Only Twin*	Triple-distilled funny—jokes, but not as we know them
Bill Hicks	*Love All the People*	The Trickster rides again
Howard Jacobson	*Seriously Funny*	Exploration of the dark side of comedy, at once lugubrious and gleeful

Ron Jenkins	*Subversive Laughter: The Liberating Power of Comedy*	Personal account from the front line of international clowning
Robert Provine	*Laughter: A Scientific Investigation*	Scientist explains laughter to nonscientists; witty and fascinating
Richard Pryor	*Pryor Convictions and Other Life Sentences*	Freebasing autobiography of comedy's other enfant terrible

LIVE PERFORMANCE

Jokes are a social phenomenon, and comedy is best experienced live—support your local comedy club if you have one.

We hope this book has whetted your appetite for British comedy. Apart from the performers we discuss in the course of the book, we can think of so many other great acts we'd recommend that there just isn't room to list all of them here. But if you're hungry for more jokes, these short lists are a good place to start.

OLD SCHOOL

The missing link between Music Hall and modern stand-up, these great comics were some of the UK's hardest-working gagsmiths when we were kids. At the time of writing, Ken Dodd is the sole survivor of the four, still on tour at seventy-eight. Some history homework for fans of British stand-up:

Tommy Cooper	*The Best of Tommy Cooper*	2004	DVD
Les Dawson	*The Best of Les Dawson*	2003	DVD

Ken Dodd	*An Audience with Ken Dodd*	1995	DVD
Bob Monkhouse	Various live shows available on VHS/DVD		

HOT TICKETS

These are just ten of the most talented stand-ups working in the UK today. Some of them have already reached your shores; the rest will surely follow.

We've restricted our recommendations to comedians whose work is available on DVD, so as not to tantalize you with news of all the great live comedy gigs you're missing. But don't forget that if you track down a DVD manufactured in Europe you'll need a multi-region player to watch it.

Bill Bailey	The love child of Frodo and Rick Wakeman. Musical genius, comedy legend. DVDs: *Bewilderness* (2001), *Part Troll* (2004)
Jack Dee	The daddy of deadpan. Elevates grumpiness to a comic art. DVDs listed at *www.jackdee.co.uk*
Lee Evans	Natural heir to Chaplin and Keaton. Pure clown. DVDs: *Live in Scotland* (1998), *Live at Wembley* (2002)
Ricky Gervais	Creator of *The Office* and *Extras*, sometime *Simpsons* guest writer/star, Gervais is no slouch at stand-up either. DVDs: *Animals* (2003), *Politics* (2004)
Jeff Green	Benevolent dictator of the kingdom of observational comedy. DVD: *Back from the Bewilderness* (2003)
Peter Kay	Local comedy with universal appeal. The man is probably funny in his sleep. DVD: *Live at the Bolton Albert Halls* (2003)
Sean Lock	Effortless balancing act between the surreal and the everyday, hilarity and pain. Audio CD: *Live* (2003)

Lee Mack	Worthy inheritor of more than one of Eric Morecambe's funny bones. "Cheeky but never blue . . ." Audio CD: *The Lee Mack Show* (2006)
Al Murray	Hideously convincing satire on "little England" attitudes. The definitive meta-bigot. DVD: *The Pub Landlord* (2003)
Ross Noble	The love child of Puff the Magic Dragon and a piece of cheese. Surreal, whimsical, unique. DVDs: *Unrealtime* (2004), *Sonic Waffle* (2005)

THE IRISH CORNER

Ah, Ireland. Land of our fathers. Land of poets, priests, and drunks—often all rolled into one cirrhotic body. Ireland produces a disproportionate number of brilliant comedians; these four are our pick of the current crop.

Ed Byrne	Who ate all the Lucky Charms? Step forward. The world's most charming comedian. DVD: *Ed Byrne Live* (2006)
Dylan Moran	The love child of Brendan Behan and Dave Allen. World-weary, crumpled, oddly lovable. DVD: *Dylan Moran Live: Monster* (2004)
Dara O Briain	Comedian, TV presenter, mathematical scientist. Funny till it hurts. *Live DVD coming soon.*
Tommy Tiernan	The love child of Samuel Beckett and Billy Connolly. Comedy as poetry—angelic yet filthy. DVD: *Tommy Tiernan Live* (2002)

INDEX

Adams, Douglas, 232
Adams, Hunter "Patch," 22–23
Adams, Orny, 156
Addison, Chris, 114
Aesop's fables, 115
Africa, 38
Alf Garnett syndrome, 199
Allen, Dave, 118
Allen, Woody, 47, 56, 96, 105–106, 134, 200, 202, 241
All in the Family (television show), 199–200
Ambivalence Theory of humor, 87–88, 95
Amnesty International, 256
Anansi (deity), 43
Anasazi Indians, 39
Anatomy of Laughter, An (Boston), 219
Anderson, Sam, 156
Anstey, E., 23, 24
Anti–Semitism, 198, 202
April Fools' Day, 44
Archetypes, 38
Aristocrats, The (movie), 175
Aristocrats joke, 173–175
Aristophanes, 145, 273
Aristotle, 16, 263
Ashanti legend, 43
Asimov, Isaac, 26–27, 29, 119
Atkinson, Rowan, 134, 244–245, 254
Attell, Dave, 56, 154, 235
August costume, 51
Augustus Caesar, 202
Austin, Audrey, 85
Authoritarian societies, 222–225, 228
Aztec Indians, 45

Baddiel, David, 231
Baldwin, James, 200, 209
Bambuti pygmies, 217–218
Bankhead, Tallulah, 265
Barker, Arj, 27, 126
Barr, Roseanne, 47, 136
Barry, Todd, 162
Batman comic books, 193–194
Baubles, 145
Baum, Bruce, 49
Beattie, James, 87
Beethoven, Ludwig van, 267
Belushi, John, 47, 48
Beolco, Ruzzante, 253
Bergman, Ingmar, 248
Bergson, Henri, 81–83, 180

Berle, Milton, 112
Bhaskar, Sanjeev, 200
Bigley, Ken, 227
Binsted, Kim, 27–28
Birdman, Markus, 162
Black, Margot, 193
Black and White Minstrel Show, The (television show), 210
Blackface makeup, 209, 210
Blasphemy, 241–255
Bliss, Chris, 56
Boston, Richard, 219
Boyle, Frankie, 56, 166
Bracciolini, Poggio, 114–115
Brand, Jo, 128, 149, 158
Brigstocke, Marcus, 57
British Academy for the Advancement of Science, 165, 166
Brooke, Henry, 229
Brooke-Taylor, Tim, 41
Brooks, Albert, 8
Brooks, Mel, 73–74, 80
Brown, A. Whitney, 201
Brown, Arnold, 121
Brown, Roy "Chubby," 152, 176
Bruce, Lenny, 47, 48, 56, 116, 125, 137, 147, 239, 246–251, 253, 254
Buddhism, 267–268
Bugiale, 114
Buñuel, Luis, 249
Burmese prisoners of conscience, 256
Burns, George, 48, 84
Bush, George H. W., 228
Bush, George W., 225

Callaghan, John, 221
Campbell, James, 61, 62, 68, 69, 72, 73
Canned laughter, 109–110
Carey, Drew, 57
Carlin, George, 10, 16, 31, 125, 128, 147, 175
Carnival, 44, 54
Carr, Alan, 213
Carr, Jimmy, 5, 10, 15, 16, 19, 27, 40, 57, 75, 80, 83, 105, 106, 119, 120, 122, 136, 141–144, 146, 152, 156–158, 160, 162, 169, 175, 179, 190, 212, 229, 245, 264, 270–272
Carson, Johnny, 50
Carter, Angela, 36
Caxton, William, 115
Celts, 45
Cerebral palsy, 30
Chaney, Lon, 53
Chaplin, Charlie, 52, 145, 172
Chappelle, Dave, 203
Chesterton, G. K., 2
Children, jokes and, 5, 61–74
Chimpanzees, 16, 17
"Christ and Moses" bit (Bruce), 249–250, 253
Christian Voice, 241–244
Christmas crackers, 190–191
Chukovsky, Kornei, 63
Cicero, 114
Circus, 51, 54, 55
Clark, Bruce, 248
Clarke, Arthur C., 26
Cleese, John, 47, 56, 119
Clowns, 36–55
  archetypal, 51
  Bambuti pygmies, 218
  dolls, 49
  evil, 52–53
  fear of, 50, 55
  history of, 50–52

Killer Clown myth, 53, 54
Sad Clown myth, 46–48, 54
trickster figures, 38–43, 54, 55, 97, 144, 246
Clowns for Christ, 49
Cohen, Sacha Baron, 155–156
Cold War, 223, 224
Collins, Phil, 15
Comedians, 71, 103–135, 117, 154–155, 181
Comedy 4 Kids show, 61–63, 68–73
Comedy for Peace initiative, 203–204, 270
Comedy Store, 117, 147
Commedia dell'arte, 54, 145
Connolly, Billy, 227
Conquest, Robert, 206–207
Coogan, Steve, 222
Cook, Peter, 56, 229
Cooper, Tommy, 33, 53, 57, 273
Cousins, Norman, 22
Coward, Noël, 275
Cox, Harvey, 246
Coyote (deity), 42–43
Critchley, Simon, 128
Cross, David, 231

Damage, Brian, 165
Danga, 218
Dangerfield, Rodney, 137
Danish Mohammed cartoons, 205–206, 255
Darwin, Charles, 15
Dasius, 45
David, Larry, 155
Davies, Bob, 31
Davies, Christie, 207, 224
Dawson, Les, 47, 137, 153, 256
Deacon, Terrence, 24
DeGeneres, Ellen, 10, 57
De Rerum Natura (Lucretius), 114
Diana, Princess, 228
Diller, Phyllis, 56
Dirty jokes, 92, 95–97, 151–153, 155, 165–167, 173–176
Dix, Gregory, 250
Dr. Seuss, 63
Dodd, Ken, 94, 95, 145
Dogon tribe, 171
Douglas, Norman, 167
Douglass, Charlie, 109–110
Dreams, 89
Dunbar, Robin, 21
Duncan, Isadora, 265

Eastman, Max, 14, 79
Éclair, Jenny, 158
Edinburgh University, 27
Egypt, ancient, 192, 194, 218
Elegba (deity), 38–39, 41
Elliot, John, 196
Ellis, A. B., 39
Endorphins, 21
English jokes, 189–191
Enjoyment of Laughter (Eastman), 79
Esquimaux people, 217
Ethnic humor, 189–211
Evolution and Human Behavior (journal), 149
Evolutionary theory, 15–16, 18

Fear, 18, 19, 269
Feast of Fools, 44, 54, 242
Federal Communications Commission (FCC), 125

Feldman, Marty, 103, 133
Female comedians, 147–148, 157–158
Feminist movement, 153
Flatley, Michael, 196
Fo, Dario, 252–255
Fool, The (Welsford), 230
Fools, 218–222, 246, 264
Fool towns, 192–194
Fossey, Dian, 16
Fouts, Roger, 17
Fox, Kate, 189
Franco, Francisco, 224
Frankl, Viktor, 203
Fratellini, Albert, 51
Free speech, 241–256
Freud, Sigmund, 68–70, 89–95, 143, 175
Frost, Robert, 271
Furnish, David, 190

Gacy, John Wayne, 53
Gaelic, 134
Gaffigan, Jim, 173
Galifianakis, Zach, 178, 213
Game of Humor, The (Gruner), 95
Gandhi, Mahatma, 219
Gender, jokes and joking and, 142–144, 146–159
Gervais, Ricky, 155
Gesundheit Institute, 22–23
Gildea, Kevin, 38, 123
Gleason, Jackie, 47
Gluckman, Max, 217
Goodall, Jane, 16
Goon Show, The (television show), 229, 273
Gorillas, 16
Gotham, Nottinghamshire, 192–194
Gotham City, 193–194
Gott, John, 246
Gottfried, Gilbert, 173, 174
Great Depression, 51
Great Terror, The (Conquest), 206–207
Greece, ancient, 40, 144–145, 194
Green, Jeff, 118, 161, 162
Green, Stephen, 241–242
Greer, Germaine, 157
Greeves, Lucy, 49, 65, 70–71, 80, 141–143, 169, 271
Gregory, Dick, 208
Greig, J. Y. T., 87
Griffen, Tom, 109
Grizzard, Lewis, 116
Grock the clown, 46
Groening, Matt, 228
Gruner, Charles R., 82, 95, 98
Guinness World Records, 26
Gutenberg, Johannes, 115

Hall, Rich, 15, 88, 213
Hamlet (Shakespeare), 269–270
Hanania, Ray, 203–204, 270
Hancock, Tony, 47
Handey, Jack, 93, 213, 217
Harijan caste, 150
Harlequin, 51
Hartogs, Renatus, 191
Hawaiian legends, 42
Hawking, Stephen, 27
Hazlitt, William, 87
Heart rate, 21
Hedberg, Mitch, 44, 132, 155, 230
Heller, Joseph, 274
Henderson, Mitch, 235
Henry, Dan, 210
Henry, Lenny, 210

Henry I, King of England, 221
Hermes (deity), 39–40, 42
Herod, 202
Hesse, Herman, 262
Hicks, Bill, 167, 231, 233, 252
Hierocles, 112
Hill, Benny, 47
Hill, Harry, 33, 207, 266
Hitler, Adolf, 204, 206
Hobbes, Thomas, 81
Hobo clown, 51–52
Holistic healing, 22
Ho'opa'apa'a, 42
Hope, Bob, 48
Hopi Indians, 39
Hortop, Alice, 24–25
Housman, A. E., 265–266
Human sacrifice, 45
Humor, origins of word, 264
Humor, theories of, 81–98
  Ambivalence Theory, 87–88, 95
  Incongruity Theory, 85–87, 90, 295
  Release Theory, 89–95
  Superiority Theory, 81–85, 89, 95
Humor workshop, 24–26
Hydraulics, 90

Idries Shah, 113
Immune system, 21
Incest taboo, 170
Incongruity Theory of humor, 85–87, 90, 95
Infant communication, 18, 263–264
In jokes, 121
Internet, 111, 146
Irish jokes, 195–197, 209
Irish language, 133–134
Irving, Washington, 193
It (King), 53
Izzard, Eddie, 28, 63, 84, 132, 135

Jacobson, Howard, 184, 263–264
James, Oliver, 73
JAPE (Joke Analysis and Production Engine) computer software, 27–28
Jeni, Richard, 162, 240
Jerry Springer—The Opera (musical), 239–245, 251, 255–256
Jest books, 111–112
Jesters, 218–222, 246, 264
Jewish jokes, 197–198, 200–205, 209
Jillette, Penn, 175
John, Elton, 190
Johnson, Samuel, 272
Joke and Its Relation to the Unconscious, The (Freud), 89
Jokes and joking, (*see also* Clowns; Laughter)
  children and, 5, 61–74
  compulsive joking, 26
  computer programs and, 27–30
  dark side of, 7–8
  death and, 265–267
  defined, 3–4
  ethnic humor, 189–213
  five basic rules, 135
  gender and, 142–144, 146–159
  humor workshop, 24–26
  offensive jokes, 165–186
  political jokes, 222–233

Jokes and joking, *(continued)*
professional joke-tellers, 71, 103–135, 154–155, 181
puns, 26, 28, 42, 190
reasons for, 15–32
religion and, 241–255
sense of humor, 5–7, 29, 80, 149, 191, 264
setup and punch line, 4, 19–20, 85–87, 122–123
statistics in, 10
structure, 19–20
theories of humor (*see* Humor, theories of)
"Jokester" (Asimov), 26–27
Joking relationships, 170–171
Jones, Milton, 9, 71
Joubert, Louis, 87, 88
Jung, Carl, 38
Jyllands–Posten newspaper, 205

Kaguru tribe, 171
Kant, Immanuel, 85
Katz, Jonathan, 90, 136, 242
Kauffman, Max, 267
Kay, Peter, 128–129
Kearney, Tom, 225
Keaton, Buster, 47
Kelly, Emmett, 52
Kelly, Emmett, Jr., 52
Kelly, Paul, 52–53
Kerr, Jean, 124
Kiley, Brian, 48
Killer Clown myth, 53, 54
King, Alan, 201, 213
King, Stephen, 53
King Lear (Shakespeare), 220–221
Kinsey, Alfred, 97
Kirshen, Matt, 69, 72
Knebel, Fletcher, 10
Knights, The (Aristophanes), 145
Koans, 268
Kokopelli (deity), 39, 42

Lampanelli, Lisa, 148
Laughter, 150–151. (*see also* Jokes and joking)
canned, 109–110
development of, 18, 31, 32
physical benefits of, 21–24
as universal mode of expression, 17–18
"Laughter and the Meaning of the Comic" (Bergson), 81–82
Laurie, Hugh, 160
Lawrence, St., 267
Leap year, 45
Lear, Norman, 199
Leary, Denis, 218
Lebowitz, Fran, 98
Lee, Stewart, 240, 242, 243, 255, 256
Legman, Gershon, 95–98, 155
Leno, Jay, 21, 24
Lent, 44
Leoncavallo, Ruggero, 51
Letterman, David, 10, 33, 192, 227
Lettslaff collection, 126–127
Levenson, Sam, 56
Lewis, David, 205
Lewis, Jerry, 51
Liber Facetiarum, The (Book of Trifling Jests), 114–115
Liebert, Danny, 174
Liebman, Wendy, 118
Limb, Jeremy, 6
Limbic system, 19

Lipps, Theodor, 91
Lock, Sean, 135
Lodagaba tribe, 171
Loki (deity), 43
Lucretius, 114

Mack, Lee, 141
Macmillan, Harold, 229
Madigan, Kathleen, 57
Mad TV, 121
Maher, Bill, 172–173, 243, 255
Maitreya Buddha, 268
Mann, John, 113
Manning, Bernard, 93, 180–181
Manurung, Ruli, 27
Marceau, Marcel, 109
Marlowe, Christopher, 113
Marsh, Rodney, 227
Martial, 219
Martin, Demetri, 3, 45, 55, 86, 104, 107, 119, 213
Martin, Steve, 33, 137, 140, 160, 161, 176, 226
Martinez, Francesca, 168
Marx, Groucho, 83, 84, 103, 145
Marx Brothers, 22
Mason, Jackie, 160
McDonald's, 48
McGrath, Rory, 160
McGraw, Seamus, 251
Mein Kampf (Hitler), 204
Mencken, H. L., 191
Meo, Sean, 42
Merchant, Stephen, 150
Merry Tales of the Mad Men of Gotham, The, 192–194
Meta-bigotry, 156, 178
Middle Ages, 145, 242
Miller, Max, 195
Milligan, Spike, 10–11, 63, 159, 228, 267
Milner, George, 87
Mistero Buffo (Fo), 253
Mitchell, Warren, 200
Mohammed, Prophet, 205
Molière, 253
Monkhouse, Bob, 33, 102, 145, 213, 265
Montgomery, Carol, 160
Moore, Michael, 230–231
Moran, Dylan, 29, 161
Morecambe, Eric, 8
Morreall, John, 146–147
Mosley, Lady Diana, 206
Mother-in-law jokes, 153
Moustache Brothers, 256
Murphy, Eddie, 47
Mystery plays, 145

Napoleon, 190
Nasrudin, Mulla, 113
Native Americans, 39–40, 54–55, 263–264
Navajo Indians, 263–264
Nero, Emperor, 108–109
Neuroscience, experiments in, 19
Newhart, Bob, 110
Newlands, Chris, 244
Newman, Robert, 231–233
New York Times, The, 146
Nietzsche, Friedrich, 238, 265
Nigeria, 38
Nights at the Circus (Carter), 36
9/11 terrorist attacks, 172
Noble, Ross, 66, 132
No Laughing Matter: The Rationale of the Dirty Joke (Legman), 95–96

Northridge Electronics, 109–110
Nubians, 192

O'Brien, Conan, 142
Obscene Scrabble, 169–170
Obscenity, 151–152
O'Connor, Carroll, 199
Offensive jokes, 165–186
Oliver, John, 247
O'Mara, Dave, 27
One-liners, 37
Oral tradition, 111
O'Reilly, Liam, 32
Orwell, George, 164
Owen, David, 229
Oxytocin, 21

Pagan festivals, 43–45, 54
Pagliacci, 51
Pain, 19, 24–26, 269
Pain, Helen, 27
Pain asymbolia, 19
Palmerston, Lord, 265
Partridge, Eric, 131
Pataki, George, 254
Patriarchal society, 157
Philagrios, 112
Philips, Emo, 17, 33, 43, 81, 88, 124, 151, 160, 162, 172, 181, 188, 194, 244, 257, 271
Philogelos, 111–112, 115
"Physiology of Laughter, The" (Spencer), 90
Pierrot, 51
Pitcairn Islanders, 170
Plato, 3, 266
Pogo the Clown, 53
Political correctness, 146, 169, 180, 181
Political jokes, 222–233
Politically Incorrect (television show), 172–173
Poplin, Sally, 137
Practical joke, 4, 37–42, 132
Pratchett, Terry, 75
Private Joke File (Berle), 112
Professional joke-tellers, 71, 103–135, 154–155, 181
Provenza, Paul, 175
Provine, Robert, 16, 31
Pryor, Richard, 47
Pueblo Indians, 54–55
Pull-back/reveal technique, 123–124
Pum pum, chi è? La Polizia! (Fo), 252
Punch and Judy, 54, 146
Punch line, 4, 20, 86, 87, 122–123
Puns, 26, 28, 42, 190

Rabelais, François, 267, 273
Race, 177, 180–183, 198–211
Radcliffe-Brown, J., 171
Radio comedy, 133
Rahere, 221–222
Ramachandran, V. S., 19
Rame, Franca, 252
Redmond, Michael, 87
Reeves, Vic, 10
Release Theory of humor, 89–95
Religion, 241–255
Renaissance, 145
Riddles, 27, 30, 64–65
Ritchie, Graeme, 27
Rivers, Joan, 31, 158, 167, 177
Rock, Chris, 177, 199, 211, 220
Romano, Ray, 107, 136
Romans, ancient, 219

Ronald McDonald, 48, 54
Rosen, Janet, 162
Ross, Jonathan, 150
Rotton, John, 47, 48
Royal Society of Medicine, 40–41
Rudner, Rita, 4, 56, 136
Rushton, Willy, 189

Sad Clown myth, 46–48, 54
Sahl, Mort, 251
St. John, Warren, 146, 147
Saturday Night Live, 31, 121
Saturnalia festival, 43–45, 54
Satyr plays, 144–143
Schaffer, Zena, 75
Schneider, Leonard (*see* Bruce, Lenny)
Schopenhauer, Arthur, 85
Sedgwick, John, 265
Seinfeld, Jerry, 7, 20, 51, 65, 106, 120, 122, 125, 137, 147, 200, 235
Sellers, Peter, 228–229
Sense of humor, 5–7, 29, 80, 149, 191, 264
"Seriously, the Joke Is Dead" (St. John), 146
Seriously Funny (Jacobson), 184, 263
Setup, 4, 19–20, 85–86
"Seven Words You Can Never Say on Television" (Carlin), 125
Shaggy dog stories, 131–132
Shakes, Ronnie, 268
Shakespeare, William, 220–221, 269–270
Shandling, Gerry, 136, 153
Shaw, George Bernard, 216, 272
Shih Huang-Ti, 222
Siblings-in-law, 170
Silverman, Sarah, 155, 156, 158, 160, 175
Simon, Neil, 132–133
Simpson, Homer, 97
Siskind, Carol, 75
Skinner, Frank, 75, 178
Slapstick, 145
Slavery, 209–210
Slayton, Bobby, 125
Smirnoff, Yakov, 147
Smith, Tom, 190
Socrates, 266–267
Sounds and syllables, 132–133
Speech-impaired children, 39
Speech rhythms, 133–134
Speight, Johnny, 199
Spencer, Herbert, 90–91
Sphinx, 42
Spice Girls, 157
Spitting Image (television show), 229–230
Stalin, Joseph, 206–207, 224
Stand-up comics, 37
STANDUP (System To Augment Non-speakers' Dialogue Using Puns) computer program, 27–30
Stanhope, Doug, 175
Starr, Freddie, 25
Steel, David, 229
Steppenwolf (Hesse), 262
Stevens, Lester, 161
Stevenson, Adlai, 224
Stewart, Jon, 223, 233
Strong, Arnold, 112
Sunshine Boys, The (Simon), 132–133
Superiority Theory of humor, 81–85, 89, 95

Surprise, as joke mechanism, 122–123
Survival of the fittest, 15–16
Swearing, 124–126
Syria, ancient, 194

Talmud, 200–201
Tamburlaine, 113
Tamil people, 150
Tavare, Jim, 171
That Was the Week That Was (television show), 229
Thomas, Mark, 230, 231
Thomas, Richard, 240
Tickling, 16, 18
'Til Death Do Us Part (television show), 199, 200
Timing, 123–124
Timur Leng, 113
Took, Barry, 133
Tooper, Virginia, 233
Tramp, 52
Travis, Greg, 143
Trickster figures, 38–43, 54, 55, 97, 144, 246
Trollope, Anthony, 23–24
Turnbull, Colin M., 218
TV comedy, 109, 116–117
Tyler, Robin, 170
Tynan, Kenneth, 248

University of Maryland, 21
University of Plymouth, 16

Vatican, 114, 253
Vegas, Johnny, 129
Verbal economy, 130–131
Vice Versa (Anstey), 23, 24
Vikings, 45
Vine, Tim, 26, 28, 108, 197

Waco, Texas, 231
Walpole, Horace, 148
Wang, Wally, 33
Watching the English (Fox), 189
Watson, Mark, 270
Weary Willie, 52–53
Wei Wu Wei, 268
Welsford, Enid, 230, 231
West, Mae, 166
Westheimer, Dr. Ruth, 3
Wettach, Karl Adrien, 46
White, E. B., 78
White, Slappy, 137
Wilde, Oscar, 266
Willeford, William, 171
Williams, Kenneth, 47, 134
Williams, Robin, 22, 47, 52, 132
Wilson, John, 148
Winnebago Indians, 39–40
Wisdom, Norman, 146
Wittgenstein, Ludwig, 204
Wolfenstein, Martha, 69
Woods, R. S., 266
World's Funniest Joke competition, 165, 166
Wright, Steven, 18, 39, 46, 73, 75, 82, 111, 263

Yiddish, 134
Yoruba people, 38
Youngman, Henny, 57, 213
Yu Sze, 222

Zuni Indians, 39